Lisa Stewart's *The Big Quiet* charts a path for all women. It's a path at once dangerous and thrilling and a path she had started down and backed out of since childhood. The resulting narrative recounts a journey not only to a point on the map but to a whole and liberated self. Stewart is finally free to trust herself and others, to survive by her wits and with the help of kind strangers of which there are still many. This is a delicious fantasy of a journey most of us deny ourselves and one taken on the back of a horse whose simultaneously terrified and fiercely loyal personality unfurls before us as the richest of characters' personalities do—on the way from Point A to Point B.

Kelly Barth, author of *My Almost Certainly Real Imaginary Jesus*

This is a book of gratitude of the highest order. Stewart, a 54-year-old woman riding alone on a high-strung, sure-footed horse across the gravel grid of rural America, is grateful each night for a place to pitch a tent and pasture her horse. But her journey, past and present, is as much about the people she meets, many of whom know how to study a horse and to trust its rider—these strangers are glad to offer water and their own stories, which, like Stewart's, churn with old wounds, hard work, family, and an abiding trust in open land. This compelling meditation reminds us that every step, fall, and missed road leads the rider home.

Gary Dop, author of *Father, Child, Water*,
MFA Program Director at Randolph College

This book is more than a log of an unusual (for this day and age) solitary horseback journey; it is also a perceptive examination of the author's own life—a well-written introspective journey of self-discovery.

James F. Hoy, author of *Flint Hills Cowboys: Tales of the Tallgrass Prairie*, Chair Emeritus of Emporia State University's English Department and professor, past president of the Kansas Historical Society

After riding more than 3,000 miles across the United States in the early 1980s, Stewart helped launch one of that country's most successful saddle companies. Yet Lisa Stewart is no salesman, eager to sell a saddle to gain a commission. She is a long rider who made mistakes and learned by them. She faced obstacles and overcame them. She was presented with ancient riddles and discovered solutions.

CuChullaine O'Reilly, FRGS
Founding Member of The Long Riders' Guild

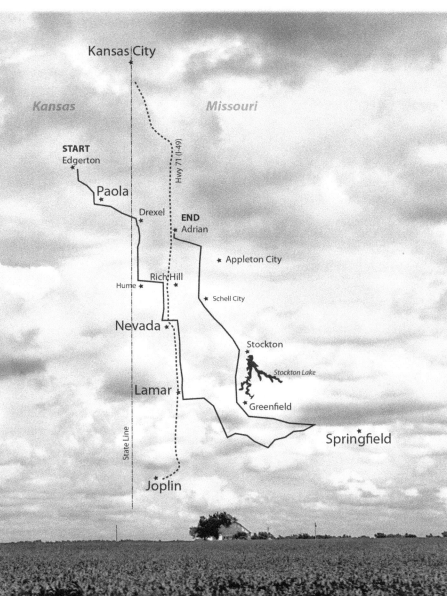

Kansas City

Kansas   *Missouri*

START
Edgerton

Hwy 71 (I-49)

Paola

Drexel

END
Adrian

Appleton City

Hume   Rich Hill

Schell City

Nevada

Stockton

Stockton Lake

Lamar

Greenfield

State Line

Springfield

Joplin

The Big Quiet

The Big Quiet

One Woman's Horseback Ride Home

a memoir

Lisa D. Stewart

A MEADOWLARK BOOK
Emporia, Kansas

Meadowlark
meadowlark-books.com
PO Box 333
Emporia, KS 66801

Cover Photo by Robert J. Stewart
Cover Design by Cynthia Beard

This book is a work of creative non-fiction; it is an accurate account of the events as recollected by the author. Conversations and details are taken from the author's mem-ories and from the author's perspective. Some names have been fictionalized, as the author felt appropriate.

ISBN: 978-1-7342477-4-9

Library of Congress Control Number: 2020936298

Contents

The Big Quiet

The man pulling radishes
pointed my way
with a radish.
~Issa

My horse, Chief, and I took right turns north and left turns west to follow our fine blue lines over hills, into bottoms, through dense growth, far away from any highway. We might have been riding closer to Kansas City, but we were riding deeper into the country, farther from Springfield and Branson, still more than two hundred miles from a major city. Our gravel road became more powder and less gravel, narrower, and with no ditch, but rusty fences abutting it, slack with unemployment, because there were no cattle to contain on this lowland that floods in spring and fall. Birds zipped past us, and deer sprang or glided in our farthest periphery. My ears buzzed with silence that was faintly disturbed by a thousand insects touching dead leaves; the leaves above lifted on a breeze penetrating in random breaths. If you weren't from here, you'd never be here.

When I was ten, I crashed through an Oklahoma wind on my aged mare, Honey, bareback, galloping. Before responsibility—other than mother's call to dinner, homework, bed—and without a father to comfort or boyfriend or husbands in succession to consider, I lived in my skin at ten, melded by sweat to my horse.

In decades since, with every life passage—two marriages, two births and a stillbirth, a husband's head injury, loss of business and home, and living without a horse for fifteen years—one vision recurred: a country road flowing under me and a horse, alone. This could never happen, I knew. I had lived in the home of a father or husband for all of my fifty-four years.

This day, I rode alone across the countryside, no one to consider, not even the wise, third husband, who had sent me on my way. My horse, Chief, and I scribed a five-hundred-mile loop through Kansas and Missouri, the summer of 2012.

For me, nothing existed but this road. I belonged here as much as anyone, and in this land, my new kin: grey squirrels and buff deer, coyotes at night, the Hansson family who fed me three days ago, and the next family up the road. Nobody else counted, because my life depended on strangers. My own family would never find me. It would take me nearly two weeks to reach a symphony at Kauffman Center for the Performing Arts in Kansas City; then where would I tie my horse? These Cedar County folks knew the way, and for now, the way was my truth and life. I would take on this tribe's language and law and religion if need be, one step at a time, pausing to eat and sleep and pee on their land. I passed into and out of worlds in the form of sections where people lived who knew the way and pointed me to it. As eighteenth-century Japanese poet Issa wrote, *The man pulling radishes/pointed my way/with a radish.*

For the first time since I was ten, I felt grounded as a bolt of lightning and just as live.

Prayer

He was the size of man who could throw open a heavy, plate-glass door with his thumb. He was wearing a ball cap, a short-sleeved T-shirt, denim overalls, and fabric-and-rubber, ankle-high work boots. My horse, Chief, followed me nicely, albeit sideways, staring at and absorbing the foreignness— and by that, I mean stench (Chief's term)—of the burros across the road. Chief, like all horses, was brain wired to believe he was a prey animal the size of a rabbit, so everything unfamiliar, like burros, probably was deadly. For that reason, I had dismounted and was leading him for comfort. I had owned him only two months. He didn't know me yet.

The man was watching me from his riding lawn mower, canted at a thirty-degree angle on the ditch he was mowing in front of his house. I strode straight toward him and smiled brightly and waved in order to melt the guarded expression he wore that told me he wasn't sure how friendly he should act toward a strange woman. Too friendly, a woman might feel threatened; but friendly means polite in this country, so I believed he was torn. A fifty-four-year-old woman leading a horse loaded with saddlebags, rope, canteen, and collapsible bucket through waist-high grass on a bar ditch in rural Miami County, Kansas, bore watching.

There was no full dental coverage in this man's world. Nor likely cashmere sweaters packed away in his wife's cedar chest while her summer things had been brought out for spring. Like me, everything she owned probably fit well enough into a six-foot-by-three-foot closet. I'd walked toward this man feeling like he was a friend I hadn't seen in years, which happens among people who've haltered horses a thousand times. You can tell horse people by the way they look at your horse. The head goes back half an inch. The eyelids drop, then click on the horse's hip, legs, chest, neck, head, back to the hind quarters. Then you. If you've got a decent horse, the eyes get serious—with respect. He gave me that look.

This man's eyes were shaded by wraparound sunglasses shaped like stretched-out sports car windows and likely cost him as much as dinner for six in Kansas City. Conservatism applies to utility out here, like his sound-but-rusty stock trailers across the blacktop that more than likely took him and his grandkids to trail rides. There was probably a $45,000 pickup backed out of the sun somewhere.

I answered his questions. I left three days ago to ride my horse alone through Kansas and Missouri. I have everything I need. No, I'm not worried about somebody hurting me on my trip. I needed to get down and dirty and see my country. We gabbed nonstop for fifteen minutes.

"Do what is in your heart to do," he said, "and you'll be . . ." What? What did he say? I'm a writer; how could I not have said, "Excuse me, I have to write down what you just said," and stepped to my pommel bag for my pad and pen? My later notes say, "He could have been a Unity minister."

You walk up to a stranger and say you're doing what you've wanted to do since you were a little girl, and conversation leaps not to what makes the car payments, but to what brings tears to your eyes. That doesn't often happen with people you know. He and I had nothing to guard. We might never see each other again.

I could see his intelligence well enough through those orange glasses, so I paid no mind to his remark about not having a lot of schooling, because I already could tell he probably was better read than me. Lord knows, I've made such apologies since I gave up hope of finishing college in my twenties, then in my thirties, then again in my forties for different reasons. We know we're smart, he and I, but we have nothing to prove it. What we do have, we can't seem to admit.

"I can't believe in evolution," he said. "Look around here."

We both looked around—toward the greening furrows that led in the distance to a bumper of newly leafed hedge, oak, and locust trees mingling their limbs. We stood in silence at the five kinds of herbs my horse snatched and chewed.

"If the big bang is true, then all this perfection and order is just an accident," he said.

"I know what you mean."

I did. Of course, I believed in natural selection. There also seemed to have to be a God, one way or another; though in truth, I think my atheist friends are smarter than I am. Maybe they would not think of me as an idiot if they could feel this presence—capital P—that I feel.

The corners of his mouth jerked down. He flicked both cheekbones under his sunglasses with the tip of his index finger. I pretended not to notice his tears.

In the thirty years I lived in the country, I never felt threatened by my dear friends and neighbors who thought there was only one way to interpret the Bible, and that my way was wrong and lethal. The worst that could happen was they'd pray for me and feel sorry I was going to hell.

The girls at the Christian Church in Hume, Missouri, where I attended high school, had never known a Lutheran before meeting me, but they knew one thing: I had not been properly dunked. Nor had I come "straight way up out of the water." I hadn't made a *decision*. I'd been given cheap grace by my church, so after trying to get me to come to their church and be saved, they invited me to a revival at Missouri Southern State University in Joplin, Missouri. I was sixteen. This was the culmination of months of prayer and discussion among them on my behalf. The dark auditorium and the music, my best friends straining toward the lights on the stage, and the call to action, lifted and carried me forward, a spirit, out of my reasoning mind to become a silent observer, above. I floated toward the stage and hovered.

I had learned to hover that way as a girl, when what was expected fell so far out of line with reason that I could do nothing else. This happened often in the home of my father, who suffered post-traumatic stress disorder from the Great Depression and having been a prisoner of war in World War II, and from being, according to some, a jerk from birth. There is not space here to explore the nature of a father who had never known security but tried to provide it for his own family in a way that seemed as if he were left-handed and all the tools given him were right-handed. I learned to hover when my father lost his temper and Mother smiled at me behind his back, "Nothing's wrong with Daddy. Don't you say there is."

I registered, and floated, in silence.

At the revival, I was given a cotton gown and dressed behind the stage curtains. I was led forward in a line of other teenagers. We approached a small pool that reminded me of a feed lot's concrete dipping trench full of liquid pesticide that cattle are run through to kill lice. Strangers held my hands on either side before the baptismal pool. I descended the three steps and went under where the water washed my nature, which, in the words of the Nicene Creed I learned in catechism, was sinful and unclean. At least I had that concept in common with the fundamentalists.

My friends at the revival cried for me. Once dressed, I even took the microphone and channeled something about having been Lutheran and suggesting that other people listen to what was being said here. That went out over the radio. I boarded the bus feeling like I had just given away my most precious possession—as precious as my horse, Honey. I didn't speak to anyone all the way home. My best friend looked out the window, bereft, when I wouldn't talk.

I had undone my religion. Three weeks later, my friend asked me, again, if I had told my parents I was saved. For the first time, I talked back to her—maybe to anyone—"No! I am so ashamed," I said. "Just leave people alone!" She draped herself over the seat back of the car I was driving and sobbed. It was never mentioned again.

I didn't hold it against her, and don't now, but I was stepping away.

Years later, at a friend's Baptist church, the minister repeated no fewer than six times, "God hates divorce!" My grown daughter put her arm around my shoulder and tilted her head into mine. I had been divorced twice.

God hates? I thought. *The Great I Am? The omniscient, omnipresent, omnipotent Love—the God-is-love, God—hates?* "People," I wanted to shout, "if we must have a god, let's not make him need anger management classes like us."

Growing up, I never viewed my fundamentalist Christian counterparts as anything but dear, regardless how they viewed me. This man on the mower was taking me back home to that time. I wanted to pull him onto my lap, wrap my arms around those broad shoulders draped with his graying hair and say, "It will be okay. Let God worry about the big bang. You and I will take care of the love."

We stood in the gradually building heat, cooled by a breeze that still smelled of morning. "What is the right-of-way like between here and Block Corners?" I asked. "That's where I'm headed, to hit as much gravel road as I can going west."

"It's not bad. A lot like this. You've got some culverts to cross along this stretch. Probably be just as easy to hop up on the road for those."

"That's a relief."

"After you turn and head west, again, on John Brown Highway, the right of way is still pretty good. You'll go through Henson. There's nothing there but an elevator and railroad tracks. I'm sure he'll have no trouble with that." He gestured at Chief. My horse made me proud, standing obediently, which he always did where two or more humans were gathered.

"He'll go through anything. He's been a little freaked since we didn't turn back for home two days ago. He's not nearly as brave by himself."

"None of them are. It's good to make them go out by themselves. You get through Henson, and you're still on John Brown Highway. In about two miles, you can cross the blacktop and ride along the bottoms. There's no fence. It hasn't rained in a while, so it shouldn't be sticky. Once you hit Block Corners, it's gravel for days."

I recognized the precision of his description as coming from one who had traveled four miles per hour on horseback. He understood the impact of terrain and distance at that speed. I was beginning to understand that he, and others like him, might keep me safe on this trip.

"You need anything?" he asked, looking my saddlebags over.

"Would you pray for me?"

"What's your name?"

"Lisa Stewart."

"What's your horse's name?"

"Chief."

"Okay."

He didn't begin to pray right then, so I knew he would do it in private.

"Be careful," he said.

I mounted up and rode the way he told me.

A Horse-loving Gene

My earliest memory was that of looking up into a closet at my yellow and pink corduroy overalls with my mother kneeling nearby. I must have been two. From that time, I had wanted a horse.

In Detroit, at age six, I gazed daily at the horse calendar ringed with photos of satiny, posed horses, their breeds printed beneath each one for me to memorize. I wanted statuettes of horses for my presents and horse stories for my books. By eight, I had wished my own horse into existence. It was true, my parents spent the money to purchase the aged mare, and yes, my father had been transferred to Aero Commander in Oklahoma City where his good friend had land to keep a horse. Wasn't it possible, though, that I had played the biggest part in the manifestation of my horse, through eight years of envisioning my arms wrapped around her neck? I saw myself as Linda Evans on *The Big Valley* television show, her tossed-back hat and thick, blond hair patting her back as she cantered her velvet mare. Might I have caused a cosmic ripple, emitted some boson particle while dreaming of brushing my future horse's flaxen tail? Honey appeared.

She was a golden palomino, dappled when sunburned, fifteen hands tall, rawboned, and earthbound. We galloped bareback with only a halter and lead rope that I looped into reins, because I was too little to lift a saddle and couldn't reach her head to bridle her.

Since the time I was in junior high, riding Honey along the blood-red, shale roads of central Oklahoma with my best friend,

Terrie Wahling—who rode her barrel horse or one of her dad's roping horses—I dreamed of riding cross-country on horseback. On day-long rides, Terrie and I braced against the Oklahoma wind that blasted over the flat plain. It whipped and tumbled and, over centuries, sculpted rounded ravines into the scaly shale. Terrie and I closed our eyes and turned our horses' butts to towers of road dust kicked up by pickups pulling trailers. We concluded our rides by tying up to Terrie's corral and entering the stillness of her father's barn. Outside, cicadas emitted deafening pulses in the trees and beyond, the horizon cut the sun in half. Inside, dust rose in the slice of light from the barn's heavy sliding door. We dusted off her notebook and sat on square bales of hay at the base of a twenty-foot stack, and we wrote a new chapter of our story about two girls who rode through Oklahoma and Kansas on horseback. In our story, we entered small towns to the amazed stares of townsfolk and storekeepers. We would be thirsty and would tie our horses' lead ropes to a barbed-wire fence behind a painted, cinderblock tavern whose two, small windows were shuttered with neon Miller, Coors, and Budweiser signs. Our horses would graze half-circle patches down to the dirt while we were inside drinking Coke and flirting.

"Let's don't drink beer," I said, as she wrote in our notebook.

"Let's make out with the boys beside the horses and then leave the boys in the dust," she said.

In the chapter Terrie and I wrote in her father's barn, our horses would brace us up in the dark, while too-old-for-us cowboys leaned in and kissed hard. My cowboy would be my favorite color combination, like the horse in pictures I drew—black hair, blue eyes. Terrie's cowboy was palomino—blond hair, brown eyes. I would be afraid of mine and make tittering excuses to pull away from him. Later, Terrie and I would giggle to each other as our horses gradually carried us beyond the reach of the town's outermost mercury vapor light, where our horses' tails vanished into the night. Chapter's end.

The First Morning—Woman at the Well

Chief and I were three hours from his home pasture, everything about us still back there, when I saw the pickup slow, then stop, on the far side of a concrete bridge an eighth of a mile ahead. I thought the driver was stopping to let me pass—and so far in advance. It would take me minutes to get there. This seemed overly thoughtful, especially after what just happened—I had asked for my first bucket of water from a stranger.

Only half an hour earlier, we had crept up the gravel driveway of a spacious, split-level home on a rise, behind which I could see the tops of neat metal buildings and loafing sheds. It was May 16, 2012. We were in north-central Miami County, Kansas, on Crescent Hill Township Road. I worried this noon that everyone would be at work. I wouldn't take water from someone's hydrant without asking. I didn't even know if Chief was thirsty. How many hours in the sun and at what temperatures would we have to ride before he would be thirsty enough to drink? I should know that. If they are home, what will I say, and what will they say?

Chief used his neck like a periscope. Each jittery leg tested the driveway like pond ice. He dipped his head and pointed an eye at large rocks around a flower bed. I thought I would say, *Hi, I'm riding cross-country, and I was wondering if I might have a bucket of water for my horse.* Then someone would ask, how long have you been gone? *Since this morning?*

We peeked behind the house, and there by the barn near a drain-back faucet was a woman my age, back turned to me, spraying off her horse with a garden hose, while her other horses casually observed from nearby lots. Her horse jerked up its head, then so did she. I made a big circle with my hand. "Hi."

Seventy-two hours before, I had left my lawyer's office after signing my first will, power of attorney, and living will. I expected to be gone at most three months, or three weeks, or if I failed, three days. Afterward, I had climbed into my husband's pickup feeling embarrassed by a certain raised eyebrow from my advisor who had tilted her head at the danger into which I surely was riding, alone. What was I doing?

My own twenty-year-old daughter had become silent when I told her I wanted to take the cross-country trip I had dreamed about as a girl. We stood in her upstairs apartment in a 1920s two-story, wood-frame home two blocks from the University of Missouri-Kansas City campus. Natalie was doing everything I wish I could have done: She had begun college, worked, supported herself and chose not to live with her boyfriend of two years. I came to her now, having saved enough money for my trip, but having released what I call "money-making writing"—my freelance business—to focus on preparing for a trip that might last all summer. "Your dad and I never had a moment's trouble with people on our trip," I'd tried to reassure her.

"That was thirty years ago," she'd said. "Things are different now. You had a man with you then." She was referring to the three thousand mile horseback trek I took with her father when I was twenty-two, which took us through seven states and four mountain ranges in the Rockies and Midwest. I had done this before, but not alone.

The truth was I didn't know if I would be safe. One phrase was repeated almost spontaneously from so many mouths before my trip you'd think the entire population of Kansas City had been rounded up to practice it: "Be careful; there are a lot of crazies out there." It was a mantra—sad and discouraging to me—that I didn't want to believe. I chose a new one, gleaned from the 2012 presidential campaign in which Missouri's congressman Emanuel

Cleaver II said at his party's convention, "Hope on, Mr. President. Hope on!" I wanted to *hope on*.

The second most common phrase I heard from friends and acquaintances was, "You gonna be packin'?"

Despite my previous 225 days of accident-free riding with Len Brown, the father of my children, in 1982, I fought to go to sleep every night the month leading up to this trip. Two scenes played over and over in my head when I went to bed: Chief shying in front of a car (with me aboard) and camping on some nice family's property when their drunk uncle sneaks in and assaults me in my tent.

Now, I am remarried, having just disappeared from my husband over the horizon, with no idea where I would wind up. I had to "hope on." Bob had gotten into our car with our dog, Sparky, and driven the opposite direction from which I was disappearing. He felt struck with confusion, he later confessed. He hadn't anticipated the shock of abandoning his wife to what seemed imminent danger. In his as-needed support position, he later said he clung to the belief that I knew what I was doing.

How could it be that at the first place I felt compelled to ask for water at midday on a Wednesday, there would stand a horsewoman my own age, holding a running garden hose next to her dripping horse?

I felt for this woman, turning to the spectacle of me in my huge, round-brimmed straw hat, black riding tights, worn, English riding boots and spurs, white shirt and red scarf. If that weren't enough, I was leading a horse wearing a mountain of packs, whose eyes were rimmed in white and whose neck was a map of capillaries engorged with blood.

"How cool!" she said. "I wish I could come with you."

"Really?"

I don't remember a word of our conversation, only that soon we were giggling like girls about our horses. Meanwhile, they swung and tried to get their noses together. The water ran around our feet until she clamped down the handle.

I didn't even know enough to get her name.

The woman at the well saved me with her admiration that day and with something else, more precious than water. It came in the form of four words.

"He's a thinking horse," she observed. Chief craned his neck at the other horses, her tractor, her plate-glass patio door, the equipment surrounding this gravel drive. He sparkled like a copper shell casing under the mid-May sun. A thinking horse.

To me, Chief was the equine version of a twitchy explosives specialist.

He was trying to comprehend a world.

We both were.

A half-hour later, Chief and I approached the pickup, which had stopped on the other side of the concrete bridge on the ecru-colored dirt road a few miles from the woman with the water. By now, I realized he had seen me but showed little interest. He was taking things out of the back of his truck. I heard him pull a commercial weed eater that snored several times before emitting a loud AAHHHhhh that soon rose and fell with the density of weeds he was cutting. He glanced from under his cap periodically to gauge our approach. I had both hands on the reins on a horse that felt like every step could launch a leap.

In the center of the groomed grass, ten miles any direction from the nearest town, on a road that hadn't been swept by a car or truck in more than an hour, this man in his late fifties, wearing a polo shirt, basketball shoes, and a KU hat, with a dusty new Ford F-250 holding its ground, opened up breathing space for a white wooden cross stapled with faded silk flowers. Hardly looking up, he cut the motor. Chief's neck was high and short, and he positioned every step to spring away from the truck if need be.

"Hi."

"Hi."

I was too shy to say, *To whom does this cross belong? How long ago?* He would have told me the story. I knew from my previous trip that people would tell us the most personal things—something about a stranger on a horse. Later, on this trip, four men would weep when they told me about someone they loved. This man might have been the first, if I had been brave enough to ask him. Only men wept. Never women.

Chief and I rode farther and farther away from the oversized, bricked, rocked homes on barren plots scraped of their history on this southwest apron of metropolitan Kansas City—close enough for privileged people to commute. We rode away from Johnson County, one of the richest counties in America, with the fifth greatest number of horses per capita. We rode deeper into pastures owned by ER doctors, city lawyers, and jokester farmers who amuse themselves with collections of exotic cows. We became a satellite speck on a straight, white path between hay fields and rows of young beans, prepubescent corn that hadn't grown its parts, much less its silks, and milo just greening up its rows. The houses grew farther apart, and many seemed to have settled their bones into elderly windbreaks as if they'd all been seeded and grown up together. These homesteads had more than one generation of farm implements positioned where they could be hooked onto and pulled to the field. This was given to me to witness, my first day. Out here a father or a grandfather weedeats around a wooden cross that only the immediate family and the closest neighbors will ever see—and who sees it isn't the point, anyway, only that the abrupt place on the ditch looks like somebody cares what happens out here.

The First Night—Women and Saddles

My biggest fear on this trip—besides getting hit by a car—was whether we would find water and a safe camp at night. By midafternoon our first day, we had ridden twelve miles from Chief's pasture near Edgerton, Kansas, thirty miles southwest of Kansas City. Far enough. Chief had tried to turn into every drive and crossroad, gesturing that now we should turn back for home—now—and surely now. He had refused water all day.

The sun lowered itself in the sky as if to get a better look at us. We came to a two-story, wood-frame farmhouse, straight as a soldier, and no landscaping, except decades-old forsythia and lilac so tall they seemed to consider the house their landscaping, rather than the other way around. I dismounted and knocked on the back door. In moments, a fair-skinned woman, whose few gray hairs mingled seamlessly with her Scandinavian blond, opened the door. She was my age, like the woman at the well.

"I'm riding cross country around Kansas and Missouri, and I have no idea if it would work for you, or if you know someone it would work for . . ." I'd prepared an elevator pitch for every job I ever had but this one.

"Sure. You can camp; how about back here?" She motioned to the lawn behind her house.

"Thank you so much. I'm Lisa Stewart."

"Andrea." She extended her hand, and I took it with my sweaty glove. She started walking in the ground-covering stride we country girls learn from youth to keep up with mothers and fathers over rough pastures. Andrea's hens scampered about her backyard in tan and black plumes, and she sang an air to them as she swung along, "Hello, girls, how are you, ladies!"

We led Chief to lush lawn at her back fence, where I would unload my bedroom, closet, and kitchen.

Andrea invited Chief to slumber his first night out with her four angus cows and calves, whose circling flies gave them a combined atomic weight of more than five hundred. Their three-acre pasture west of her house was ringed by dense woods, which I knew would keep Chief sleepless all night, on guard for what only he knew might emerge in the dark.

This elderly Kansas homestead was set back off the road just enough not to catch too much dust from the occasional passing car and truck. Three large trees shaded the scene like towering thugs within this alley of tornados. All this was partitioned off from pastures silky with fescue in the afternoon light. The place was proportioned to cinematic beauty, bordering on cliché. We forget. Homesteaders often were gifted architectural designers, without the papers to prove it. I explained where I was from, that I was a writer, that I'd wanted to do this since I was a little girl, and that at my age, I better do it while I still can.

"That—is—for—sure," Andrea said.

She showed me a drain-back faucet poking up from the ground near her wellhouse, and she bent over and unspooled a garden hose.

"I'd better get back to my centerpieces," she said. "My daughter's getting married in two days."

That was the first hint she gave that I had interrupted a major production with a tight timeline, which I would learn included floating silk flowers in dozens of mason jars of pink-tinted water.

When she left, I returned to the pile of my life in the grass. I became still for the first time all day, maybe for years. What to do first, second, and third? I hadn't horse-camped in thirty years.

A routine emerged like tail lights in fog: First, spray Chief clean with the garden hose; second, hide behind the barn and bathe from our collapsible bucket and change into t-shirt, shorts, and sandals;

third, wash my riding clothes; fourth, massage fly repellent into every inch of Chief's coat; and fifth, set up camp and eat.

The nylon saddlebags in the grass looked like overstuffed couch pillows. When installed, the top pack rose behind my saddle so high, I had to kick like a ballerina to clear it. The side compartments draped behind my legs down Chief's flanks.

The top pack contained light things, like the cylinder of my one-man tent, blow-up sleeping pad, silk mummy bag, extra set of riding clothes, red silk pajamas, seven silk panties—each embroidered with the day of the week (donated by Mary Green Lingerie, thank you), shorts, and sandals.

The side compartments contained a gallon Ziploc bag of Nutrena Empower Boost supplement for Chief. In another gallon bag were nuts, seeds, jerky, packets of tuna and salmon, and Kind nut bars for me. A third Ziploc contained toiletries and ophthalmic ointment for Chief. Sealed in a waterproof envelope were signed documents from my veterinarian, proving Chief tested negative for equine infectious anemia and noting his recent vaccinations. The saddlebags also contained bootlace for repairs, a collapsible bowl, a Goal Zero solar charger, which I would use to charge my phone, and The SPOT Personal Tracker—a satellite GPS that could provide location-based communication to family, though I hadn't yet figured out how to use it.

I'd brought a feedbag for Chief, my bottle of biodegradable soap, a five-inch bowie-style knife with serrations along its spine, a spare four-inch-by-eight-inch spiral steno pad, spare giant plastic garbage sacks and Ziploc bags, and a gallon bag with an inch-thick pile of baby wipes, not to mention miscellaneous items that at the end of my first day I soon would have scattered in the grass, while looking for the one thing I actually needed. Small side pockets held hairbands, sun block, my all-purpose tea towel (used for washing myself, Chief, and my fork) and Chief's special treats: individually wrapped prunes, his favorite.

Strapped around my thigh was a flip phone in a holster (so it would be attached to me and not in a saddlebag in the event Chief decided to divorce me), and in my bra was a brand new iPhone, which my stable owner had urged me to keep against my skin. That morning, as I was loading up to leave, my pasture landlord, Mary, spoke to me over her arm through the window of her pickup. "You won't be able to hear an AccuWeather tornado warning when you're riding in the wind. You want it against your skin so you can feel it vibrate." So I put it in my bra. Then she told me about a lady she knew who got hit by a car and killed on a trip like this.

That evening I sat alone inside my tent on another woman's land, unmoored on a becalmed prairie, without a barometer or telescope. I called my best friend, Tatiana, in Nevada, Missouri. She was the only person I wanted to speak with that first night of my trip—not even my husband. Tanya sounded surprised to hear my voice. She had forgotten I was leaving on my trip that day.

None of my friends were thinking about me. They would see me again weeks after I returned and comment, perhaps, "Oh that's right! How did your trip go?" I decided that tonight and every night, I would zip my tent and pray alone, and record in my notebook gifts too intimate to share: a cross in a ditch, a bucket of water, and a three-acre pasture for Chief.

The world turned its back to the sun so slowly I began to realize no amount of straining my eyes would help me find my headlamp in the jumble of bags and boots inside my tent. I felt for the items that I had removed from my pommel bag earlier. The pommel bag would remain tied to my saddle. Its two sections held my most immediate needs: extra baby wipes, pen, headlamp, reading glasses, this week's map, coin purse with ID and credit card, snacks, notebook, and my twenty-seven-year-old son's Ruger .38 caliber handgun, which he insisted I carry. These things I had tossed into the tent earlier, and now I felt for my headlamp in the dark. I squirmed into my silk pajamas and clean socks, blew up the small, heat-reflective sleeping pad, and began arranging the mound of bags and boots that filled my tent.

I scooted and shifted up and down, side to side, until the lumps in the turf corresponded with muscle, not bone. There was no barrier between me and night birds. I pulled on my silk eye mask and squeezed foam plugs into my ears. An hour later I awoke in pain from a rock under my hip, and the cold, and turned and pulled on my riding tights. Sometime later, I awoke and dragged my saddle-bags under my knees and lay on my back to relieve my hips and shoulders. I pulled on my sweatshirt and windbreaker. Later, I awoke to pee in the wet grass behind the wellhouse, which shaded me from the yard light. I dragged into my tent the dew-damp rain poncho that I'd used for a doormat outside the tent and curled under it. I awoke and found my top pack and pulled out my extra clothes for a pillow and dozed, shivering, until just before dawn.

I was stuffing away my tent at 6:00 AM when Andrea came out and proclaimed I would share breakfast potatoes and eggs with her and her mother.

I entered her home through the back mud porch—for friends and family. Andrea had replaced ancient cabinets with walnut modern cousins, which by now were twenty years old and sur-rounded two sides of the square fifteen-foot-by-fifteen-foot room. Her counters were arranged not with decorative lanterns or ceramic pineapples, but with the implements of cooking and canning and freezing and office work in a farmhouse of the vintage before there were closets. I had walked past the chest-style deep freeze on the back porch, like mother's had been on our own back porch, full of beef I had helped calve and vaccinate and castrate.

I felt snugged at Andrea's table, the nerve center of this single-woman's farm. Another woman, showing me the way. Andrea's thin mother sat across the table from me. She had freshly dyed black hair through which I could see her scalp all around. She had little to show for eyebrows and a fair, unlined face punctuated by red lips that either she or Andrea had painted. Her brown eyes looked bright with the mystery of her world, which she seemed to be observing for the first time. In other moments, she regarded her daughter with familiar dominion. "Mother is staying with me now. She has cancer, and she needs to be here for a little while." Andrea glanced to my eyes with a look that said, *for the rest of her while*, and said in the same breath, "I would certainly love to do what you're doing. I've always had horses."

"You're lucky to have this property," I said. "I always say I traded seventy-five acres for 75th Street when I moved from Nevada, Missouri, to Kansas City for a job. I miss having land."

She raised her eyebrows as if I clearly had forgotten what *that* was like. "I had a manufacturing operations management job near Paola," she said. "I got laid off five years ago in '07."

"I'm sorry," I said.

"Thanks. I'm one of many. Fortunately, I'd already restored and paid for this place. I've had to sell all my horses, though. I make a little from the cattle—and we have the beef. I'm doing contract office work and bookkeeping around the county," she said. "It's not where I expected to be."

Five years after the Great Recession, rural Miami County, Kansas, had not begun to bounce back, or slink back—nor was it likely to.

After we ate, my host led me into her small living room, which contained an overstuffed, suede sofa, recliner, and a wood stove. She wanted to show me her saddle. In the corner of the room sat a custom western saddle on a polished, wood stand.

"I'm sorry for the dust," she said.

I touched her arm. "It isn't as if you'd expected me."

Her name was engraved across the Cheyenne roll of the saddle—the leather binding that topped the back of the seat. Deeply carved oak leaves trailed down its fenders. The leaves had been worn shallow by her calves. The suede seat had been burnished in a V by her seat bones and thighs. She crossed her arms and tilted her head, a finger over her mouth, as did I. We might have been praying.

In the weeks before leaving on my trip, I had kept my own Ortho-Flex #002 Paso Royal saddle on a polished stand in our small living room, just like Andrea Miller's. She and I would glance at them from our kitchens as if they were babies that might at any moment roll over for the first time.

"It's beautiful," I said.

"It fit me like a glove," she said. Past tense.

Outside, I finished saddling and loading Chief. The farmland stretched away to the horizons. The sky had opened its doors—a soup kitchen of light. I filled my canteen from the hydrant in front of Andrea's house, half-full so it wouldn't pull my saddle off center. I stood on Chief's left side, known to horsemen as the "near side," from which one typically mounts. I gathered his reins and lifted my foot to waist height to gain a toehold on the stirrup. Andrea watched to see whether Chief was well-trained—would stand still for me to mount. He rocked, forward and back. I lowered my foot, slid his reins through my left hand to tighten them. I grasped mane and reins, barely able to reach his wither while I raised my left foot again.

"Stand," I said. If Chief could have rolled his eyes, he would. Instead, he started walking. I hopped on one foot. He swung to get out of there, away from Andrea's disgusting Angus cows, away from the woods where he'd spent the night. Get out of there, to find a reasonable person with a horse trailer to take him home, or to fly back up the road to his pasture. *Move,* he said, *let's move; I'll run all the way home.*

I swung my right leg up and over the top pack, fished for my off-side stirrup while he took his first steps, butt-tucked, suppressing a twelve-mile dash. I forgave him this dangerous act, because of what I had put him through on his first day and night, because he knew what to do, and because, as with any kid, you pick your battles for a time and place where you know you can win. At our first crossroad, Chief forced me to tell him three times to turn south, away from his pasture, instead of north. Giving and taking with reins, squeezing legs, step by step, I insisted we would not go home, which confused and revved him, lacking a herd, or a bond with the woman in charge.

My fellow horsewoman didn't tell me to be careful as I rode away. Good horsewomen don't do that. They know it's a risk every time you mount up, regardless how far you're going.

The Wreck

Chief and I rode away from Andrea's house so expanded by our first night's good fortune and the question of whether we ever would find such a generous camp again on this trip, we could have popped with the slightest prick.

We toured farmland whose black soil had been groomed in straight lines by planters pulled by tractors as tall as my house, and pastureland converting its air and light to cellulose fit for king and queen cattle. Our roads for today—as represented by thin, red lines on pages torn from the *Kansas Atlas & Gazetteer*—led us plumb-line straight east and south, plotted in the late 1800s to scribe 640-acre sections of land.

Though stereotypically thought of as flat, Kansas's eastern edge tricks travelers with its plateaus, hills, deep valleys, and rivers. Chief and I crunched along a stretch of flat gravel road under the massive blue compass of a sky. The wind acted coy for Kansas, and little by little my horse's suspension relaxed; his head lowered, and his ears slackened a degree.

I cleared my throat. Chief pounced to a stop, which convulsed my heart. "It's just me, for God's sake!" Chief took a breath, swallowed, and continued.

By 1:00 that afternoon, we came abreast an assortment of Brahman-mix cattle, some with horns, others with long, lax ears and leather collars hanging beneath their necks, arranged under the shade of two Civil-War-era trees. They lounged about one hundred feet from the fence beside our road.

A bull rose from the shade and began looking hard at Chief. I learned in that moment that stern eye contact from a horned bovine was all Chief required to issue a lightning-quick, 180-degree spin, followed by two great leaps, the third of which, if it came, I thought might produce a mad runaway. In my fantasy, this always ends in a collision with a school bus or five-strand, barbed-wire fence. The one-eighty didn't loosen my seat, but the two great leaps did, and I lost my near-side stirrup before catching Chief up by the bit and regaining my stirrup. He swung to face the bull in the pasture one hundred feet away.

I thought I had Chief settled and I could swing off and lead him to the fence to start "desensitizing" him to horned cattle. (More on the idiocy of that idea later.) The moment I started to dismount, the bull rushed the fence and shook its horns at Chief, whereupon Chief spun again and leapt at the exact moment I swung my leg to get off, and—let the record show—I was unable to reverse my *intentional* dismount. It was like trying to get off the space shuttle.

It seems impossible that the mind could consider such a thing at such a moment, and yet I noted with detachment how hard a gravel road is—I felt like I'd been hit by a car. I tumbled length-wise and slid on both elbows through the limestone rock for several feet until I came to a stop. Involuntary, palliative grunts and pants did their job and eventually stopped.

Through my gathering and drifting dust, I could see Chief standing a quarter of a mile away at an intersection with another gravel road. Chief faced me, head lowered and ears forward, as if he'd scampered off after having given birth and just turned back to look at it. Good boy, I thought, he's scared and needs reassurance; he'll hold still as I walk toward him. The moment I stood, Chief swapped ends and took up a strong trot in the opposite direction.

At this stunning moment, when I was abandoned by my horse—who, unlike Spielberg's War Horse, will not have a movie made about his devotion to his master—I knew I was alone. We were not a team. If we were to survive this trip, only my will be done.

I was astounded to find that my only injury, besides bruised hips, was chewed forearms. I limped east along West 319 Road, gaining speed, regaining my gait, my sleeves now drenched and growing cold from my blood, a clear view of Chief trotting toward his far-off home pasture over the farthest hill. From this physical and psychic distance, I was able to observe that his saddle and saddlebags rode perfectly centered on his back. Everything was balanced and fit. This meant something. Barring a car collision, the one factor that could end a horseback trip was saddle sores on the horse's back. From the way Chief's rig rode on him now, I knew this trip was going to work.

I fell into a long-legged walk, likely to help my bruising. I was struck by the presence of gravity. After lilting through Miami County for two days on my horse's nervous suspension, I now felt like an ant, not a warrior or explorer. Gone were my four legs. Mother Earth held me close and reminded me I was her particle. The gravel shimmied under my heels.

I trusted that Chief eventually would wear out his flight reflex and become fearful of being alone. Not that he would look to me for safety. He would enter a yard and start to graze or pause near a fence where other horses raced to greet him. He might run all the way home. I would walk, like an idiot, all the way there if I had to. I would catch him, and I wouldn't tell anyone but my husband. I would turn Chief around and point him away from home again.

Without slowing my pace, I dialed Bob from the phone in my holster. I knew he would be leaving his office in a couple of hours to come check on me this second day. That was our agreement. He would come to me wherever I was on the second and fourth days. Then he would find me roughly once a week, if he could, to bring me supplies. I would have him take back the bowl and plate, the satellite locator, the mascara and eyeliner and lipstick, and anything else I could jettison. He would bring full-strength DEET for Chief.

"I've lost Chief," I said into the phone.

"Oh."

The way Bob said "oh" told me he thought losing a horse might be like losing a dog. You might never find it.

"He'll be up here somewhere. I'm walking. I had a wreck."

In the horse world, the term wreck is a catchall phrase that means you got dumped, or your horse got his foot caught over the rope and hurt himself or some structure, or your pack horses bolted and scattered your belongings down a mountain trail.

"Are you okay?"

"I hurt my elbows," I said. I searched the horizon for any movement in the road ahead. "I didn't break anything." I could tell my call was exploding Bob's finely calibrated series of tasks that would put him in my vicinity sometime around 5:00 PM, as planned. It now was only 1:30.

"Could you come pretty soon?"

Bob was still wrapping his mind around Chief's being lost and the search mission that might require.

"I think I need to go to the emergency room."

"Really?"

"I might need stitches."

"Oh."

"You start heading my way when you can, and I'll call you when I find Chief so you know where to go. I'm walking north on a gravel road the way he went."

"You sure you're okay?"

"It's no biggie. Don't tell anyone."

I kept walking north. A westerly wind scraped my ear. A tractor growled out of sight, except for its dust, like our neighbor discing in nearby bottoms when I was a girl, a 245-horsepower presence beyond the bluff—someone down there working—so nobody ever feels alone in the country, though there isn't a house for miles.

My crunching gait, and the wind, and the patient task of following my horse erased the words in my head and supplanted them with a continual motion that lacked any sense of body, face, name. I noticed that red-winged blackbirds both chirp and whistle as they bend the tops of woody stems. Lisa, the commercial writer, salesperson, mother, wife—was gone. I had not known it before, but I knew it now: This was why I left my home, my husband, my grown son and daughter. I wanted to see with my own eyes, and control a course with my bare hands, and learn for myself what land and people are made of. I knew what I was made of. I would take the ankle turns on roadbed rock, waves of dust from coated cars, the calculations and orientations, and every half-halt of my frightened horse with the increasing strength of my own grip.

Except, there was nothing to grip.

I heard gravel popping behind me. I moved over to the long hillock of rocks that tires spray to the edges of all such roads. The popping grew louder and slowed. A two-year-old Chevy mini-van held its coat of dust like a magnet. A sandy-haired woman in her thirties looked at me with eyes that already had assessed the oddness of my clothes, my dustiness, and her own clear responsibility.

"Do you need a ride?" she asked.

"I think I've got it."

"You sure?"

"I got separated from my horse. He's probably up here a little ways."

"I'm going that way, if you want a ride."

"If you don't mind. I'm sure he's stopped running by now."

In the van, she turned up the air conditioner, then her head jerked toward me, having seen my left sleeve drenched from elbow to cuff in blood. "You're hurt!"

"I think it's about stopped bleeding. I slid on my elbows."

She widened her eyes.

"I can bend my elbows," I said. "He got scared by a horned bull, and like an idiot, I thought I should get off and introduce them."

Within a mile, at the back of a long yard near a modular home, we spotted a young man about the age of my own twenty-five-year-old son, Derek, in the shade of another Civil-War-era tree, holding my sweat-drenched, riderless horse. The woman eased her van into the driveway.

"Are you sure you're going to be okay?" she said.

"My husband is coming. He's only a couple of hours away. Thank you so much."

The young man holding my horse, serendipitously also named Derek, had seen me riding along John Brown Highway earlier this morning. When he saw Chief trotting past just now without me, he drove out the driveway in his pickup, caught my horse, and led Chief back down the lane through the driver's side window of his truck.

"I used to take care of horses," he said.

"Sweet."

"Do you need anything?" he asked. "Food? Water?"

After two miles walking within this mass of wind and light, without a plan, without a strategy—no water, no makeup, no meetings, no transportation, bloodied and dirty—a nice lady in a van picked me up, and Derek stood holding my horse in the shade.

"I need nothing at all," I said, "except to sit down here in your shade."

ER

An hour and a half after I found my horse, Bob eased our Toyota Corolla into the drive where Chief dozed, tied to the brush guard of Derek's truck. Derek had displayed the manners of a country gentleman who wouldn't leave an injured woman to wait alone for her husband. He stood nearby as Bob and I discussed our strategy, and to watch me get back on my horse, as if the act deserved a small crowd, if not a ceremony.

According to Bob's and my agreement, he would follow me in the car while I rode to find a place to turn Chief out for the night. Bob then would take me to Miami County Medical Center in Paola, Kansas. We would eat, get a motel, and in the morning, push the reset button.

I was still trying to depart on my trip, steeling myself for it, but suspending all that for the feel of my husband's arms and the air-conditioned car, and a sensible trip for professional wound care. Bob felt hard and slim and ridiculously tall in my arms. He offered no passion, just a polite, professional embrace, as always in public. His dispassion told me he refused to insult me by questioning my judgment—even now.

I pulled up my unbuttoned sleeve and showed him my left elbow and forearm, now nearly twice their normal size and looking like a layer of hot asphalt that hadn't yet been rolled out.

Bob blinked and turned his head. Neither of us was sure what could be stitched.

Next, the litmus test for the rest of this trip—getting back on Chief. The question wasn't whether I had nerve enough. I knew the horse had a good mind ninety-eight percent of the time. Besides, how humiliating would it be to go home my second day? The litmus test was mechanical: Could I mount without touching my forearms to anything?

Chief stood obediently, and behold, both elbows cleared everything when I mounted, and the strain of gripping Chief's mane didn't much hurt. Chief and I glided out of the yard on his quick, smooth amble and back down the gravel road the way we'd been headed as if nothing had happened. After passing only two houses, we came to a brick, ranch-style home surrounded by freshly painted black-pipe corrals and red accent posts with a wrought-iron gate header declaring that this patch belonged to the Kilpatricks. I could imagine a farm wife in her sixties with buckets of paint and spray cans working over the place. Dignified-looking cattle dotted the acreage, a bovine characteristic that implied good management.

I heard a sound like thirty children blowing toy clarinets—actually guinea hens somewhere out of sight. I dismounted, and Bob parked in the drive. We approached the door, me first, while Bob stood behind, holding my horse. Mr. Kilpatrick looked over his wife's shoulder, first at me, then my horse, as the couple absorbed not just the story of my ride, but the wreck, my planned trip to the ER, and whether they could keep my horse for the night. After sweet clucks and murmurs over my bloody sleeves, Mr. Kilpatrick said, "Let me close a gate, and you can put your horse in this field north of the house. He can't get into anything out there."

The phrase "get into anything" in this world means falling into a well, tangling himself in loose wire, or reaching over a door and killing himself by eating too much grain. People in the country who have cattle invariably have had horses, if they don't now, and handle them with the fondness of pulling a favorite novel off the shelf. That's how Mr. Kilpatrick looked at Chief. Once safely behind the pasture gate, Chief strode off through luxurious grass, head down, looking for a smooth place to roll. I assured Mr. Kilpatrick I would be back in the morning to continue my ride.

"You sure you want to do that?"

"I can get on and off without touching my arms to anything," I said. "There's no reason to stop."

Within twenty minutes we were checking me into the ER. My clothes looked like I'd stumbled and fallen in an industrial bakery. I felt as suited to this chrome and white-tiled triage suite as an electrician on a ladder in a fine-dining restaurant. I had driven away from my horse as easily as from a bad job but longed to be with him now. I wasn't supposed to be in a car, with my husband, in civilization—not yet. I was supposed to be riding farther and farther away from home and looking for a second safe camp, if there were any more to be had. My good luck could be coming all at the beginning, I thought, like Andrea Miller last night, the lady in the van today, then Derek, followed by the Kilpatricks, only two doors down.

A male nurse, whose name tag read "Jeremy RN," poked his head in, and he immediately looked relieved to see me sitting up in bed and talking to my husband. Jeremy would have looked more at home on a Kansas City Chiefs defensive line than wearing royal blue scrubs. He inspected my left arm and returned with a pan of water, bandaging, and a sponge. He sat beside me and held my arm gently and apologized over every stick and rock he scrubbed from the wound.

I focused on my breathing and waited for the Tylenol #3 to take effect. "After I have it cleaned up so the doctor can see what he's dealing with, he'll be in. Were you trail riding?"

"I just started a ride around Missouri. I'm camping along the way."

"So, you didn't come in off on one of the trails around here?"

"I'm road riding."

"How long are you planning to be gone?"

"Two days from the looks of it!"

He glanced up at me.

"I'm just kidding. Unless the doctor has some reason not to, I'm going to keep going. The most I would want to be gone is three months, but I'll settle for less. Just not two days!"

Jeremy grinned and glanced toward the door. "This doctor does not like horses."

I knew what he meant. My daughter's godmother was an RN, and her godfather a physician who routinely worked the ER in our hometown hospital in Nevada, Missouri. He and his colleagues generally hated motorcycles, trampolines, and horses.

"Injured riders come in off the trails nearly every day," Jeremy said. "The doctor says they always say the same thing: It wasn't the horse's fault. It was something the rider did wrong." Jeremy chuckled. "He just has to leave the room."

"Well, don't tell him, but I figure if you get hurt riding, it's your fault for getting on a thousand-pound creature that's scared of anything it hasn't seen before. I've always said, if a sport requires a helmet, you probably shouldn't do it."

"I would agree with that," Jeremy said. "You gotta live, through."

"Nothing bad enough ever happened to make me stop riding horses," I said. "But I don't ride motorcycles anymore, after my former husband wrecked his. So there you go."

When the doctor came in, he hardly made eye contact with me. He rolled a stool close and inspected my left arm. The doctor had me bend my elbows, grip with my hands, and agreed I didn't need X-rays. My right arm needed only a few bandages, despite its swelling. He wasn't sure what he was going to do with the frayed flesh of my elbow. By now, I already had explained I was riding long distance, alone.

"I've never had stitches in my life," I said.

"Well, you're getting them now."

"I've actually never gotten hurt on a horse."

"First time for everything."

I knew better than to say what was going through my head—
that if I hadn't tried to get off Chief when I did, none of this would
have happened.

When the injected anesthetic had numbed the wound, the
doctor began sewing.

"I was surprised it didn't hurt much to mount again," I said.

The doctor glanced up at my husband. Bob kept silent and
serious.

"My elbows don't touch anything when I mount, believe it or
not."

"You'll have to change this bandaging every other day. Keep it
clean."

"At least it's my left arm. I can wash it with my right hand."

"You'll need help bandaging it. The stitches need to come out in
ten days."

I didn't voice my next question—will a rural convenience store
have tweezers?

"So, is there any reason I shouldn't keep riding, since it doesn't
contact the horse?"

"You don't need to bang this again. Go home and rest up. Let
this heal."

We ate that evening at Paola's We B Smokin' Barbecue restaurant
that occupies a converted building at the town's airport. President
Barak Obama dined there the year before, having descended in one
of two Black Hawk helicopters—the second a decoy. After dark,
Bob and I pulled up to the Paola Inn and Suites, a new, two-story
hotel on the west edge of town. I walked into the hotel barefoot,
carrying my boots and all my belongings in a three-part saddlebag
over my better arm. The Tylenol #3 was wearing off, and my arm
throbbed, and I felt hung over. I fell asleep with my back tucked
into my husband's front, under a down duvet. I saw Chief
becoming dewy, alone in the dark.

CHIEF

I bought Chief from a horseman I'd trust with my life, Rick Bousfield. He had been one of the best saddle makers and salesmen in Ortho-Flex Saddle Company, which my husband and I founded. Rick now owned Huckleberry Stables in the southwest Missouri Huckleberry Ridge State Forest, and he was the first person I called when I knew I had to take this trip. "He's harder than a pine knot," Rick had said of Chief. "You can't wear this horse out."

Rick also remarked that Chief had been used for cowboy shooting competitions, until it looked like they were starting to screw up his otherwise good mind with all the running around an arena, shooting out balloons with slugless black powder rifles and pistols.

Rick had bought Chief as a three-year-old and raised him on the rocky, tree-covered Ozark mountainsides, with deer gliding through his pasture, log trucks grinding up the grade, sleet pelting, lightening knocking out transformers, and blankets of wet heat in the wiggle-waggle shade of summer. I drove three hours south from Kansas City to the Ozarks to test-ride Chief two months before we left.

Chief was red all over but for two short, white stockings on the back and a few white hairs in the middle of his forehead. His hooves were in perfect shape, and he let me catch him in the pasture. He was at least two inches shorter than most of the tall, leggy, gaited horses I had ridden over the years, and I liked this a lot, because I am only five-feet-two. I hesitated at his eyes at first. They weren't warm. Chief was all business, ready for work, and he wasn't used to, nor did he require, some woman hanging around his neck. All this was good, given what I was about to ask him to do.

"Don't grain him," Rick cautioned me three times. That meant he was hot enough on hay. "The only thing he ever did," Rick said, "was one time he pulled away from me and ran off a hundred yards when he saw a bull with horns. But then, we'd ride in the Bandera, Texas, parades. I could practically ride him up the back of a fire engine with its sirens going."

Chief is a grandson of Missouri Traveler E, one of the most famous, gaited Missouri Fox Trotting show-horse lines ever to stand at stud. Gaited horses have an ancient gene mutation that causes their medium-speed gait to be broken—instead of the bouncy, two-beat trot—making the broken gait smooth to sit. Traveler E was line bred for show. As the saying goes, if it works, it's called "line breeding." If it doesn't work (meaning the horse turns out nutso), it's called "inbreeding." Missouri Traveler E was line bred, and his progeny sometimes had quirks. When you're on a thousand-pound horse, riding cross country, a quirk is not what you want. I bought him for $2,500.

Bob and I hauled Chief in a rented stock trailer from Rick's place to Classic Tango Stables, near Edgerton, Kansas, under a thunderous front. There, I would stable Chief two months before the trip. When we arrived at Classic Tango, I stepped into the trailer beside Chief to untie his lead and encourage him to back out of the trailer. He was sweat-wet from nerves. Chief pointed his right back toe toward the ground and bunched his left haunch to lower himself, touching down tentatively, one foot at a time. Despite his thick winter coat and hay belly, Chief looked regal, defiant, and in possession of some ancient intelligence—a sensible mistrust.

When he cleared the trailer, he blasted the air like an elk. He sucked a long rattle, pulling in the wrong tree pollen, wrong grass, too many horse smells from the big barn, all made more intense by the lightning-ionized rain that was draining away down the drive and dripping from everything.

This wasn't the same horse I rode with Rick. This one, at the end of my lead, had an edge.

I pushed him away from me and started walking him smartly toward a stall in the barn where he would stay one night before I turned him out in a pasture. *Pay attention to me, Bud.* I would not learn until morning that he never in his life had been in a box stall in the interior of a closed barn, and that the sweat would pour off him all night long. He wouldn't kick or whinny or chew the wood like a stable horse driven to psychosis. He would stand alone in the dark, lightning flashing through the skylights above, negative ions lighting his heart, his mouth too dry to eat the hay.

Early the next morning, I stepped inside his stall and slid the door almost closed behind me. His ears pointed back, not flat or angry, just: *Who are you, and why are you nervous? Should I be nervous?* He didn't face me, but he did not turn his rear to me. With his new halter over my shoulder, I bent at the waist slightly, hands clasped in front of me, and spoke quietly. In a moment, I reached into my pocket and pulled out a carrot. His eyes watered and his ears swiveled forward. I cracked the carrot in two, as Rick had cracked a carrot for him after Chief had loaded politely into the trailer. I usually just let my horses bite off what they want, but I wanted to do one thing that was familiar to Chief—crack the carrot. He stretched his lips for it.

The pieces of a seasoned, working horse were there, but they were sprung apart with mental shrieks and boogiemen, and a dangling chainsaw or two, after being ripped from his home. I led him out across the driveway and through a pipe gate into a two-acre field where I planned to keep Chief on the lead and brush him while he grazed. His breath rattled long and loud. He took frantic bites and walked away from me. Tall grass soaked our legs, and fog obscured the source of a scent that tugged him toward it. I knew there were goats hidden in the fog one pasture over, but he could not categorize the scent—therefore it was a threat. I pulled him up and made him eat beside me in his hard, red body, arched neck, straight back, gently sloped croup, and that blocky engine of a rump. Chief's neck flowed straight up out of his chest, rather than at an angle in front of him, allowing him easily to raise his head. Not so good for roping, but very good for being able to lighten his forehand, round his topline, and travel with less stress to his forelegs. The heavy bone of Chief's lower forelegs (cannons) and large feet were as tough as the Osage orange wood that has held down this part of Kansas since someone during the Dust Bowl got the bright idea to quilt the land with squares of those indestructible trees. Chief wasn't warm; he was hot. Not a trickster or spoiled, but tough, and every nerve a live wire. Already, I was falling into mature love with him; not the infatuation of attraction, but a conscious choice, because for this trip, he had the right size, right bone, right hooves, and the right references.

To the Core

At 8:00 AM, the morning after our wreck, I stood beside my saddled and loaded horse on the gravel road where Chief and I had inelegantly parted ways. United-friendly skies stretched over the lukewarm plain that seemed purposely to deliver a soothing breeze.

I had asked Bob if he would help me get past the field of horned cattle before he returned to Kansas City. I would lead Chief on foot while Bob drove between us and the herd. This was a humiliation. Many horsemen would spank a horse if it wouldn't go exactly where pointed, or they would get off and literally back up the horse as fast as it would go a few hundred feet until it was too tired and scared of the person to look for a cow over a fence. I already knew Chief wasn't the kind of horse you could smack around, and I didn't want to make a point with him right then. I wanted to walk safely past the place of my trauma and into new territory where I could call on my old reserves of confidence to manage a different set of scary obstacles.

On this road, Chief stood rock still, eyes huge, and by the ridges in his cheeks, I could tell he was clenching his teeth, all of which meant his mind was nearly blown. A blown mind in a horse can result in a sudden crouch, then a spin or dash that lasts the length of an adrenalin dump, approximately one hundred yards. Think autistic meltdown: when too many sights and sounds and textures get crammed into too few filing cabinets in the brain. That's what

happened yesterday. If I didn't push him too hard today, it
shouldn't come to that again.

Today, better I lose my self-respect by leading him than act the
tough guy and lose the trust of a horse whose only problem was
fear. Besides, I didn't know how much fear Chief was picking up
from my own lost nerve after landing in the ER yesterday.

Thus, we trembled together, the third day of our trip, where I'd
taken my first bad fall from any horse in forty-six years of riding. I
led Chief, while Bob drove three miles per hour beside us. Chief
began to relax and lower his head. We passed the herd. Chief didn't
seem to remember them or the wreck. The cattle were nearly out of
sight in the field.

I knew that Chief and I would soon strike the first blacktop of
our ride, which we would follow until we reached the next stretch
of peaceful, gravel roads. I dreaded the blacktop. Would there be
enough shoulder? Would Chief see something in the trees and jump
onto the asphalt and shoot his four slick shoes into the air? *Stop it,
Lisa.*

At the next gravel crossroad, Chief stood calmly for me to
mount, then walked off just as I had my seat, a bad habit to let him
get into. We would deal with that later. He held his head high, ears
tightly pricked to scoop sound. By the time we had traveled another
mile, his head began to drop. The Toyota still hummed behind us.

For no reason, I drew a deep breath and let it all out. Chief
expelled a deep breath, too, which made me smile. I remembered to
bring my shoulders back. They were crimped forward like I was
expecting a bomb. As a dressage instructor once explained, drawing
the shoulder blades together "shortens the back" and lifts and
opens the chest. *Opens my heart.* I relaxed my tight ankles. An early
teacher once took my foot from the stirrup and rotated it back and
forth, "Relax your ankle," she repeated. I had no idea it had been
tight. "The right heel is always hardest to drop," she said, "because
people have their foot on the gas pedal all day." When she loosened
my ankles, my entire body relaxed.

I let my heels sink toward the core of the earth. I imagined myself tethered there by my heels, one on either side of my horse. I saw the line of my spine flow down into magma and fuse. I mentally locked my elbows to my hips, as I had been taught. No horse could pull my hands by the reins when they were tied through the anchor of my seat to the core of the earth.

Chief and I seemed not to move at all, though the fences unspooled, and the fields scrolled past. A butterfly beat us. We walked in one place it seemed, rolling a benevolent earth beneath our feet, anchored to its heart with the cadence of our own footfall: *lub-dub, lub-dub.*

Bob quietly passed us, and in minutes, the small, white car melted into the next rise and vanished.

Sailor on Horseback

The third morning I met the man on the riding lawn mower, who had prayed for me. Since then, Chief had balked at a liquid-eyed Jersey cow with a sparkling chain around her neck, and he nearly jerked away from me when I led him across a crazy intersection of railroad tracks in Henson, with pickups blamming over the rails. Those two behavioral hiccups (or rather upchucks) notwithstanding, Chief bravely walked wherever I pointed him.

At 1:30 PM, we padded along the edge of a bottomland field, which encompassed 120 acres. A curve of tall trees clung to a distant riverbank like the ruff on a collar.

I rode light on the balls of my feet, heels down, eyes soft. (Soft eyes calm a horse.) I checked Chief with the reins just enough to hold him to a fast, smooth gait, but gave to his bit the instant he accepted my government. Imagine a sailor on a forty-two-foot ketch not quite small enough for him to handle alone. See the wind stretch his clothing, his hair; the banging lines; the constant shift of boom from tack to tack, his tying and untying, adjusting his course. A boat, or a horse, stays on course only a fraction of the time. The pilot's job is constant correction. Think how the sailor's soles follow the odd heaves of the deck, his knees and ankles loose. He becomes the center, and what the waves will do is anyone's guess.

A horse's middle swings like a pendulum, to the left when his right hind leg steps forward, and to the right when his left hind leg steps forward. My calves swung left and right with the bell of his barrel. My hands moved forward and back with each nod of his head—up when a hind leg moved forward, down when a front leg moved forward. I supported Chief's head by the bit in his mouth with constant contact—not unlike a gentleman's hand on a lady's elbow. He needed to know I was there. I became a tedious job with benefits he couldn't quit.

I didn't choose a dead-broke Quarter Horse for this trip; I chose a horse that was "forward," in equestrian lingo—could go eight hours straight and be ready for more. Like choosing a rich husband, there would be a price to pay. With my heels roped to the core of the earth, and my spine connected from heaven to hell, all I had to do was match my bottom to his top. I gigged him lightly with my spurs to keep his walk peppy and remind him to pay attention to me.

Not a moment could I relax, not on this third day, but soon, I hoped. In a few days, he would be swinging along with his head down. Our reins would be tied in a knot, and both my hands would hold my notebook as I rode and wrote. Or, I would pull out the first four pages of "The Eve of St. Agnes," by John Keats, whose 378 lines I determined to memorize on this trip. "Ah bitter chill it was! /The owl, for all his feathers, was a-cold." I wanted that cadence and rhyme of the poem in my brain to help me write more beautifully. Imagine memorizing while riding a horse! The cerebellum speaks to the frontal lobes to make the iamb not just a part of my memory but embed it in my body. Clip-*clop*, clip-*clop*, lub-*dub*, lub-*dub*, "Ah *bit*-ter *chill* it *was!*"

In a week, Chief would be calm.

For now, I was at code orange and too busy for any sense of fatigue or to notice more than my elbow's regular throb. Where would I stay tonight? Had my luck so far been a fluke?

Chief lilted along the trampoline of bottomland we skirted, and the sun tried to penetrate the soil and succeeded with our flesh, raising our core temperatures to match the day. The creek belonging to this bottom necessitated a bridge. We would have to climb up a steep ditch bank and onto the pavement to cross the creek on the bridge. I leaned forward and gripped Chief's mane with one hand, and he thrust us up the bank.

The concrete bridge crossing this small river was eight car-lengths long. I couldn't bear to get off again to lead him, though I was afraid of him slipping and falling on the pavement if he shied. I knew horses well enough to know he didn't want to fall any more than I did.

I kicked Chief up to a quick, flat-foot walk, and his shoes on the bridge reported like a machine-gun. When we cleared the bridge, the shoulders were steep, and both sides of the road were dense with undergrowth and tall trees for several "blocks" if you could judge distance out here that way. We had to stay on the pavement a quarter of a mile. I couldn't hear any cars coming, and it was hard even to turn and look behind me and keep a good handle on my quick-stepping horse.

The land opened up again, and I leaned back, and we slid down the ditch and onto the edge of an open field. We were low, so it took several minutes to see that the field was actually someone's front yard. A new, two-story, brick home blessedly appeared in the distance to our right at the end of a long, curved stripe of fresh gravel. We would stop and ask for water.

I could see that a few juvenile shrubs garnished the fresh mulch at the home's footing. The young house graced this old land with a kind of hope. We crunched up the lane and, *behold*, a garden hose had been rolled neatly among the shrubs.

Who would be home on a weekday at two? I rode right up to the front door, dismounted, dropped the reins, hopped up the steps, rang the doorbell, and dashed back down to pick up Chief's reins in the grass.

In a minute, the etched-glass-and-oak door swung open upon a pretty, slender brunette in her early forties, wearing fresh makeup, designer jeans, darling bow flats, and the kind of top you'd shop in.

"What a treat!" Her first words.

I hadn't had time to pull off my hat and sunglasses so she could see my eyes. As I stripped them off and handed her my card about riding ninety days on horseback (you can put anything on a business card), I began to refine my elevator pitch: "Hi, I'm riding cross country, and I wondered if I might have a little water for my horse. I have a bucket."

"Oh, I'm sure I have a bucket around here."

"No really, mine's right here," and I untied my wadded-up bucket from the side of my saddlebags.

"I wish my son were here to see you!"

"I can't believe I found you home in the middle of the day. My horse was getting thirsty."

The hose cleared out its air before exploding its contents in three or four bursts into the bucket. Chief didn't flinch. He drank two full buckets. The swallows of water ran up the underside of his long neck like a cartoon garden hose. Meantime, the woman told me about the table centerpieces she was making for her daughter's wedding this weekend. Another woman at the well.

"I'm taking the week off work," she said.

"You, too! A lady I spent the night with two days ago was making centerpieces for her daughter's reception."

"It's that time of year," she said. "How far are you riding?"

"My long-range plan is to ride a circle around Missouri. We'll see. I had a little mishap yesterday," I held up my arm, thick with edema and layers of bandage.

"I was going to say!"

"I was stepping off my horse when he bolted. I got my first stiches ever at age fifty-four."

She grimaced. "Doesn't it hurt?"

"When I stop and let it hang, it does. When I'm riding, I'm too busy concentrating on Chief to notice it. I don't know how I'm going to turn over when I sleep tonight, though," I said. "It was bad enough last night on a soft hotel bed. But I'll have my new best friend, Dr. Hydrocodone."

She laughed. "Where are you staying tonight?"

"I don't know."

"Oh."

"There are so many wonderful people. I'll find something."

"I guess that's right. I should think that way more."

I wished I could have written all the words she said that moistened my eyes with relief at her care, but my gloves were wet and full of reins, and Chief was starting to pull away to graze. I do remember one thing she said.

"I can't thank you enough."

She said that to me.

Sometime in the flurry of two women joined by need and fascination, I had mentioned my hormone replacement therapy. How did we go from, "Hello, I'm riding my horse cross country," to, "it's a cocktail of progesterone, testosterone, and estradiol. One dose at night and two in the morning. It's wonderful. I can't even tell I had a hysterectomy!"

How do you get to that in ten minutes with a stranger?

This is what happens, I was learning, when you ride across someone's yard on a horse and ask for a bucket of water.

Within an hour, Chief and I stepped off the blacktop and directly onto gravel at Block Corners, nothing more than an intersection and sign where the pavement ended. How to express my relief at finally achieving traction on a township gravel road. We rode west on 343 Road another hour toward Missouri. The land under bright, blue skies seemed to become higher, with belly-deep pastures and fence rows of trees. Our road narrowed, only wide enough for two cars to pass. The ditches were earthen gutters with the fences only a horse-length from the road. More birds, more insect sounds, more wind, and not a car in over an hour. With every step we left the city farther behind, and the trees grew closer and the fields wider and lusher, and our presence began to diminish within it.

We weren't turning back. Chief seemed to behave as if what lay ahead deserved his full attention, while he gradually dismissed the lifelong pattern of riding away then returning home at the end of the day. I felt I was swinging from a string in the air. I must spin my web wherever I rode and make a rectangular pattern in which my tent would fit tonight and wait there, the breeze flexing our guy wires, and insects, perhaps, lodging with us.

Kansas Rises—an Osage Cuesta

I t was a dry, blue noon in Miami County, Kansas, four days into our trip. West 343rd Road pointed us east. With a few jogs, it would convey us momentously across our first state line into the town of Drexel, Missouri, population 962, and my first cup of coffee. I normally would have had a crashing, caffeine-withdrawal headache for the past four days, but on this ride, not a trace. Drexel's high school basketball team had played my own, Hume, Missouri, population 350, in tournaments thirty years ago. Both towns had fought off school consolidation and survive today because they kept their schools.

This part of Kansas reminded me of west-central Missouri, where I spent my high school years, with its persimmons, blackberries, and wild grapes. Eastern Kansas now has germinated dozens of boutique wineries. Twenty-first-century autodidact farmers seemed to be reawakening the spirits of nineteenth century, German-immigrant vintners, like R.W. Massey, who must have whispered into their sleeping ears and set them dreaming of grapevines until they began to study and plant the slips, now by the thousands on this strip of border-war land. Massey began growing grapes just after the Civil War near the Marais des Cygnes River, not far from Paola, Kansas, whose surrounding township roads I now traced with my horse.

Chief's quick gait made a striptease beat on the chat. For hours we rode through woods and open land, loose fences draped with wild grape and blackberry vines; and despite the powerful sun, I felt grateful for the clear skies and purposeful breeze. As hours passed, our road softened, narrowed, and grew a young beard in its center as if it had slept late and lazed ungroomed between the fields. The world seemed higher and lighter. A shelf of rock beneath us was taking the breath of a lifetime, lifting us toward the sky.

A buckeye butterfly winked its brown eyes at me by closing its wings. It sailed a rollercoaster of drafts beside us. In time, I realized it followed us a full mile, then handed its relay baton to another butterfly just like it, who brought us the next mile. Then a third took us up. A small, brown bird sat on a fence wire and watched us so close I could see its white throat. It flitted ahead to the next and the next stretch of fence until its twin took over a mile down the road. What next, the Seven Dwarfs?

It was time to find the "powder room," that place in the ditch coated by cars with white gravel dust. I swung my leg high over my bags to keep from catching a spur. Chief took sideways snatches at weeds in what was becoming his herb-tasting tour of the Midwest. I unclipped the bit from his bridle so he could eat freely.

We rested together like fellow roofers at lunch. Behind me, the corn flapped its hundred thousand flags in a new wind I'd just begun to notice. I stood and looked at the corn. We'd had a wet spring. The young stalks, up to my chest, stood shoulder to shoulder like Muslims at prayer against the powerful gusts. Their fingers flicked sunny glints that hypnotized me as well as any sparkling lake or fire.

I pulled my notepad from my pommel bag and wrote for twenty minutes. I stood and ate walnuts and raisins from a quart Ziploc bag. Chief took three-inch steps, ten grinds of his teeth between each.

The wind bent back the brim of my hat. I would have to fashion a stampede string from a spare shoelace to hold it on. My black tights and boots were striped in white dust from standing in the tall grass. I unclipped Chief's bit from my saddle and reached down gently and pulled him by his bridle. He took three stubborn last bites and chewed before raising his head, expectant of his bit. I placed the copper against his teeth and waited for him to unclench his jaw. The wind was pushing his mane to the wrong side in a roller breaking on the beach of his glistening neck. A high wind makes horses skittish. He seemed to be bearing into it, instead. I pushed my thumb into the corner of his mouth where the bit would rest and slid the bit home.

I led him to the center of the road like an elderly woman, to show my respect, allowing how he'd kept my company and didn't try to depart from our newly formed herd of two.

"My Sweet Person Horse," I said. I had christened him. This would be his name for the remainder of our trip.

Before I mounted, we stood in the road together. The fields sloped away, leaving Colorado's breath of wind unimpeded across Kansas. How had we climbed so high without my noticing? Missouri stretched below us at nine hundred feet above sea level; in the distance, Drexel's water tower was a turquoise bead on a quilt of green and brown. Draped down the eastern side of this plateau should be ovals and rectangles of grapevine plots and white dots of German and Italian immigrants planting their new hearty hybrids in this former land of buffalo swarms. Thanks to Prohibition, rectangles of corn and wheat, instead.

We stood on an escarpment of limestone, the distillation of millions of years of sea life dying, sinking, layering, absorbing, and eventually turning to stone. Over the course of three hundred million years, that mud became lane shale on the edge of a sea that lapped here once. Meanwhile, the earth's crust pitched upward at the speed at which I seemed to be learning what to do with my life. Between the layers of shale are thick slabs of Wyandotte limestone that tilt toward the surface like a raft on a wave that, for all we know, still is rising.

The wind that now was on a tear, had, over time, eroded the shale from the south and west, leaving high ridges of limestone, later blanketed with soil that supported bison and Osage Indians, eighteenth-century vintners, and now, us. Chief and I had climbed the back of what formally is known as an Osage Cuesta, one in a series rising just west of 69 Highway south of Kansas City that nobody notices from their auto-bubbles. Chief and I stood on this crest overlooking Missouri, where thousands of men and women died—to free slaves or to keep them enslaved—on this Civil War border between abolitionist Kansas and Confederate Missouri. (Today's urban shootings here seem surgical in comparison to border-war times.) The wind seemed to be shaking Chief and me free of what made sense, and we became content simply to hold our hats, right ourselves, scan the horizon, and thrill at the thought of a drink and a snack in town.

My own disbelief at having ridden away from my home seemed to be raising a white flag to the wind's insistence that nothing in the world mattered but this road and what held it up.

If that on which I stood were once as soft as silt, then hard as rock, then worn away by wind—I could be, too. I had been silt-like, when I was a girl. At fifty-four, my neck and shoulders felt brittle with tension. Yet, here I was, my body almost blowing away, the wind shaking me to my senses. What sense? The common sense I'd worked all my life to acquire? As a girl, I *was* sense, neither common nor good. I loved to run, to swim, to wrap my arms around my horse's neck. I loved to record my voice announcing the news while sitting on my bedroom floor. I loved to practice my trombone for hours—to double-tongue, triple-tongue.

In my teens, gradually, like climbing the back of this Cuesta, I leaned less and less on my horse's neck. I turned away from sixteenth notes played to perfection, while the milo out front shivered its dry leaves on a frosted night. How could I continue to muse and play at marriageable age, with Depression-era parents, no money for college, and a proposal on the table from the best farm family in the county? At eighteen, I did not know how to walk (or ride) away on my own. Thirty years later, the original girl neared extinction, like the wild grapes we were farming away.

I stood beside Chief in the middle of the road. I didn't touch his reins. They dangled in long loops from his bit up to their knotted ends at his wither. I didn't say, "Stand." I put my foot in the stirrup. Chief waited. I grasped his mane and hopped up. He let me find my off-side stirrup. Only then did I touch the reins. He began to walk.

She's Something, That Woman

C hief and I entered Drexel, Missouri, from the west side on a gravel road. A gust of wind cuffed a stop sign beside us that twanged and quivered. Chief dropped his front end at the sound, then kept going, like driving into a pothole and bouncing out. We turned the corner at a fast, flat-foot walk on the powdery road and approached rows of ten-thousand-pound, double-axel anhydrous ammonia nurse tanks and applicator tanks shaped like white torpedoes. To Chief, these could not be explained in the natural world. They would be hooked onto by farmers in pickups, rolled to fields, and pulled by tractors to inject nitrogen into the soil. Anhydrous is the kind of stuff you want to stay upwind of, because it will burn water-rich tissue like eyes and lungs. I've never seen a farmer wearing safety goggles as recommended, but I did once see an old Mennonite farmer who had white eyeballs after getting a face full of it. If you ever see a young pickup that looks like it has a pealing sunburn, you know it probably was downwind of an application. We approached a small, metal building with two front windows and three trucks parked outside—the locus of fertilizer in this area.

The land surrounding Drexel proper was flat as a lakebed. Houses ranged from neat, ninety-year-old frame structures, to new modular homes, to bare-yarded, clapboard boxes on a slab. Did it look desolate—this back-end gravel road on the edge of a tiny town that abuts the border of Kansas in Missouri? No. Not if you're from here. It's not what a metal building looks like that matters. It's who's inside: your kids' Little League coach, your daughter's teacher's husband, your mile-to-the-north neighbor, Kevin, the alderman. The building is what it needs to be for the purpose, as are the houses, and yes, it would be nice if the township paved the road, but there are bridges elsewhere that need to be replaced. Drexel is a "fourth-class city"—not a putdown, a fact, that in Missouri law determines what type of city government it can have. It's bigger than a "village" but not as big as a third-class town. Like metropolitan Kansas City, its electricity comes from Evergy, its gas from Spire Energy, and its trash service from Waste Management. Drexel also is home to InnovaPrep, LLC, a high-tech start-up whose many clients include NASA, which has tested its microbe detection equipment on the International Space Lab. Who would have thought? I rode the grassy right-of-way in front of the fertilizer business.

A culvert over a small creek ahead soon would force us onto the road. I pulled Chief up and swung off to get a drink and let him grab a bite of grass before we walked through town. His rear swung every time he looked in a new direction. He was too lit by the approach of yards bristling with bird baths and barking dogs to put his head down and eat.

My gallon canteen hung against Chief's shoulder and waggled with each contraction of his triceps. It hung from a long strap tied with a bootlace through a bracket on my saddle pommel and annoyingly bumped my knee all day. I worried that its edge might be bruising Chief's shoulder. I drank from it from the ground by tipping it up and bending my knees and leaning into Chief, who stood still for me to drink. The cap was attached to a keeper, so I couldn't drop it into the grass, thank heaven. I always took eight gulps without stopping each time I tipped it up. I wiped my mouth with my sleeve and mounted again.

A 3:15 PM bustle of traffic descended on us. I call this phenomenon the "rush-five-minutes"—the one time each day in small towns when cars line up ten deep at the stoplight and make you wait. This happens daily before and after school. We rode past the grain elevator with its centrifugal fans roaring at 1,750 revolutions per minute to keep the grain from molding before it could be shipped for processing into flour or high-fructose corn syrup. The fans provided soothing white noise for a good night's sleep three blocks away. Up close, they made us point our ears away and walk through the blizzard of noise as quickly as we could. Soon, we found the paved main drag that became Route 18, but before that, I dismounted again.

Chief seemed relieved to walk behind me, past the rear ends of cars parked at angles on Main Street and facing store fronts that looked like a western movie set. Some held silent space in hopes of adoption; others, spruced with colorful trim, contained a clothing boutique, an insurance agency, and a copy shop. The traffic diminished.

I headed for a grocery-store sign on a brick building ahead but didn't know what I would buy in any case, since Bob was coming tonight with more food, sunblock, and fly dope for Chief. I stood in the road wondering if Drexel didn't have a convenience store for the coffee I craved, when three stringy-haired, snaggle-toothed people emerged from the grocery store and headed for the car I knew was theirs, an old, gold LTD with decades of nicotine staining the windows. I'd be writing a letter of complaint to a movie producer if I saw these three in a film depicting rural America. *Why do you have to make them look so stupid and dirty?* I would write. *Nobody dresses like that.* I am that defensive, but here they were, and they weren't wearing costumes. I recognized them. Not them in particular, but their kind. I smiled, and they came over and asked me where I was going.

"I don't have a plan, per se. Riding a circle around Missouri," I said.

There's nothing like the open-mouthed joy of a person who has no teeth and stopped caring about it long ago. I could sit in this man's kitchen and relax with every shred of pretense understood-away.

"Where you staying tonight?" said one man.

"I have no idea. My main goal is to string together enough gravel roads that I can stay off the blacktop. I'm looking for 14001 Road. I'll head south on that."

"We live over down by Milford. You should ride down there. We'll put you up for the night."

How to respond? The only security I felt right now was believing I'd selected a route for today and tomorrow with the fewest miles of blacktop, that would keep me safest.

Since I first decided to take this trip, everything I'd done had seemed to be as a passenger, not the driver. Some little girl inside had written a screenplay, and I acted it out for her. I was getting my script handed to me minute by minute. I'd invested $2,500 in a horse, had my husband driving all over the country worrying about me; and I wasn't about to start questioning my little movie director now. I trusted only one thing: She must have wanted to do this for a reason, and I wasn't going to let her down. This offer, from sweet folks, threw me off my precarious balance.

"My husband is meeting me tonight. I'm trying to stay on my route. I truly appreciate the offer."

"We'd sure love to have you."

What might I be missing?

"Thank you, anyway."

They pointed me back a block and north five blocks for the Casey's General Store. Coffee. The wind had calmed down by half in town, so I could feel the heat. The walk to Casey's ended with my heels getting sore, yet I did not feel tired. I tied Chief to a pealing, Rust-Oleum-painted sign pole. He fidgeted but didn't threaten to circle the pole and snub himself into a panic attack. I threw my hat and gloves on the grass beside him. As I walked across the parking lot to get my first blessed coffee with cream and sugar, a pickup pulled in behind Chief pulling a long stock trailer loaded with cattle that were nervously pooping out the openings. I glanced back, and Chief's eyes were huge, and he was chuckling loudly to the trailer that surely had come to deliver him at last from this crazy trail ride with no destination. I was sorry to disappoint him.

Inside the convenience store I asked a high-school-aged girl behind the counter for directions. Nobody who lives in the country knows the names of the smaller roads, not even the blacktops. They drive them every day and identify them by the owners' names of abutting fields, or the church that faces them, or the town that used to be there. The blond, straight-haired teenager at the cash register had never heard of my target, 14001 Road, so I told her that on my map it appeared to be the first gravel road going south out of town off Highway 18. Her chin jerked up. "Ball Diamond Road. It has a ball diamond on the corner. Go east on the main road out of town, and you'll see it."

Bearing my precious insulated cup of sweetened coffee, I returned to Chief. He ignored me and chuckled loudly at the departing stock trailer. I blew into the square hole I had bent back in the lid of my cup and took two sips. I took a third sip, then a fourth, just to make sure. Then I walked across the lot to the trash can and threw it out. Drinking it was like taking a hot bath on a ninety-degree day. I drank more canteen water.

We turned around and headed back to the main drag, down Route 18 to "Ball Diamond Road." We rode the edge of a two-acre lawn in front of a VFW hall in mid-afternoon. The parking lot was full. Something was going on here. Behind the VFW, I spotted a group of beautiful young women in long mauve gowns wrapped around their legs by the wind. Thank heaven the bride had all her hair pinned up and sprayed tight. The bridesmaids held their locks in their fists and arranged themselves as directed by a photographer on one knee in the light of a descending sun. Out here, wedding photos often have a stand of young corn in the background—what more promising scene could there be?

Ahead, I thought I could see ballfield lights on tall poles. Suddenly, I could breathe. I was where I was supposed to be, which demonstrated how lost I had been feeling. We turned the corner at the ballfield. On weekends, this place would be crammed with cars and trucks, while parents who farmed or worked in the city sank into sling-back folding chairs where they released to the games their frantic commutes and cultivation. They chatted or called encouragement to the field, like parents at soccer games everywhere, except these folks would know the lineage of everyone there. If a stranger did climb into the stands, the parents would surreptitiously stare, and if they were near, would lean over and ask, "Are you related to . . . ?"

We achieved Ball Diamond Road, and Chief put his head down and took swinging, mile-eating steps. Soon, the gravel road became hilly. Scrub oak clogged the woods that grew up on either side, and the houses became scruffy and close together. It's a joke between us border dwellers that you can tell when you have crossed from Kansas into Missouri, because the roads get narrow and rough. Kansas has a better tax base than Missouri. At least, it did until Governor Brownback's tax cuts. Now the roads and schools are becoming more like Missouri's.

It had been easy for me to feel safe in Kansas, with its roomy sky and high, open land. Most of the homes in Kansas were trim and well kept. Here, I rode into short, scrubby hills where elderly mobile homes seemed to regard me suspiciously from their dark, metal-framed windows. Every house we passed looked paycheck-to-paycheck.

My phone rang. I pulled Chief up, got off, and unstuck my iPhone from the skin inside my bra.

"Hello!" Even out here, I sang my greeting like a saleswoman, as was my habit.

"Wherey'at!" Bob barked. That was how he jokingly called through the house when he came home at night—as if I might be hiding behind the dryer.

I was too hot and tired to joke back, just relieved to hear his voice. "I'm on 14001 Road, just off 18 coming out of Drexel."

"Okay. I'm probably an hour away," Bob said. "It took me longer to get everything than I thought."

"Did you bring plenty of food?" (I meant for the next week of riding.)

"I'm hoping to get sandwiches at the Mennonite Café in Rich Hill on my way."

"Okay, but I need food for the week."

"I got it."

"Thank you, Sweetie. All I can tell you is to aim toward 14001 Road, and I'll let you know where I've stopped. Call me when you start to get close, because I don't see anything good around here. It's creeping me out a little."

"Be careful."

"Love you."

I became more uneasy the farther I rode into the scraggly hills. Perhaps my luck so far finding safe places to camp had not been a benevolent condition of the world. I knew that if I had to, I could sneak down a field road and tie my horse to a fence and camp. Having lived most of my life in the country, I knew how people felt about trespassers. I wouldn't get shot, but it would hurt my self-respect not to ask.

By 5:00 PM, I came to a curve where a modular home sat jauntily on its lot in a wreath of flowers, with a neat metal barn containing an antique tractor and a mowed, meadow-of-a yard flowing behind it into trees and a creek. A man was in the drive, so I rode up and gave a big smile and wave. Jerry, as I was to learn, walked toward me with his hat cocked and a look like he was about to tease his little sister. He had emerged from the wide metal door of his lit shop that contained a red, antique Farmall tractor surrounded by homemade wood workbenches against the walls, rows of neatly hung tools, and a band saw, drill press, and belt sander.

"Hi. How ya doing?" I asked.

He grinned. "No good." He walked up close and stood with his hands on his hips.

"Looks like you're busy," I said, pointing to his shop.

"Got to, or you'll die."

"That's a nice-looking shop."

"I retired last year after thirty-five years—maintenance supervisor." Jerry stood trim and fit and in possession of this bend in the road.

"I'm riding cross-country, and I wondered what it was like up ahead. Do you think there would be any place where folks would have a pasture where I could put my horse and a tent? I wasn't expecting to see so many houses without land along this road."

"Oh, they keep putting up trailers. It's not like being in the country anymore. I'd like you to stay right here. I'd need to ask my wife."

A man asks his wife if she minds. And tells someone this? This struck me as sweet and manly. "She's awfully sick," he said.

I wasn't asking to stay. There were no fences, nothing but a groomed back yard. Where would I put Chief? And his wife was sick.

"The only thing I worry about is Chief will tear your yard up with his shoes."

"That doesn't matter. I'll be right back."

Of course, his wife, Sharon, wanted us to stay, he said when he returned. "I'll see if she's up to a visit later. She wants to meet you."

Whatever was driving me, or pulling me down this gravel road said, *stay here*. I obeyed.

"I could tie him between those trees."

"Sure. We let family camp back there all the time."

"My husband is supposed to meet me tonight and bring me supplies. Will that be all right?"

He brushed off the question as he turned to walk back to his shop. "Make yourself at home," he said without looking back. He pointed to the spigot on the back of the house and the coiled hose.

"Thank you so much," I called. He waved it off.

Two hours later my husband's truck was pulling down into the meadow. I hadn't told Jerry what kind of truck my husband drove. He had never seen that model and color of Silverado on his road before—especially with a man driving slowly, sitting up, looking around. Jerry waved my husband into the drive. (In the country, a different car on your road is a legitimate topic for dinner conversation.) Bob later told me that the only words spoken between the two men when he pulled in were from Jerry: "She's back there; pull your truck on down."

Our legs dangled off the tailgate of Bob's truck in the night. He had brought a bottle of cabernet. My shrinking cells soaked it up and thickened. Bob also had bought a mosquito net to cover us with in the back of the truck, but he said he was not inclined to try it out tonight. I panicked an instant. I had strained toward his arrival all day. I hadn't seen him in two days. He didn't want to stay the night with me. I knew it would be uncomfortable and cold for him. I had put this barrier between us—my ride, my discomfort. I needed to be on my way without him.

I sat in the dark with my thigh pressed into his and my head on his shoulder. We both were employed by this road show, but we had different tasks: performer and grip. In the dark I could see Chief's head hang straight in front of him. It dropped a few centimeters with every breath.

I would be cold again tonight. I would undress, crouch behind the tent—the only place out of sight in the dark—and bathe from a bucket and get perfectly clean in cold water. In the morning, I would bend my head under the garden hose and shampoo, as I now did every morning.

Later, I lay in my tent and heard the orienting thump of Chief's hooves. A hydrocodone tablet numbed my throbbing arm and let me sleep.

My phone alarm woke me at 5:00 AM, and I got up, damp from condensation under the plastic poncho I'd covered myself with. By the time I was nearly packed up, Jerry emerged and invited me in for coffee, and my "yes" had such force behind it, I seemed to startle him. Sharon was able to sit up this morning, and she had come into the kitchen. The night before, she lay propped on pillows on the couch, a cloth over her forehead, drugged to relieve the violent nausea caused by vertigo from an unknown origin, and yet she had asked all about me. This morning, at the kitchen island, before a bright window diffused by white, eyelet curtains, we drank coffee and talked about our families and histories. I held my cup with both hands and drained it embarrassingly quickly. I felt swaddled.

Jerry led me to a china cabinet that contained his antique model car and truck collection. He told me stories about many of them. We released Sharon to the living room to be still, then Jerry brought me into a bedroom that doubled as Sharon's sewing room, where her two machines resided. "She can make anything," he said. I studied her quilt-show winners hanging on the walls and folded on a chair. He lifted the hem of a white and floral quilt coverlet on the bed. "She even made this," he said, looking up at my eyes to note my reaction.

Soon, we stood in the driveway. "She's something, that woman in there," he said.

His eyes filled with tears.

After a pause to let his emotion land, I said, "I know you're worried about her."

He took in a sharp breath and swiveled on his heel. His arm lifted to point toward a bare patch in the ground. "There used to be a big tree there before the storm last year." He flicked a tear while his back was turned. I imagined the ground becoming saturated and then the right burst of wind to upend the tree, roots and all.

I returned to saddle and bridle my pawing horse and fasten down everything I owned for today's ride.

When I reined up to say goodbye to Jerry in the drive, my steering column came loose. (The bridle broke.) Chief froze. I dismounted and unbridled my horse, so Jerry could take it to his shop and hammer it back together with copper rivets. My favorite bridle was almost thirty years old. Jerry used a nylon zip tie to reinforce the joint, then gave me six extra zip ties for the road.

How had I wound up at the home of a career maintenance supervisor with a complete workshop on the morning my bridle broke?

I imagined Jerry and Sharon saying to each other, "She'll be lucky to make it another ten miles." That may be what they thought, but that's not how they made me feel.

"Call us if you need anything."

"I will. Take care of that girl in there," I said.

He raised his arm and walked away.

Type-A Farmers

Leaving Jerry and Sharon's, I saw dark lines crisscrossing damp pastures like evidence of aliens. The tracks of rabbit tummies, instead. This was purple-poop season in Missouri, when birds gorge on mulberries from the indigenous trees. Back home in Kansas City, mulberry trees stand fifty feet tall, too high for me to reach the syrupy berries I crave. This, and every day so far, I discovered along the road young trees that farmers hadn't bothered to clear out from their fences. I easily could reach the mulberries from Chief's back, each tiny fruit tan with road dust. They fell from their ringlets into my cupped glove when touched. The dust was so fine it did not crunch in my teeth and had no flavor, and I ate as many as I could reach. Chief was so accustomed to my berry picking by now that when I rode him beneath a young mulberry tree, he dropped his head to graze.

Sticking out from under the roads were snarling mouths of bent, corrugated metal culverts. Last year's leaves lay like old women's hands, filled with dust. Clusters of pink blooms the size of pinecones stood erect as we walked past. I wanted to pick and keep them. The best I could do was fill up with the sight of them and hope they made me a more beautiful person.

I watched the land change gradually, surprised to discover we were leaving the belt of scruffy hills near Jerry and Sharon's home and entering flatter farmland where my diaphragm began to relax. This country looked familiar. When I was in high school, I rode Tabasco, my Quarter Horse stallion, through land like this, trotting bareback for miles and swatting green-headed flies in post-rain, sauna-like heat that smelled of damp firewood. The fifth day of my trip, I hadn't yet realized that the terrain and available gravel roads would funnel me straight south—not east, as planned—but in a forced circumnavigation of lakes and busy highways that would send me back to the township where I lived in high school. There, my horse Tabasco had carried me from puberty into young womanhood.

I hadn't planned this route.

During the two months Chief and I prepared for our ride, the untilled fields had gone from bed-head—last year's crop stubble—to black, combed lines with seeds sprouting under each peak. Now the wheat was up and had formed green heads, too young for beards and still able to reflect glints of light. Yesterday's winds had quickly disbursed dust from trucks, but today's calm left dust billowing behind cars like quarter-mile-long caterpillars that drifted, whole, across fields and between window jams. Or the dust lay in the road and swelled into a formless haze.

Chief and I passed green harbors of fescue grass that undulated in swells of potential hay. The expanse was tinged with red and gold ripening heads. These fescue seed heads were long, slender fronds on the ends of tall shafts of grass. When waved about, each field became a phosphorescent surf. Between these bays, hedgerows formed seawalls of green fluff, followed by stripes of green corn or milo, tall as my knee. I had never seen so many wildflowers in the ditches. We'd had a wet spring, yet it had not rained in three weeks—odd for mid-May. I would learn that this land had seen all the water it would for the rest of the summer. I studied the roots of corn stalks as we passed. They were beginning to peek out of the soil like little elbowed pipes, still green. If it didn't rain soon, the corn would begin to "fire"—the roots would die of thirst, and the lower fourth of the stalk would be baked to death. The corn would turn to brittle statues in tribute of their fourth week when growth stopped. It would have to be cut and ground for silage to feed cattle—a loss. The young corn stood beautifully on the brink of ruin.

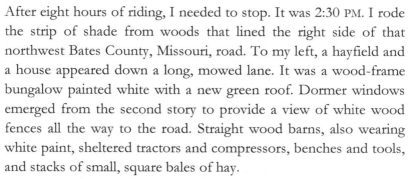

After eight hours of riding, I needed to stop. It was 2:30 PM. I rode the strip of shade from woods that lined the right side of that northwest Bates County, Missouri, road. To my left, a hayfield and a house appeared down a long, mowed lane. It was a wood-frame bungalow painted white with a new green roof. Dormer windows emerged from the second story to provide a view of white wood fences all the way to the road. Straight wood barns, also wearing white paint, sheltered tractors and compressors, benches and tools, and stacks of small, square bales of hay.

A certain light surrounded the homestead that had nothing to do with the gold eye that had watched us all day. *Let this be the place,* I thought. As I had every night when I asked to camp, I would break two rules I had been raised with: Don't ask for things, and don't put anybody out.

I was swinging off in the yard and taking a couple of stiff steps toward the door when I saw a pickup on the gravel road miraculously slow and turn down the lane toward us. My clothes clung to me. My horse had long stripes of sweat in the shape of muddy sickles from the rear of his saddle pad tracking down under his flanks. I could smell the heat off his engine. He took ten snaps of grass in a row before beginning to chew.

In the pickup, a boy and girl of high-school age pulled even with me. I imagined her leg pressed against his, her thumb and fingers wrapped around the hard muscle above his knee. He leaned forward to look around her through the window at me. I was jerking my hat off so I could look more normal. There were dents in my forehead from a missing brow liner in this cheap hat. The top and sides of my hair had come out of my ponytail. These two would never imagine my sleek figure in a cocktail dress and heels. All I had for credibility was my smile and an articulate explanation.

"I'm riding cross-country, and I was looking for a pasture or a lot I could put my horse in for the night. Do you think they'd have a place here, or somewhere else close by?"

The handsome pair was too young to be able to disguise their apprehension at the sight of me. I was surprised by the young man's hesitance. The teenagers poised on their bench seat as if they were sitting on firecrackers. My guess was they had to rush back to the field with a topped-off fuel tank that took up a fourth of the pickup bed. They became serious with the awesome responsibility of helping a strange woman, alone on a horse.

Seeing this couple reminded me of an interview with the actor Richard Gere, who referred to people he met at a rural movie shoot as "people of the earth." I had felt embarrassed for Gere. I don't know anyone who farms or lives in the country thinking they are "of the earth." Farmers are some of the most up-tight, type-A people I know, because they have to watch their fields like grilling steaks or baking cakes. Everything depends on timing: discing after the rain, letting cut hay cure the right number of hours in the sun before turning it over. It depends on the art of implanting embryos at the right moment, so a prize-winning cow and bull can parent a herd of progeny in one season. Minnesota farmer's daughter and author Judy Blunt referred to a farmer's work ethic in her memoir *Breaking Clean* as "stopping just short of insanity."

This couple studying me through the pickup window could have been brother and sister. Their children would look like both of them. *Stay together*, I thought. *Against all better judgment, stay together.* Who says you should date around, go to college, have a career before marriage—though I wish I had been brave enough to do it that way. This couple's love, squeezed together on the otherwise empty bench seat deserved a marriage, a piece of land, and a new, queen-sized bed.

"My uncle lives across the section," the boy pointed with a tilt of his head. "He's got a lot of horses. He'd probably have a place for you."

People always think I want to stay with horse people, which I don't. They usually have every spot on their place taken up by their own horses, and you can't put strange horses together because they beat up the newcomer. This young man didn't seem inspired to make a call to find out if my perfect place here were available. I knew one thing—there was a good reason I was not to stay here. I'd proved it by stumbling upon heartbreaking hospitality for the past four nights in a row.

Silence

Thirty minutes later, we arrived at the home of the boy's uncle and aunt. Chief and I had come nineteen miles through eastern Kansas and western Missouri, our longest day yet. We circled behind the ranch-style house. I caught my reflection aboard Chief in the storm door. How silly my big, crooked hat looked—and necessary. How round and puffy my face. I seemed tiny surrounded by our packs.

At the age of nine, I had studied my shadow like this on the front of a barn in the footlight of a setting Oklahoma sun. I'd preserved that girl through the years and today reconstituted her with this sweat and the endless rocking of my horse's walk. It was as if all my life I had floated above my body, and now, hot, homeless, and horseback, I'd snapped back into every original cell.

I swung off and rubbed Chief's wet neck, and I pulled him by the reins until the tips of his hooves touched the edge of the walk. He would come no closer to the patio table and chairs and his reflection in the door. I could barely push the doorbell without letting him go. I knew someone was home; a newer car sat parked with the attitude of one who had just hurried in from somewhere. Also, the interior back door stood open.

Shari, I soon would learn, probably couldn't hear her dog bark at us over her blow drier. She came around the corner within the polished dark of the house and rose an instant at the sight of me through her door. As soon as she comprehended what she was seeing, she leaned into her approach. She pushed the door open, and the light touched her brow from the dark like a nineteenth-century portrait of a young lady in twenty-first-century jeans. I detected random molecules of perfume from my place at the edge of the walk. Perhaps Aveda hair product, the kind I'd used a week ago. She wore an expensive, shabby-chic haircut and polished nails. Her clothes don't remain in memory, only the recollection that I wished she would help me shop. She lit her features with a hint of foundation, shadow, liner, and mascara—accoutrements no longer part of my world. Shari recently had whisked her car home over the gravel roads from work in Butler, Missouri, to get ready for a relative's birthday party, she told me.

She greeted me as if she'd been expecting me all day. I was in the middle of my qualifications: "I only need a couple of buckets of water. I have my own food. I just need a little lot or pasture, or perhaps you know of someone else down the road."

"Mark is going to be so jealous when he meets you. My husband would *love* to do something like this. I'm sure he can find a place for your horse."

At once, I felt cooler and not a bit tired.

Mark rolled into the drive in a beefy dually from his job ninety miles away in Lawrence, Kansas. Shari must have called him, because he didn't look shocked to see me. I can't tell people's ages. He was a fit, handsome man wearing western boots and belt and a nice dress shirt and seemed at least ten years younger than me, though I tend to think of myself as younger than I am. He strode toward me with a half-embarrassed grin, which I took to mean he was excited to talk to me but didn't want to look too smiley. I decided that he managed a lot of people, because of his steady gaze and polite confidence.

Without peppering me with questions, he led Chief and me toward his powdery lots where well-bred Quarter Horses pointed themselves toward big, round hay bales in metal rings. A mule and a few other horses stood in an adjacent pasture. Through a gate and behind a metal garage stood a hitching rail and, nearby, the door to his tack room where I unsaddled.

Describing Mark's horses as "well-bred" might seem a literary cop-out, unless you know that well-bred means something specific. It means that the forehand (forelegs and shoulders), hindquarters (hind legs and hips), and mid-section (barrel and back) are virtually equal in proportion—they conform to each other, as in "good conformation." The neck comes high out of the chest, and the junction between the head and neck is fine, so the horse can easily tuck its chin, which is both beautiful and functional for proper posture. It means the back is relatively flat, not a ski slope toward the front. The legs are straight, and the eyes are warm and wide set. You should know that, to a considerable degree, the excellent body shape was sculpted by this man's training. In his book *The Way to Perfect Horsemanship*, Udo Berger, German veterinary surgeon and riding master, who died in 1985, calls it the "modelling of a living animal." The horse is sculpted by its work, like a weightlifter. Correct riding forms a more perfect union of parts, and Mark's horses had it.

"I think we'll put him in that little lot out there." I watched Mark's eyes fondly catch and release each of his horses we passed. An Australian shepherd jumped and yipped around us. "Get down!" Mark scolded, but his words held no hammer. "Don't let him jump all over you. He's a mess. Not a year old yet."

Mark opened a metal gate to a small, overgrown paddock in the backyard attached to a cinder block building. "He can tromp this down for me." Mark spoke as if everything had the potential to be a punchline. Rural men I've known all my life made jokes at their own expense—a male code of politeness that prevented the worst offense out here—egotism. While a Chinese businessman might present his business card with the fingertips of both hands and a slight bow, men like Mark showed respect with self-effacing quips. He motioned to the white-painted block building.

"We used to raise rabbits in here."

"It seems like everyone in the country has buildings where they *used* to raise something for extra money," I said, "and now they raise something else."

"Isn't that the truth," Mark said. "About the time you start making money, everyone else gets in, and the price goes down."

"I remember when they tried to start farmers' unions," I said.

"In the '80s."

"They'd rather run themselves out of business than cooperate with each other."

"Farming is complex," Mark said. "What's good for me isn't good for somebody just fifty miles down the road. Do you have food?" he asked.

"I have everything I need right here," I pointed to my bags.

"Don't let him take anything from you," he said of the dog. "Sorry about this mess. He steals everything." The dog had found and carried into the half-acre-wide yard a single sock, a shop towel, a collapsed soccer ball, a wood slat, and a leg bone from a calf that probably had been stillborn in a field within roaming distance.

Mark apologized for having to leave for the birthday party. He walked away from the place in his yard he seemed now to consider mine, then turned. "Maybe you can come up to the house later. I'd like to hear more about your trip."

"Definitely," I said.

I've never been good at relaxing around strangers. I never lack for charming conversation, either, but that comes at the expense of tense shoulders and short breaths, both of which began to ease when Mark went inside the house and left me alone.

I put my bags on a trampoline nearby to keep them safe from the dog that now was in the tiny pen with Chief, barking at him incessantly to get him to run. I called him out and tried to calm him down, but it was like trying to pet a trout. I studied the lawn for the least lumpy place on which to pitch my tent and began to calculate in what order I should tackle the tasks: laundry, bath, tent, organize, eat. I couldn't comprehend where to start. It was as if the sudden absence of worry had shut off my hot brain too quickly, and it vapor-locked. Had I been still today? Ever, really? My eyes fixed on a tuft of grass, which eased out of focus. My muscles buzzed from their bones. I entered the gap between perpetual self-preservation against Chief's next bolt—and a safe place on the ground. A nearby horse blew its nose, clopped its foot in front of it, and rubbed the side of its mouth on its leg with a smacking sound. Colors brightened, as if I were looking through tears. A mockingbird became a cardinal, then a robin. The dog's bark insinuated itself into me. Kansas wind wrestled the tree above. I was aware of everything in this land, and at this moment had not a single word for any of it. Perhaps this gap is where the Hopi Indians lived, whose language contains no past or future tense, and neither do they.

"Silence is the absolute poise of mind, body, and spirit," said Ohiye S'a, Santee Sioux writer, national lecturer, and reformer who lived between 1858 and 1939. "The man who preserves his selfhood is ever calm and unshaken by the storms of existence," he said. "If you asked him, 'What are the fruits of silence?' he will say, They are self-control, true courage, endurance, patience, dignity, and reverence. Silence is the cornerstone of character."

Riding five days alone in the wind and sun, not knowing where or if I would find a safe place at night, or if my horse would spin out from under me, I had stumbled upon my own kind of meditation. In it, I could be still, under a tree, absorbed out of my life and into the wide world. I was not alarmed when sounds became louder and colors brighter. A faint, white noise in my ears began and grew louder—a hint, I thought, of the roar a shaman hears when leaving the body in flights of astral travel. I ceased to be a namer and became an observer of things—each perfect. Perhaps this is how ancestors discovered prayer. They walked until they were too tired to think and just saw. My body seemed to dissolve—into God, I believed. Crackling of tires on gravel emerged as if from within me.

A pickup pulled into the drive. Shari looked out the back door, waved, and came to the end of the sidewalk in her bare feet. Mark was talking through the truck window with a couple, friends, who happened by. I was aware they were talking about me. I wrenched my mind out of the silence and into the requirements of a verbal world and wandered over to join them. These kind souls on a farm in eastern Bates County, Missouri, gathered around me like cattle sniffing a stray child. If Shari had called them over to see who she had in her yard, perhaps I was not such an inconvenience.

By the time I had pitched my tent, Mark and Shari were headed to their truck to go to the birthday party. I met them in the drive.

"Use this shower in here while we're gone," Shari said. "It's right here by the back door." She paused and turned. "Let me show you." I could tell it was no use for me to explain I could take my bath behind a barn with my bucket. I stepped into her house on the toes of my dusty boots. I felt for her, leading a stranger inside before tidying up, but she seemed not to care, probably because she apparently kept the place spotless. She showed me the towels, the soap. I admitted to her that my stitched arm deserved a soaking wash, and she made a face at the news of my stitches only three days before.

Soon, the couple was climbing into their truck to leave.

"You drink coffee?" Mark called out his window.

"Yes!" I thought he meant for morning. I had been poised to accept an offer of a cold beer tonight, which I craved. A beer would come only once in twenty-nine days riding through this Bible belt.

"Mind if I call my sister and her husband to come over for coffee tonight?" Mark asked.

"I would love that."

"She won't believe me when I tell her about you." With a smirk, he put the truck in reverse and checked his side-view mirror. "She doesn't believe anything I tell her." Shari shook her head.

One moment, I am a stray. The next, I am rounded up and claimed.

I still had several hours of warm wind to dry my clothes on the nearby fence. Bob had brought me sliced ham last night that I'd saved for my supper, with my dried fruit. I was desperate to eat.

By the time my clean laundry was drying on the fence, and I had taken my blessed shower and re-bandaged my arm, the dog had jumped on the trampoline and eaten my ham. If that weren't enough, it stole Chief's feed bag (which I never found) and had taken a bath in the muck over the septic tank in the pasture. I had to yell at him to keep him from jumping on me with his slime.

I spent the last of my energy pitching my tent and arranging my tools for living. I felt lusciously alone, the way one might feel at a noisy family reunion, having retreated to a quiet, upstairs bedroom.

For safekeeping, I carried my saddlebags inside the little, cinder-block building attached to Chief's paddock. The building was fifteen by eight feet, I guessed, and painted white inside and out, with a small window and a door. Cobwebs in the corners contained dehydrated flies, but otherwise, it was clean and neat. Next to the door hung a small sink with a mirror above it. I had enough light to see. I had jettisoned so many toiletries they now all fit into a quart Ziploc instead of the original gallon bag.

I looked at my face carefully, perhaps for the first time since I left. This is what people saw: a lined, thin, red face with high fore-head, high cheekbones, thin nose, and short-lashed, small, gray eyes. My aunt said my eyes were deep set, which made them fleshy, like some Germans and Natives'. My children look like Inuits. My maiden name is Dawes. My grandmother reportedly was born on a reservation in Oklahoma. I am one-fourth German and the rest mostly English, according to our papers. This face in an out-building mirror, one hundred miles from home, wasn't the one I left with.

I can like you this way.

How completely I had depended all my life on makeup and a pretty figure for a sense of myself—for power. Self-protection. While I was married, fighting the fat produced by three babies ranging in weight from 8 pounds 13 ounces to 10 pounds 11 ounces in five years, I had peered hundreds of times into the side-view mirror of my company's cab-over truck to see if I was pretty enough.

The red, worn face in front of me seemed to mark my next epoch at fifty-four.

What did Mark and Shari see? Certainly not a writer of federal grants or broker of tons of food to major corporate buyers. Not the writer of business plans and financial models for investors. They saw a thin woman in her fifties trusting the world, riding into the unknown, blindly—perhaps clueless. My identity had been scrubbed clean this week with a thousand beads of sweat on the washboard of my horse's walk. Starting with makeup. This person here cared only to make the next mile and fall softly on those she met.

Rounded Up and Claimed

At dusk on the fifth day, before Mark and Shari returned from their birthday party, I zipped myself into my tent. It stood in the hoop-skirt shade of an old yard tree. I lay still on my back. Mark and Shari would not return until after dark. The dog obsessively darted back and forth behind my horse in the lot and barked. The mockingbird repeated its repertoire. The muscles in my face slackened. Then in my neck. A large breath washed through me. How long I had dozed, I don't know. Then came the thought, *my face looks ugly like this*. I felt my forehead and cheeks tighten to a shape I'd practiced in mirrors since junior high. My breath became shallow.

Stop it. Nobody cares.

I thought of tomorrow. I needed to plan my route for the next two days while it was light, before my new friends came home. I pushed myself up with my good arm and sat with my knees bent in front of me for a map table. The backs of my bent knees produced beads of sweat that ran down each thigh. I ciphered my map through my dusty, precious reading glasses. Plotting my course was like piecing together cross-cut shredded paper. First, I traced a gravel road that headed the right direction. I followed it with my finger and discovered that over time, it would lead to eight miles of blacktop before I could hop on another gravel road. Not good. I tried following a different gravel road with my finger. It led to twelve miles of pavement. No. Suddenly, my path for the next four days rose off the paper into plain sight like a deer against the trees when you've stared so long, you quit looking, and there it is.

All along, I had been trying to ride southeast, but every route in that direction led to major highways required to cross rivers leading to Harry S. Truman Reservoir, Lake of the Ozarks, and Stockton Lake. The path of least resistance now led me straight south, to the only bridge safe enough to cross the Marais des Cygnes River. Route V.

Route V was *my* road. I stared at the map, trying to comprehend it. This route would take me directly to the land where I lived on the farm with Mother and Dad in high school—where I had loved, married, and left my childhood sweetheart. I had never returned until now, other than to whisk my car through my old hometown so quickly no one would see me.

During my high school years, Mother and I had driven "V" weekly over the Marais des Cygnes River Bridge to church and to the laundromat in Butler. I drew a pen line from Mark and Shari's to Route V not five miles from my father's farm. I turned my pen right, at the fine line that led past the house where I lived in high school with Mother and Dad. My stomach flipped with joy at the thought of riding the road on Chief that I had ridden on Tabasco so often. But divorce from my first husband had been a scandal, and those folks lived nearby, too.

An hour after dark, I heard Mark's diesel engine growl, then shush in the drive. I gave them time to go into the house and regroup. Soon, Mark's sister and her husband arrived. I emerged, and we gathered on the patio in the heavy metal chairs around a large, oblong patio table purchased, no doubt, for its weight and open-work to let the plains wind pass through.

The evening's molecules seemed to slow, and the nearby trees seemed bathed in calm. Though the wind had ceased, the country was in no way quiet. A high-pitched tinnitus of crickets and frogs permeated the scene. Gold light shone from the house. I glimpsed through the door gleaming granite counters and a stainless stove and hood. A pole light in the driveway lit us and attracted its looping lovers, moths. The night absorbed our words so I no longer can remember them, exactly, just the feeling of adoption by this family and the cool metal under my thighs and my gratitude for a warm ceramic cup.

I heard a story about a little boy, a relative of Shari's, who had cancer. She had prayed for him many times. She seemed to need to talk about him and believed that I, sitting in this group, should not be ignorant of him. She told about one night when she couldn't sleep and was praying her hardest for him, because his cancer was irascible. Something compelled her to throw off her covers and go to the computer, again.

As Shari spoke, I could see into her house from my chair. I imagined her face reflecting the blue glow of her computer that night—a point of light surrounded by miles of beans and corn, growing. Again, she googled the boy's cancer, and this time the name of a doctor who specialized in the disease appeared. She created a path between him and the boy's parents. Around the table there were looks of shared humility and reverence, and one breath-held suspension of fear as she said, "He's fine now."

The group then tried to place me. I explained that I had gone to high school in Hume, Missouri, and my father's farm was near Foster. I told them my former married name. It hadn't occurred to me that they would know my first husband and in-laws. Mark mentioned names of people in my former family. I caught my breath. I already had ridden that close. The subject came and went. If they knew the story of how I left my first husband and the shame I still felt, they didn't seem to care. I was a woman on a horse, doing something I'd dreamed of since I was a girl. They treated me with admiration. We all stayed up late, even though Mark had to leave for work by 5:30 AM.

In my tent, after coffee with the people who took me as I rode in, without judgment or question, I wept. I squished foam plugs into my ears against the mockingbird that tried to drill a hole in my brain. By 6:30 AM, I was packed, mounted, and riding toward the farm where I grew up.

Saddle—Seat of Power

I tightened my buttocks to hold my tender crotch above Honey's aged backbone when I was nine years old. Bareback, I trotted her in straight lines, learning with every bounce how to tuck my tailbone, let my core absorb the shock. I practiced through hours and miles, movements that never reached my reasoning mind, to follow the shift of her weight and tempo—minute muscular responses to minute muscular changes. My seat and limbs talked to my reptilian brain, while her serratus muscles under my thighs bulged left-right-left-right, or when her neck bent slightly, or her head rose an inch. Not my mind but my body learned the pressure to place on my left or right seat bone when Honey curved her spine to turn. Repeated over hours and days and months, flesh to flesh, in wind that crashed through my thick, gold hair, while dust lifted from red-dirt fields and stung my eyes, I made a home in her center, a gyroscope of human and horse learning to stay together. Ground blurred beneath, and I let my lower legs relax and gripped with my thighs and knees and prayed for my horse to aim straight. I scooped my pelvis under and up, under and up, a ladylike horse-woman's twerk to keep bottom joined to galloping bare back.

I had dreamed of owning a saddle when I was six, in Detroit. I imagined myself an adult, driving down the highway with my saddle in the back seat or in the back of a pickup, and people who passed by would see that I had a saddle—I must own a horse. I was eight when Honey—a fresh-cut-hay-and-merlot-fragranced apparition—came into my life. Dad bought me a man-sized, forty-two-pound saddle from a Sears and Roebuck catalog. He reasoned that I eventually would grow into it, which I never did. On the rare occasions my parents had to transport my saddle in our car, and if we chanced to stop at a service station, I would stand beside the car near my saddle in the back seat, my face stiff with self-consciousness, averting my eyes from people who must be staring at me, a horsewoman.

Only a year after Dad bought me Honey, he moved us away, to Lynnfield, Massachusetts, and then to Cincinnati for his work. In the four years that separated me from Honey, while she lived on a friend's farm in Oklahoma, I sometimes descended the basement stairs to clean my saddle with linseed oil or saddle soap. I massaged its leather-covered horn, wide at the top with a two-inch-high neck made to anchor a rope with a calf on the end. I worked oil into the fork, whose swells someday would keep me from spilling over the front. I oiled the seat jockeys where my thighs would grip when I got big, and the fenders that would protect my legs from Honey's sweat—if I ever rode her again. I dusted the Cheyenne roll—the top of the cantle where I would push back my seat if my horse ever took off fast. I would never learn to barrel race or rope a calf. You would have to be born into a family that did that. Maybe I could show, I dreamed. I had read stories about city girls who worked at stables for free and learned to ride and one day were asked to ride the best horse in the biggest show ever.

Meanwhile, Honey grazed with cattle a thousand miles away in horizontal wind that pealed up hanks of hair on her rump—as if I never existed. In summers while I was away, I wrenched my saddle onto a deck rail and mounted it from a lawn chair. I positioned my legs under me: ankles, hips, shoulders, ears aligned vertically. I held twine for reins, fists lightly closed, backs of my hands to the sky, as I had seen in books.

Horse Drawn Like a Bow

By 8:30 AM the day I left Mark and Shari's, Chief and I stepped onto the straight and narrow, paved Route C, which by now had been drained of going-to-work and going-to-school traffic. The sky had filled up with blue, and the sun seemed full of itself today, and so did I, having made up my mind to trust Chief not to plant all fours and go down on the asphalt. We easily could see cars coming from either direction, leaving ample time for us to consider the easiest place to step down into the ditch and onto safe, flat turf by the fence. Route C would take me to a dot on my map called Virginia, a four-building town. Remembering it, I felt sixteen again, riding beside Mom in our green 1965 Volkswagen Beetle, sixteen miles each way with two weeks of laundry in hampers in the back seat. I sat on the cusp of womanhood then, already having dated my boyfriend for two years, desperate to go to college.

Today the celebratory toll of Chief's hollow hooves on the pavement flowed up my spine and into my chest, and if there is a spirit, mine extended to the clouds, straining against its seat in my heart. I rode with a horse for a body. Chief stepped from springy fetlocks. I drove him forward with my seat, so he knew his job was to keep a quick, steady pace. I held his reins firmly, but I gave to his mouth the instant he gave to my hands—not too fast, not to slow, not too round, not too long—an equine version of the Buddhist Middle Way.

My body sank safe in my horse while my vigilant mind flew—no different from a Tartar warrior who centuries ago crossed a verdant expanse in early morning. Those horses could feel their riders merely turn their heads, so when their riders brandished bows, the horses shortened their strides and lifted their backs. Their heads rose, and their ears froze, and their necks formed arches. As the muffled mass of warriors topped a ridge in breathless ritardando, the commander would raise his bow, and the warriors' eyes would harden at this last day, last hour, last moment of a thousand-mile march to surprise an enemy.

How does a horse prepare to fly? It contracts its abdomen, which raises the suspension bridge of its back between its anchors at the withers and croup. This creates a bow of strength that can raise the rider as much as four inches. The tightened abdomen rounds the loins, tucks the croup, and draws the hind legs under the horse's body. The bridge no longer absorbs the rider's weight but sends the impact of every step directly to his seat. The horse is drawn like a bow.

Every instant, I knew Chief's abdomen might bunch to raise his back and thrust the two Cs of his hooves under him to spin our world like a top. But what bad could happen beneath this great blue spectacle of a sky on docile Route C? My right hand stroked the side of Chief's neck. His relaxed back swung as we neared the shed skin of Virginia, Missouri, which tickled my tummy at the first sight of it in thirty years. Between the ages of fifteen and twenty, I had turned at the approaching intersection every week on the way to St. Matthew Lutheran Church in Butler, Missouri.

I guided Chief down from the pavement and onto the edge of an acre yard in front of a manufactured home. The house had blue siding with about fifteen years' worth of sun bleach. The neat place had the attitude of a home that had been trucked in and assembled by a family that worked so hard to pay for it, they had no time for landscaping—only built a deck off the front, three feet off the ground, which doubled as a twenty-foot-long porch with a single rail, all weathered the color of split wood. Lattice hid the crawl space under it through which dogs had shoved gaps to create a cool, summer cave for sleeping.

I could see across the deep yard that three dogs soaked in the sun that morning on the deck. At the sound of my horse they opened their eyes and jumped like they'd been tasered. They rocketed off the edge of the porch and tore across the yard, yowling and barking up their lungs, and slamming on their brakes at our hooves. Chief bunched his abdomen and thrust his hind end under him and drew himself up like a bow. He stopped our sliding force of eleven hundred pounds on thirty-two square inches of hoof horn and spun us around, then leapt three lengths before I could shut him down. I jabbed his right side with my spur and spun him toward the dogs and screamed at them *get-outa-here*, which shocked Chief. I jabbed him hard with both spurs, and he bunched again and launched himself at the dogs, head down and ears back, forefeet pounding. The hounds tucked their tails and streaked across the front yard and disappeared under the deck. I slowed Chief in four lengths.

We circled the yard, headed toward the junction where C became Route V, where it crossed Missouri Highway 52. *Good boy,* I said to Chief, and patted his neck and waited for an oncoming semi, after which we would tap across the highway, toward the land I rode when I was a girl.

Route V and the Road Home

I held Chief at the junction of Route V, a county two lane, and Missouri Highway 52, a sixty-five-mile-per-hour state route that carries traffic from Butler, Missouri, into Kansas and back. We stood in a memory of a town. Byrd's Pecans, famous for three generations, still had its sign in the darkened window of a seasonal store with silver paint on the parapet above its serious face. I wondered if Mrs. Byrd still lived on Route V.

I held my horse firm and watched V slope out of sight ahead and in the far distance reappear at the top of a hill. A semi was coming from our right on 52. I could tell it was slowing and would be turning the same way we would go, down Route V. The truck harrumphed through lower and lower gears. Chief rocked forward and back like he was trying to ease out of a rut. Another semi appeared on a rise, coming straight toward us on V, blathering and clearing its throat as it downshifted to stop at the sign across from us. It looked exactly like the one meeting it from the west. Its blinker was on to turn in the same direction its counterpart was coming from. The two cleared out while I held Chief back, and they wound up their diesels over and over through their gears, one quickly, because it was empty, and the other slowly, because it was full. It was not unusual to see trucks on normally tranquil Route V during harvest—but coming and going in May, that was odd.

Route V formed a twenty-four-mile connection between vacant Virginia and slightly-less-vacant Stotesbury, Missouri, a village of eighteen that still had its post office, and where lies the most beautiful stretch of highway in the United States of America. The section of road immediately before me—leading to the Marais des Cygnes River Bridge, which we had to cross—was considered by many the most dangerous road in Bates County. It had only a foot or two of shoulder that dropped to steep ditches four to ten feet deep. It was built in the 1930s, rated then for forty-five miles per hour. Now its occasional pickups whistled up it like they'd been lit and shot out of Coke bottles. V draped itself over the popcorn hills and banked through several hairpin curves. Add to this the occasional farm tractor roaring along at twenty miles per hour with the right triangle of a folded disk wavering behind it, followed by a wife in a pickup with its flashers on, and it could eat your lunch. I had expected my ride to be tricky on V, much of it spent in the ditch, but not overtly dangerous with frequent semi traffic. Then came a third semi.

Lake of the Ozarks, Stockton Lake, and Warsaw Lake shoot holes through western Missouri for through-travel on horseback, as I discovered this week. In a car, no worries, but for horse travel, these man-made lakes had dams that swelled tributaries and produced dangerous four-lane highways over long bridges to cross them. Gone was the network of ancient streams and thousands of steel and plank bridges on secondary roads that our great-grandparents used to cross. Here to stay were recreational lakes and submerged ancestors' farms. I only now fully comprehended why I kept piecing together gravel and secondary roads that led me straight south—I had to skirt the lakes.

"Marsh of the Swans" in French, the Marais des Cygnes is 217 miles long, spanning eastern Kansas and western Missouri to become a major tributary of the Osage, which flows into the Missouri River in the central part of the state. The Marais des Cygnes is prone to flash flooding, and for this reason the combination of levy and bridge I would cross was high and long.

I strategized our impending crossing of that bridge. The levy spanned the bottoms for half a mile as high as twenty feet, with no shoulder. Once we started to cross (me leading Chief to ensure control), I wouldn't be able to see oncoming traffic until it was too late to get off the bridge because it is that long and convex. We would have to time our crossing so two vehicles didn't meet next to us. It would be impossible to calculate such timing, only divine it. With the normal sparse traffic, this wasn't a major risk, but I hadn't planned on a semi every five minutes.

Once over the bridge, we would ride another quarter mile to the gravel road that led to the farm my father bought fifty years before and left when he grew ill. There, we would retrace the tracks Tabasco and I had made during my teenage, day-long rides.

But that was miles ahead. For now, I relaxed into riding a wide bar of land along Route V, past lush pastures and bungalow-style, 1920s farmhouses. I would enjoy this spacious path, because soon enough, the road would gnaw into hillsides, forcing us into deep ditches.

Chief's legs and belly shushed through fleeting, lavender-fringed daisies with yellow centers and lacy doilies on woody stems, as big around as plates, which I let Chief grab as we went. Ten other varieties of flowers grazed my horse's knees, which I had never noticed from my mother's Volkswagen Bug, flying to Butler for church, groceries, and laundry. A feathery feeling filled my chest. I had driven Route V every week from ninth grade to twenty years of age. Back then, I had my mind trained on the radar blip of a journalism career, somewhere, someday. I emerged from the car in summer with a sweaty print of a bucket seat on the back of my dress. In winter, I scraped frost off the inside of the flat windshield, while a frozen land scrolled by.

We only had one good well on our farm, and it could not support a washing machine. Every two weeks, Mother and I filled the back seat of the Bug and drove our laundry to town. We worked in the laundromat light that blared through the thin curtains on a wall of windows facing Business Highway 71 in Butler. We filled seven washers at once, one of us shoving in pre-sorted clothes while the other followed with quarters, jamming them home and hearing the water spew. I stayed to watch our machines while Mother went to the grocery store. Before she returned, I would hear the machines quiet a few decibels, meaning one or two of them had stopped spinning. The summer heat cooked the shoebox of a building; the two air-conditioners built into the walls on either end ground a tinny hum and dripped their moldy streams outside. Inside, it was only a few degrees cooler, with a breeze produced from two box fans on the floor. I pulled out the laundry and rolled it in metal carts to the dryers and began filling them, one by one, dropping quarters, clicking doors shut to start them, hoping to pull my sweaters out before they melted.

That was the end, the eastern pole of my highway, then.

Now, I rocked along, the sun beating down, the birds trilling or chirping, the wind a pestering sibling. All I felt was my body. Never had I been more inside it. To balance, to feel, to hear the whine of trailer tires, to steer, to grip, to feel my pulse, to smell my horse's oaky sweat. I felt enormous. And minute. It would take me a week to ride back home from here, eighteen inches per step. I felt bound to the earth by my slowness, caught between the sanctity and stupidity of crossing the state one step at a time on a horse.

All was blue, and a dozen shades of green, and lavender, yellow, white, brown, Chief's red coat, his undulating shoulders in front of my saddle, the glints on his red mane as he walked, his ears like frogs' eyes swiveling, wet on their backs. A fly shaped like a MIG fighter landed on one ear, gripped, then lifted away from the drop of blood it couldn't hold.

These trees were as old as my mother, in her nineties now. The fence posts flowed, a row made of cracked locust trees, followed by orange metal posts driven into the ground by a man who, I can say, had to open his mouth when the post driver struck to keep it from bursting his ear drums. I rubbed Chief's neck with my fingertips as an old cowboy once advised, to let him know I cared. The semis assaulted our ears but became as much a part of nature over time as the weeds we passed. Chief turned the backs of his ears to the trucks. Their turbulence flipped my hat brim up, then down, so I canted my head to stop it. For the first time in my life, I had achieved balance—in the center of this horse—focused only on the next step.

Soon, Route V cut into the side of a hill leaving us only a deep ditch to ride in. I dismounted, and we slid down where the weeds grew nearly as tall as us. We walked the narrow path of the ditch bottom, only a boot wide and booby-trapped with chunks of rock or bottles. Tracks like snakes were embossed on the powdery surface by runoff. The trucks labored toward us beyond the hills with soft snores, which rose and fell with the curves and dips before they rolled into view, mouths open, pallets flapping, oscillating on their suspensions, taking their last loud gulps before blasting past in an exhalation of diesel and heat that twisted our hair.

Chief followed me like a baby duck. Horse paths are barely wider than a boot. He was suited to this. There was little breeze here but for the churn of air from the trucks. I waved when I could, but finally let the drivers be. We walked and walked, me stumbling. I began to feel the skin on the back of my right heel give, too numb to hurt. I knew the pain of these new blisters wouldn't start until after I stopped the rubbing tonight. At length, I stopped and lifted my right boot behind me and looked down. Most of the heel had come off.

We rode and walked another hour in and out of ditches. I had mounted and dismounted twenty times since this morning. In the grass flowing beneath us, a glint of blue. I stopped Chief to dismount and see what it was: an ancient glass phone-pole insulator, half buried, waiting all these years for me to find it. I fished over my head in my pommel bag for my pad and pen and wrote a note in fatigued script. I tucked the note in the transparent hollow of the insulator and walked it to a farmhouse mailbox by the road fifty yards ahead and placed it inside. "I found this while riding my horse. I hope you like it."

Again, I clunked into endurance gear, my wool sock stuck to the wound on my right heel. Then suddenly, my spirit bobbed back to the surface. We topped a familiar rise, and before us now, a mile-wide flat, black river bottom stretched away to the banks of the Marais des Cygnes River.

I wanted to call my mother.

On this hilltop, I led Chief across the blacktop to a triangle of grass formed by a wishbone graveled drive. I sat on the hard ground next to my horse's hooves to place my call.

"Hello?" Mother's voice sounded like she was drunk and surprised. A dozen years earlier, she had been diagnosed with cere-bellar atrophy, shrinkage of the cerebellum and was given, at most, seven years before it took her life. The disease left her sharp wits intact but gradually would take her fine motor coordination, so at first one foot didn't move correctly, then she lost her balance, the ability to grasp her cup well, focus her eyes, speak properly. Next to go would be swallowing and breathing.

Mother chuckled awkwardly when I identified myself.

"Mom, I wanted to call you. I just realized yesterday I would be riding past our old farm. I'm on V Highway now."

"Oh, you are? That's nice."

I wanted to say, *No it's not nice, it's profound; it's a miracle. How could I not know I would ride straight south to the same gravel road where Tabasco carried me into adulthood?*

I was in my thirties before I realized Mother always chuckled nervously on the phone. I recognized that she—and I—crafted our sentences from a collection of polite clichés and supportive murmurings, each poised to conclude the exchange as quickly as we could. I turned my head so the wind wouldn't distort my words. I wanted Mother to see this scene with me.

"I hadn't planned it, Mom, but the best way to get around the lakes was to come south—straight toward our farm. I'm going to ride past it today!"

In my most hopeless moments over the decades—after my second child's stillbirth at term; my husband's head injury; the loss of our business, marriage, home—when I allowed myself to imagine my future, an impossible scene unfurled in my mind: me riding a Midwest ditch, alone for a while. Not once did I envision riding back here. Yet here I was, six miles from home, calling Mother as if I were sixteen and had stopped Tabasco at the Bisby's farm to say I rode farther than I meant, not to worry, and I would be home in an hour. Through my life, Mother always listened, never judged or advised. I had been there for her: trips to her apartment several times a week to bring her snacks and supplies, fix her TV remote, toilet and bathe her. She continued to survive, growing clumsier and blinder by the year, until I realized I couldn't wait until she was gone to take my trip.

"It's pretty hot and windy. I'm at the bend in V above Nation Farms. You know the curve I mean, when you're coming from Butler and it curves hard right, and then you come to Mrs. Byrd's and then the river bridge?"

"I think so." I could almost hear the neurons wrenching their attention away from hours watching CNN, now reaching deep to retrieve an image of the sign high above me on a pole bearing the family name, Nation. Did she remember the farmhouse at the bottom of the drive near which I sat? The house stood neat in its white paint and four rooflines that represented additions designed by practical men, which produced the architecture of a pair of sensible shoes. The house stood beside a miles-wide bay of dark earth that four-wheel-drive tractors (built for fields the size of seas) churned through four times a year.

"I'm going to ride past our farm, Mom."

She became quiet.

Mother and Dad left their farm in 1995 after twenty-two years—I moved them off it when they grew elderly—tools, equipment, and auction.

I wanted Mom to feel this earth rising up under her feet, and smell the ripe fescue, and have the wind tousle her hair, which was the color of cherry wood before it grayed.

I no longer looked like myself, with this Swiss-dot rash on my angular face; I must not have sounded myself, either. Before, I would have spilled a torrent of newsy bits in the charming air she taught me. Today, I was honest as a fence post, and as steady. The wind had caught me up like a grain of pollen, like all grains of pollen set free by their mother cells. I left long spaces in which each of us had time to think and feel.

"I forgot how beautiful this country was, Mom."

"Really?"

"I'm going to stop at Mrs. Byrd's, a few miles from the bridge."

"Oh."

"I wonder if Ira Conner is still alive," I said. I pictured the Conner family's green, square, two-bedroom house, under century-old trees across the road from where we once lived. Mother would sit at our kitchen table with her unsmoked cigarette burning, soap opera playing, rubbing the table in long strokes with the flat of her hand as she talked to Ira, who stood in the front-porch door. One day in my teens, I realized that Mother must be nervous to talk to visitors, rubbing the table like that.

"I'm so glad you're having a good time. Thanks so much for calling."

All I had to tell her—about Jerry who put me up near Drexel, and Mark and Shari—must wait until I sat beside her wheelchair again. Perhaps nobody could understand where I was on this hard earth. Perhaps Mother had the greater awareness that I no longer stood on a geographic coordinate but on a different plane with new kin—the birds and the insects and our mutual wind, the herbs I brushed through like any cow or bug. In my mute trudgings, I had left some precious heft along the trail: my cells, their drops of sea; my mind, its strings of syllables. I was thinning to nothing but silent appreciation.

Mother *was* glad I was "having a good time," which to her, I believed, meant a host of things she couldn't say: "I'm glad you're finding meaning today; glad you can return to those we left behind; glad you're a grown woman."

"I don't have good coverage, so I may not call again for a while. I love you, Mom. Goodbye."

"Thanks for calling."

I shoved my phone into its holster, gathered Chief's reins, and mounted. Our road took us around a bend, away from the bottoms along a high, tree-covered bluff above the bottoms. I thought Chief must be thirsty, so we turned up a drive I knew, which curved atop a rise. It brought us in front of a 1970s, partially in-ground house whose front door and two garage doors peeked from under the earth. High noon always brings high wind in the summer here. Tall oaks and pines dipped their limbs. A sixth grader riding a bicycle out front dropped it and ran in the front door. Soon, Mrs. Byrd appeared through the door looking bright, quick, round-shouldered, and slim, as I remembered.

She waved, "Hello!"

I called across the yard, "May I get a little water for my horse?"

She stepped farther outside her door and motioned to me, "Go on around behind!" (We Missourians often couple our prepositions.)

I led Chief to the rear of her house, which faced a mowed pecan grove. A bank of plate-glass windows gave me a view of her slick, updated kitchen on one end of a family room and fireplace on the other end, with a comfortable sectional between. The windows offered a view of acres of pecan trees spaced so tractors with shakers could move about them. The grove draped the top of a rise behind the house and out of sight. The pecan trees' nearly branchless, dual trunks leaned into the sky like Maasai tribesmen. Around here, the Byrd family represented generations of successful farming. Would it be too clichéd to say she had just pulled chocolate chip cookies out of the oven? It was true—for her great-grandson, staying with her after school. My day was nearly half over, and I was anxious to get across the bridge and down the road.

"I know I have a bucket around here," she said, and walked back and forth looking for it.

"It's fine, I have a bucket right here!"

She was determined I should use her bucket, and she disappeared through a rear door that led into her garage and eventually returned with a plastic mop bucket.

"Here, let's get this turned on," she said, walking to the faucet on the back of her bricked house. The end of the hose was in a flowerbed near Chief. It erupted in several hot gushes. Chief's ears snapped toward it.

"I'll get that." She wouldn't let me fill the bucket. She worked like she'd been helping out since she was four and wasn't about to let someone fill her own bucket now.

"Lisa…"

"Stewart now," I said.

"You were married to . . ."

"A Yarick from Hume."

"That's right, but your maiden name was Dawes."

"I can't believe you remember that."

"I remember your folks." While Mother tried to picture Nation Farms, this woman remembered a teenager like me and parents who only lived here twenty-two years, a blip compared to everyone else's history.

As if Mrs. Byrd had nothing else to do the rest of the day, she stood flat-footed, arms crossed beside me in the strong breeze.

"Where are you living now?"

"I'm in Prairie Village; it's . . ."

"I know where it is," she said.

I forget—country people know everything about their regional city—it's city people who usually are ignorant about the country that surrounds them.

"I remember when your dad died. He was in his seventies, wasn't it?"

"Yes, seventy-eight."

"Was it heart?"

"Heart trouble, but stroke did it."

"I hate strokes," she said. "Is your mother still living?"

"Yes, she's ninety. She still lives on her own in a nice independent-living apartment. She goes to the dining room, and they have a company that provides care for those people who need it. She's in a wheelchair now. Her mind is good, but her motor skills are shot because of a brain thing."

"Who are you married to now?"

"His name is Robert Stewart. He teaches at UMKC and edits the university's literary journal."

"I remember you had that saddle company quite a while."

"Yes, almost twenty years."

"Your husband had that wreck."

"Yes. That pretty much messed everything up. To ask him, you'd find out I was to blame!" I laughed, so she would know the topic was not sensitive, though I had a feeling she wasn't worried whether it was or wasn't. With her gray eyes, she held me firmly by my own gray eyes, no nervous chuckle, no airy phrases, no hand on her blowing hair.

Mrs. Byrd was the role model I sought in every female gathering: a woman older than me who spoke in purposeful sentences, after thinking. I have for the past twenty years tried to look steadily into other people's eyes, like her. I grew up clicking my eyes from person to person to "read the room" as I spoke. I wanted to stop my nervous gesticulations, laughter, and interruptions. I discovered some time back I could silently say, "I love you," to whomever was speaking, and this quieted me. Mrs. Byrd's presence seemed a shelter from the wicking sun and the miles that piled up behind and ahead.

"They've reopened the Walnut Creek strip mine," she explained of the heavy truck traffic. I had accommodated myself so completely to the roaring trucks every five minutes, I had stopped wondering why they existed. "It's a wonder nobody's been killed," she said.

In the early 1930s, Peabody Coal Company strip mines around Hume had left knobs of tree-covered earth and deep alkaline pits, many now fresh and full of fish, after coal mining stopped. Walnut Creek Mine, south on V, and others, had re-opened in the late '80s, then closed again. This one had sprung back to life when the price of oil rose. These trucks would shuttle coal like honeybees between the open bloom of earth and the power plant in La Cygne, Kansas, for the next two years, until the forty-two-inch vein of coal had been scraped clean, or until the price of oil fell. The eighty-thousand-pound trucks massaged moguls of asphalt into Route V that wouldn't be repaired until they were done yawing back and forth at sixty miles per hour.

Mrs. Byrd brought me a cookie and Chief an apple. I bent my manners to ask for another apple for me to eat later.

"You be careful!" she said, before we hugged goodbye.

Chief and I were only a mile away from the levy road and our dash across the Marais des Cygnes River bridge. We rode away along the edge of her yard until a hill thinned the right of way on both sides, and we plunged back into the ditch.

Another truck rounded the curve ahead. Its dark windshield contained a beacon—the light of a man's face. I could see a smaller light below it, his massive hand on top of the steering wheel, with which he gentled his screaming rig like a baby's cradle, back and forth over his uneven half of the road. Then I saw his other hand, fat with muscle, fisted around the mic over his mouth. I realized then that he was telling the others where I was. I could see the cant of his horseman's head assessing my rig. He'd probably passed me before. I had never been alone on Route V.

The mine dispatcher knew me. The power plant dispatcher knew me. Every beefy or skinny driver who rode horses and farmed part-time around here, and had kids in my old school, and who would trailer their horses and wives to a roping this weekend, and would tell their nephews it looked like I was gone for good from wherever I came—knew me. These men had been murmuring over me all morning, praying that my horse stayed where I put him. This driver lifted his chin as he passed.

Marais des Cygnes Levy

We arrived at the start of the levy and bridge. It stretched before us and out of sight, nearly half a mile long. Ahead, the earth steeply dropped thirty feet from shoulderless Route V on both sides to bottomland below. The bridge arched high above the water, above the flat black fields on either side. We rested on a field road, where Route V began to rise to form the levy. I was calculating when to step out and attempt our run. Once we did, there would be no place to get out of the way of trucks.

Field roads, like the one on which we rested now, cross ditches to link blacktops with farm fields up and down rural America's asphalt capillaries. These had become oases in this truck traffic for Chief and me along Route V. I unclipped the ring snaps on both sides of Chief's halter-bridle. He lowered his head and opened his mouth for me to remove his bit. I clipped the bit to the saddle.

The heat had reduced me to a mindless swirl of atoms that mixed with spinning shapes and hues appearing as trees, fences, and weeds. Chief and I relieved ourselves together. I squatted and held myself up by his foreleg. The one time I needed it, the wind had disappeared. Heat lay undisturbed over the tacky asphalt. I leaned against my horse to crane my neck under my canteen for eight warm gulps. Chief jostled me as he jerked bites of grass.

I rested with my hands on my knees until a faintness from heat went away. I was so still, I could not ignore the endless, gnawing ache of my left forearm and elbow. We would divine when to step out onto the levy, to jog—I hoped—me leading Chief, and pray that two trucks didn't meet beside us.

In time, I pulled Chief's head up and slid his bit between his teeth. We poised beside Route V, dripping wet, as if we'd already swum half the river's girth and were panting on a flat rock in the middle. I led him in a slow circle around this field road. The ground flowed under us. We clipped the edge of the pavement. My mind was as devoid of words as Chief's, but tweets and beeps filled the space, along with the muffled attempt of a hundred thousand drooping leaves to clap. We circled. I let Chief snatch a bite. We floated in the mercy of the moment. We circled again, aware of the importance of our timing in this crossing—and how utterly out of our control it was.

The pavement's edge passed under our feet. We stepped onto the road, where our trucker had been, where trucks were passing north and south every five minutes, and I tried to run—me and my horse in a current of road, sky, and sweat—and somewhere, that trucker or another watchful man soon would loom on eighteen bouncing wheels. Better be on foot for that. I never had run while leading Chief before.

Come on. I was running in place, pulling Chief, who was too confused to trot. His neck stretched straight, and he took halting steps behind me. I bounced and clucked and kissed and sang, *come on, Boy, come on.* My socks squished with sweat. I couldn't feel my heels. *C'mon, Boy, c'mon.* I sprang in front of him. He responded by walking as slowly as he could, laying back against the reins. I couldn't hear any sound but his clopping hooves, my tapping boots, my clucking and kissing and panting, and my pounding heart in my ears. *Come on, Chiefie, come on.* The road had emerged from the trees, which gave sway to the gaping bottoms that let the breeze through. The land spread out black and lined with new shoots. Random, shiny coins of earth below marked spots too low to drain or plant.

Come on, Chiefie. I dragged my horse and bounded in place toward Dad's upland pasture, toward the woods where my first horse, Honey, folded her knees and flopped to her side for the last time—where two years later I collected her ant-scoured skull. I clucked and cheered, *come on!* toward the pasture behind the house that had dipped and peaked under me and my galloping, copper-penny Quarter Horse, Tabasco, when I was sixteen.

Then he got it, and Chief broke into a strong trot beside me. Now we could fly—as I'd flown to the window the nights my boyfriend picked me up for a date. The end of our long lane would glow when his headlights neared their turn at our drive. In searchlight style, his high beams swept our milo field in front of the house. When they reached the potholes half-way down the lane, they nodded up and down to me at the window. His car rushed up in a cloud of invisible dust in the dark.

The Marais des Cygnes River appeared ahead in our jerky, trotting view. I ran and glanced behind me for the next truck. Still nothing. The water's surface formed a textured wall of cocoa in a deep section under the bridge, following a rush of chocolate froth over rock riffles upstream. The bridge's arches loomed. We trotted toward the metal expansion joint—clop, clop—then onto the bridge, clink, clink, clink. So high and round was the bridge, we could not see the road in either direction. We ran exposed; a truck could appear in front or behind to be shocked by us. I focused on running and the clear awareness that my life might end in this hot, precious, gorgeous moment with my horse. At last, we cleared the far expansion joint, then ran and ran along the high levy, curving past fishing shacks on stilts, and the luxurious soil that seemed made to steal a farmer's heart, then flood.

We jogged and trotted together along the curve of the levy south of the bridge. Still, no truck ahead. In the distance, I could see the road to my old farm a half mile off. Gradually, upland pastures rose to meet the bed of Route V, and finally we could hop and jump into the ditch and through it to a generously wide bar of land along a fence, safe and tired. I pulled Chief up in grass and mounted for, I guessed, the thirtieth time that day.

At last, we reached the old gravel road that led to my father's farm. We rode toward the only patch of shade we could see in an otherwise treeless expanse of tilled fields—a small gathering of ash saplings in the ditch ahead. As soon as we reached it, I dismounted and crumpled onto the gravel in the shade a quarter mile from Route V.

Hidden in shade, seated in rocks, I could see a truck gliding north on Route V, the first in twenty minutes. The road was not visible from my seat on the ground. The truck appeared to glide through the fields. The driver couldn't see us. None of the truckers who had watched over us today would know where we went. In five minutes, another truck came. I rested five minutes more. Another truck passed. How, in the twenty minutes it took us to run the length of the bridge and levy, had not a single truck passed?

Father's Farm

Dad's land came into view one step at a time, as Chief pulled us over a rise in southwest Bates County, Missouri, on day six of our ride. First, we saw the tips of trees in the distance, then trunks, then an inch of pasture, then the whole velvety green vista. My father's upland pasture spread north and south before us, all hips and shoulders under a plush throw. The long, narrow 120 acres made the road go around it, creating a jog below us where we soon would ride.

Dad first tried farming in Oklahoma in the early 1970s. He had retired as a manufacturing executive in jet propulsion with General Electric at the age of fifty-two, due to narcolepsy, which had required amphetamines to stay awake, sleeping pills to sleep, and another drug to combat catatonic spells caused by the narcolepsy. His retirement had brought me back to my beloved Oklahoma plains and to Honey after four years of transfers for his work. It was to be our last move. Two years later, Dad announced we would move to Missouri, to a farm he had bought with his brother.

Heartbroken to leave my best friend, Terrie, and my boyfriend, Tedd, I found my purpose over time on the farm in Missouri: to support Mom and Dad by never asking for anything. Money was short. I was a born conservative. I loved to mow, garden, help cut wood, gather and "work" the cattle. I loved doing a man's work. I had Honey and Tabasco just outside my door.

Back then, I rode down tire tracks into a cut in the bluebird-flecked trees that emptied us into the bottoms. The slough of a shallow lake to my left was bounded by a steep, rocky bluff. To my right, corn grew in soil barely dry enough for us to tread without sinking between the rows. At sixteen, I was frightened of disturbing even one stalk and hoped Mennonite farmer Wesley Dirks, who leased and farmed Dad's land, wouldn't see my tracks. I couldn't bear to displease him. It was bad enough I wore shorts and danced at school and watched television. At least I could have manners on the land the Mennonites worked so hard to farm.

The trees Tabasco and I rode through smelled of bananas—locust wood—that was bright yellow when cut. Pawpaws hung like three large testicles under leaflets in lowland woods. In fall, I picked up persimmons from the ground and squeezed their syrupy, apricot-colored mush into my mouth and spit out the two, slippery, brown seeds the size of oblong dimes.

I had a trail along the bottom of the bluff and another along the top arranged with deadfall—dead tree trunks and branches that I'd pulled across to create a jumping course. Tabasco and I would ride the top trail bareback, take our jumps at a lope, then slide down the bluff, his undercarriage and rear axle scraping the rocks as he slid down among the tumbling stones. I would grip with my thighs to hold myself off his withers as we slid, and then ride back along the bottom of the bluff, taking our little jumps at a lope. Beside us was a permanent slough, and I often could see faintly patterned, charcoal-colored snakes swirling in the black water—non-poisonous but aggressive water snakes, some more than six feet long. A trail took us back to a soggy, plywood-and-tin fishing cabin where we would climb the slope of the bluff again to race bareback across the pasture all the way to the house.

One day, Dad drove his truck slowly through the pasture, carrying Vic Koenig, the cattle buyer, to look at the calves before Dad took them to the sale barn. When I saw the men in the truck in the distance, I galloped especially fast across the pasture despite my fear Tabasco might stumble and fall. Vic asked about Tabasco and me every time he saw Dad after that, remembering the flaming red horse and sixteen-year-old girl with long, golden hair galloping—like

Linda Evans. Dad told me later that Vic said he'd never seen a more beautiful sight.

Within a few years, Dad's brother sold off the bottoms when it didn't make enough money and left Mom and Dad only the upland pasture for cattle and the one-hundred-year-old uninsulated shotgun farmhouse where we lived—no central heat or air—and two old barns. The transaction permanently ended their relationship. Dad quickly farmed his savings away, due in part to a flood our first year that had wiped out a record corn crop in the bottoms—which would have paid down the mortgage.

The three of us subsisted on proceeds from cattle sales produced by a herd of forty-five cows. Our gross income must have been below the poverty line when I was in high school, but so was the income of many other families where I went to school. Where once I attended Indian Hill in Cincinnati, a college-prep public school attended by the children of GE and Proctor & Gamble executives, I now attended Hume High School, one of twenty-two in my class, with broken books and no college counselors.

Dad had experienced poverty as a youth of a sort he wouldn't describe. He was born in 1918 and was raised in hilly, tree-covered eastern Oklahoma. I heard stories of his grandfather owning a coal mine and Dad driving coal trucks as a boy. Then he lived in Louisiana. I remember talk of hunger, alligators, and he never would eat rice again. He never would return to Oklahoma, he always said, though he did, twice to live. Among the legends are his going to work in a CCC camp (Civilian Conservation Corps) and sending money to his mother. He eventually moved to Detroit to find a job in the auto industry. He consciously rid his diction of any Oklahoma drawl. He lied and said he graduated from the University of Arkansas and got his first job with Timken Axle doing time studies. Then he worked for Chrysler. He enlisted in the Air Force, hoping to be a pilot, but he washed out of that dream, he learned later, because his vision for distance was poor.

In his Air Force photo, Dad is a handsomer version of Frank Sinatra. He was trained as a radio operator/mechanic/gunner with a crew that would carry out Operation Tidal Wave from their base in Southern Italy to destroy nine oil refineries around Ploieşti, Romania, on August 1, 1943. His plane was shot down on its first mission, and as far as I know, he was the only survivor. He parachuted and was taken prisoner. The rest of his life he had a bump on the wrist he broke when he landed. Dad was a prisoner of war for several months, and though terrified and malnourished, he was not tortured, as far as I know. He earned the Bronze Star Medal awarded to members of the armed forces for acts of heroism, meritorious achievement, or meritorious service in a combat zone. He earned the Purple Heart and was honorably discharged from the Army on February 12, 1945, with a neuropsychiatric disability. Apparently, he wasn't alone. A 1944 Army report states that between July and December 1943, 132,959 servicemen received such a discharge. Neuropsychiatric disability means post-traumatic stress disorder, battle fatigue, shell shock.

Everyone in the family knew Dad had a temper. He was serious, articulate, intelligent, depressed; he loved to expound on politics, was inordinately cuddly one minute, could explode the next, then want a hug minutes later like nothing ever happened. Legend has it, he was one of the best jet engine manufacturing consultants in the country, though he was relieved of several positions due to insubordination, which resulted in moves from Michigan to Oklahoma City when I was seven; to Lynnfield, Massachusetts, when I was nine; to Cincinnati when I was ten; to Cashion, Oklahoma, when I was thirteen; and to Foster, Missouri, near Hume, when I was fifteen. That year I started dating the boy who would become my first husband when I was twenty.

Not long after I was married, and I was home for a visit, Mother confided that Dad had gotten in the pickup and taken his shotgun down into the pasture. "He couldn't do it," she said. "He couldn't do it—to us." He did not.

Years later, I read a line in a poem by Robert Hayden, "Those Winter Sundays." I understood what Hayden meant when he wrote about the difficult, hard-working father who rose early every morning to start the fire before the children went to school, just as my father had done for me: *"What did I know, what did I know/of love's austere and lonely offices?"*

I rode Chief slowly past the place where my house had been. I knew the old farmhouse had been torn down after Mother and Dad sold it in the early 1990s, but I hadn't been prepared for what I found. The son of Wesley Dirks, who had farmed our land those years ago, had bought the land and replaced the shotgun structure with a two-story, likely four-bedroom house on a green lawn as pretty as any Midtown Kansas City home. They had cleared out the remnants of our completed lives. They ripped out the old fences and wisteria, cleaned the long, straight lane, leveled it, and rocked it properly. The last of the half-rotted trees on the lane had been removed, leaving only a few sturdy centennials. The pasture to the north of the lane lay weedless and lush. The same creek bisected it to fill the same small pond, where I had chopped ice six inches thick so the cattle could drink. The same trees shaded its bank. Across the lane, the forty-acre field in front of the house was planted to beans now nearing adolescence.

I would not walk my horse down the lane. I would come back, announced, clean, another day, and thank the young couple for loving our land.

People Who Knew Me

It felt like days since we rode away from Mark and Shari's, yet we'd left them only this morning. The risk and rigor, riding, and remembering among the semis on Route V already had exhausted me, but we had four more good hours to ride. We continued south along the same gravel road over which the school bus had bounced me thirty minutes to school and back, past Larry's and Connie's houses—classmates who fell in love on that bus and who still live on this road. Chief and I passed a large, groomed pond and a McMansion that would fetch half-a-million dollars if it were in the city. Chief attracted a sudden, crazy swarm of flies, an indication of cattle lying in nearby shade. Sturdy stems stood in the ditch, engorged and translucent. They terminated in blushing buds, long as a man's finger, soon to become clusters of orange tongues, all of them edible lilies, opened or closed. I picked eight of them to eat with olive oil and salt when I camped.

By late afternoon, I was so hot and tired, I cried. I guessed it had reached ninety degrees. Two blue silos stood an inch high on the horizon. I knew I had ridden twenty miles that day, my longest yet. We were on a straight, flat road, trying to stay in the shade of the hedgerow that bordered one side. Chief and I had ridden later than I intended, but the homes had grown far apart, and I couldn't stop until I reached whatever was under those silos. I needed a hydrant, to strip off this saddle, hose down my horse, peel off these sweaty clothes, and bathe. I swallowed, and my throat stuck together deep down, which made me cough unproductively.

At last, we arrived at the ranch-style three-bedroom home, barns, lots that fronted the silos. We turned into a driveway. A couple of horses grazed with cattle beside the house in a pasture. In the driveway behind the house, an elderly man had just plunked his walker up the rough wood step into the barn's dark hallway. A blond woman watched him with apprehension, then turned to see me and called, "Lisa!"

I had swished so long in this sea of wind, I was stunned to hear my name. I hadn't realized I'd ridden nearly to Hume, my old hometown. It was Carol Deitz.

"Dad. Hold on!" Carol called to her father.

"I can't believe you recognized me," I called to her across the driveway. She was straining, first toward me, then toward her father.

"I just need a place to put my tent and two buckets of water!"

She batted the air and turned toward her father, "No problem."

I walked Chief to shade under an enormous tree beside the house and disburdened him. Nearby, just over the board corral, was a small stock tank and a hydrant with a cut-off garden hose bent into it. I helped myself to the water for Chief, while Carol emerged from the barn, having redirected her father. She now walked slowly beside him, fighting the urge, I could tell, to take his arm while he jerkily rolled the front stubs and back wheels of his walker over the gravel. She spoke to him in such gentle tones, I didn't need to hear her words but could imagine them.

"I'll be right over," she said without looking up, loud enough for me to hear. When Mr. Deitz was headed toward the back door of the house, Carol circled toward me. She wore the same calm, fair countenance I remembered from high school.

After a bear hug, she asked, "What are you doing?" as if she'd walked into a kitchen and discovered a child emptying a silverware drawer onto the floor.

"Right now," I said, "I'm not sure! I couldn't believe it was you."

"I'm home helping Mom with Dad for a couple of weeks. She just came home from shoulder surgery." Carol said this as if I might have known I had ridden up to her parents' house, which I hadn't entirely realized.

"Is she okay?"

"She's sore. But she's fine. She just can't do anything."

"Your dad looks pretty helpful."

"Right!"

Just then the pickup behind the house roared to life and clanked into reverse.

"Well, now I've got him in the truck!" Carol turned and walked quickly toward the fifteen-year-old pickup. Mr. Deitz already had angled back and now was pulling out of the drive and onto the road. The truck pulled itself in low gear past the house and back into the driveway on this side, where Chief and I stood. When he got close, he turned off the engine before he'd even stopped the truck, so the wheels locked, and the truck slid six inches. He addressed me through the window over his elbow like nothing. Mr. Deitz was sinewy and bright-eyed. By this time, Carol had circled the house and rejoined us. This is how Mr. Deitz should address a visitor—through the window of his truck, not clinging to a walker. Besides, this way, he could sit.

"You remember Lisa Dawes," Carol said. "Sorry, what is it now?"

"Stewart," I said to Mr. Deitz. "I've ridden from where I live in Kansas City. Just taking a trip around Missouri on my horse."

"Well that's quite the deal," he said.

"Carol said it would be all right if I pitched my tent here. I only need a couple of buckets of water. I have food and everything."

He looked at Chief not with the bright, big-picture stare of a non-horseperson, but with the minute appraisal of firmly held opinion. He owned two well-put-together Quarter Horses just over the fence.

"Let me go check on Mom," Carol said, entrusting her father to me. She resumed her quick gait, useful for keeping track of two adults on a farm.

"There's hay in the lean-to behind the barn. You can put him in there. You want me to help you get the hay?" Mr. Deitz said.

"No, I'm sure I can handle it. He won't need much."

"Carol!" Mr. Deitz yelled.

She hadn't quite made it to the back door.

"We need to get those calves out of there."

She hadn't heard exactly where he wanted me to put Chief, but she knew what he meant.

"I'll be right back!"

"I'd always wanted to take a horseback trip alone since I was a little girl, so I decided if I waited any longer, I might not do it."

"That's for sure," he said. "Do it while you can."

"I had no idea I'd be riding up to a house tonight where I knew someone."

"That's kinda handy."

"When I saw your silos in the distance, I thought, I'm stopping no matter what. The houses out here are starting to get farther apart. Thanks so much for letting me stay." His lack of response reminded me that too many thanks might insinuate my benefactor might have made a different choice, which could be insulting out here.

"How far did you ride today?"

"I'd think about twenty. A total one hundred so far." He widened his eyes as if suddenly remembering I said I'd come from Kansas City and not from a farm down the road.

Mr. Deitz caught sight of Carol coming out of the house, headed toward the back lots.

"Move those calves out of that back lot, will you?" She climbed the board fence instead of bothering to open the pipe gate, and within minutes had sent three four-hundred-pound calves scooting in front of her and out a side gate into another lot. She buttoned it up for Chief, climbed the fence again, and rejoined us.

"Anyway," she said, picking up the thread of what she was about to say before her dad rolled up, "I live in Monett now." She listed the ages of her children and grandchildren, which I promised myself I would remember, but the heat apparently had dissolved my brain's adhesive for facts. She told me where her husband worked and she, as well, but all I could retain was that she'd been married only once, had beautiful children, a good job and life, and now a week's task of caring for her parents—one that probably would be repeated often in the coming years.

"Mom wants you to come in for a visit. You can use the shower."

"Oh, I can take a bath out back with my bucket. I hate to bother you."

"You might as well take the offer while you can. I'm sure you can't shower everywhere."

"That's true. Thank you."

When I had ridden up, I was at the lowest point in my trip, desperately hot, worried about finding a camp, then stumbled onto a home where I not only was recognized but joyfully received. The imposition I dreaded daily, as always, seemed to bother only me.

Chief's lot was formed by weather-checked wood boards and a long, three-sided lean-to extending back from the rear of the barn. Chief slashed at the spiny thistles and chalky-tasting lamb's quarters growing from the powdery dirt like a small meadow of weeds. I broke open one of the recommended small, square bales of hay in the lean-to. They looked like they had been baled ten years earlier, and I carried three flakes of the brittle, old stuff and tossed it on the ground. Chief sniffed it and returned to the fresh weeds. I longed to turn him into the lush field with the other horses, but that was not the offer. I would graze him by the road later. He would get three handfuls of Nutrena Empower Boost tonight and three in the morning, a supplement that I discovered hyped him—which he didn't need—but provided essential nutrition for a trip like this.

I stood still beside my horse. The earth moved under my feet to the beat of his walk, like getting off a subway and feeling its phantom movement on the platform. Chief circled the lot methodically, his nose six inches from the ground. The dirt puffed where he blew it. He stopped and began digging with one front hoof, eventually walking his hind feet up under himself and bending his knees. He tipped his front toes forward and gently descended onto his right shoulder and his right hip almost simultaneously. He lay his neck flat and kicked up his legs to rock onto his side, then rock again onto his back, and wiggled his spine deliciously into the dirt. He sat up like a dog and rested a moment, straightened his front legs, then shoved himself up with his rear. He shook the dust into the breeze, then he pawed with his other front foot to repeat the act on his other side until he was covered in dust.

After my blessed shower (I had started referring to all showers as "blessed," like "The Blessed Mother"), I stood in the Deitzes' kitchen, leaning against the doorway into the living room. Their house was updated, unlike the one I grew up in, containing the quality furnishings found in family-owned local stores, rather than disposable versions from big-box furniture marts. Mrs. Deitz's arm was in a sling, and she sat on a stool, as sensible and grounded as Mrs. Byrd. She was as bright as I remembered.

"You haven't run into any trouble?" said Mrs. Deitz.

"So far, everyone I've met has been very kind. I've done this before."

"Yes, you did." She was referring to my long trip with my children's father, which everyone around here old enough had read about in the *Nevada Daily Mail* thirty years before.

"There are so many more good people in the world than bad."

"I know that's true," she said.

"Not that I wasn't worried before I left, going alone."

"You've been gone from this area a long time."

"Since '80."

"We followed your saddle company in the paper." Nevada was the nearest town to Hume with any shopping, and the *Nevada Daily Mail*, the nearest paper. It ran stories about Ortho-Flex Saddle Company when I remembered to send press releases. After Len's motorcycle accident, the paper regularly reported on his condition during the three weeks he was in the neurosurgical ICU at St. Luke's Hospital in Kansas City. He had been flown there on a life-flight helicopter from Nevada City Hospital after he ran off the road on his motorcycle going an estimated fifty-miles-per-hour with no helmet. I remembered finding old clippings from the newspaper. One day the front page reported Len Brown was in serious condition. The next day, stable condition. The day after, serious condition, again. That must have been the day a new bleed had formed in his brain.

"I've been wanting to thank you ever since I was in high school, Mrs. Deitz. I remember I was at a gathering at someone's house, maybe a shower or something. I can't remember what you said, but you said something really nice to me. I think it was just that you acted like you cared about me, by actually talking to me when I was just a kid. Anyway, I've always wanted to thank you."

"I can't imagine what you're talking about."

"I know, that's all I can remember, too! But it meant a lot to me."

"Well, you're welcome."

First Marriage

Perhaps Mrs. Deitz had caught me feeling lost that day, thirty-seven years ago. Her words had imprinted a point of confidence in my mind, while the world around me said I must marry, and I looked for any excuse to make the world right. Later, I would leave this country at twenty-two, having been married barely two years to a good, handsome, hardworking boy. I would leave behind the silver half dollars my mother-in-law had given me for a wedding gift. I left the flatware, the wedding gifts, antique dining table, chairs, and buffet I had stripped and stained. I drove away that late afternoon with the sun at my back, a rooster tail of dust behind me. The young man I had loved seven years could find someone who deserved him. I told him this in our basement that day. It was not self-serving. I meant it, because who but a truly bad person could leave such a good one? I must, however, or die, I believed. My little pickup was being sucked into the air as I drove away, into the vortex of an older man who was holding open the door to the world. I let him pull me through, just as I had been pulled through my revival baptism, my voluntary wedding. I had not a clue where he would take me, just that I had to go, then or never.

When I was ten, I climbed into a car with my oldest sister, Nancy, her boyfriend, Jim—now husband—and his brother, Jack. We drove to a rise in Kingfisher County, Oklahoma, and rolled down the windows. Jack extended his bare arm out the window. A strange breeze ruffled the hair on his arm. I put my arm out, too.

In an instant, the hot air turned cold. The sky was light overhead, but in the not-far distance—five miles or so—was a black horizon of storm above a tan horizon of land. We sat with the engine off and watched tornados descend from the belly of their mother cloud. Some touched the ground and dug it up.

I no more could have resisted the pull of such freedom as Len Brown offered in 1980, when I was twenty-two, than the dirt could resist those funnels on the Oklahoma plain. I had been introduced to him at KNEM-KNMO radio station in Nevada, Missouri, where I chose to work, instead of breaking free from my young marriage, figuring out how to flee to college as I had dreamed. There was no money, and I was too timid to find a way. Len was an advertising customer of the radio station and a buddy of the station manager, my boss, who introduced us.

I had driven away from the farm of my first marriage—more than a thousand acres of deeded and rented row crop land, pasture for cattle, and hog breeding and raising facility. I breathed hard, my chest filled with aspiration, my heart full of dread and hope. I believed that if I drove through the panic, I would reach something better on the other side that would come hard at first, then more easily, and finally, I hoped, right. I would take stock, dazed, and rebuild with the ecstatic emotion that had provided my escape. During that drive, I tucked into a fold in my mind all the sorrow I had for my young husband, and with it, a fear—that I would never expose to anyone—that there must be another, and another choice I might have made instead. These feelings abided thirty years. The farm and husband I left lay only a few miles away from the Deitz farm, where I lay in my tent now.

Abandoning my husband for an older man felt like yesterday, for all the shame that washed over me in Mrs. Deitz's kitchen—as it did even now at odd times, when I least expected it. I stood firm in her presence that day, brought through the moment by these people, who seemed not to care about my past, but did care about me.

Hollow and Free

I sat cross-legged in my tent. I was still fighting the trucks on Route V and reliving my past, and trying not to let on to the people who lived here. Outside my tent, the sun seemed to blush and cover its head with the earth. My lids drew down and my breath relaxed. Thirty feet from my tent, an Australian shepherd jumped against a heavy chain and yipped its heartbreak under a tree.

I ripped open a packet of tuna and emptied it into my collapsible plastic bowl. I added a half-dozen wild lily buds I had gathered for my salad that day. The tender buds tasted like young, sweet celery. I thanked the earth for my dinner.

Later, I returned to the house with my maps to get Carol and her mother's advice about where to ride next. Chief and I were due for a rest after tomorrow's ride—our seventh day of continuous travel. On the kitchen table, we gently unfolded the sweat-softened creases of my map and spread it flat.

"It takes a moment to get accustomed to the scale of this map," I said. "These finest red lines are gravel roads."

"Oh, here we are," said Mrs. Deitz.

"I'm looking for the best route to go west, then continue south and get around Stockton Lake before heading east into the Ozarks."

"Okay, so here's Hume," she said.

"Yah, I was thinking about riding into Hume just for old time's sake."

"They have a café now," Carol said.

"You're kidding."

"The Swarens girl is running it. It's good."

"Really? I think I'll stop there for early lunch tomorrow then. Now that I've made it six days, I'm getting into a little bit of a rhythm. I think I can make it a month. Then maybe another month."

"If your husband doesn't miss you too much," Mrs. Deitz said.

"Believe me, I can't wait to call him every night and every morning. This wouldn't be worth it if I didn't have him to share it with on the phone."

We all studied the fine lines. My finger kept returning to one. "This one looks the easiest from Hume, don't you think—a B-line into Rich Hill. Then, rather than crossing 71 Highway, I can just stay on the west side of 71 until I get down to Nevada and cross it there."

Carol and her mother nodded.

"Or this one," I pointed. "It isn't quite as quick to get to from Hume, but it also leads to Rich Hill."

"That would be a good one." Carol seemed more enthusiastic.

"But this one seems a little easier," I pointed to the previous road I'd mentioned.

The pair bent over my map, oddly quiet.

"But. Oh!" I said. "I just realized what road that is."

They continued to look at the map without comment.

"I probably shouldn't go down that road," I said.

Mrs. Deitz chuckled.

"Probably shouldn't go there," Carol quipped.

That gravel road would have taken me past my first husband's house, where he and his wife have raised three children and still lived. Where he and I had lived.

"OKAY then," I said. "This one instead!"

We all drew back from the map, and I folded it away.

It was nearly dark when I lay down on my pad in my tent, wearing my red silk pajamas. Carol and her parents watched television. The dog barked. I'd been instructed to come in and use the bathroom as needed that night, but I knew I would hide beside the barn instead. I positioned my baby wipes beside my door, as usual, near my toiletry bag, headlamp, pistol, and pillow of clothes.

Suddenly something exploded within me. I grabbed my baggie of wipes and ripped open the L-shaped zipper of my tent and raced barefoot beside the shed out of sight of the house. It was the first of seventeen eruptions, every ten minutes or so, that had me ripping open the zipper and closing it against mosquitos to dash and struggle to keep my pajamas clean and not step in anything I had left in the dark. I had not known the lilies would prep me for the fussiest gastroenterologist. The final eruption came from above, not below this time, in three vomiting heaves from which I felt completely relieved before the third was complete. I made it only halfway to the shed that time.

I crouched on my hands and knees in the grass. The dog continued its mechanical "Rarf, rarf." I pushed myself up and wavered toward the small stock tank in the moonlight and ran the short hose into it to wash my hands and face. The night air cooled my perspiration. I hid the twenty-five used baby wipes in a spare, gallon Ziploc bag under the edge of the tent. I tumbled back into my bed, raw inside, heels oozing from the walk on V, and elbow raw and bandaged tight.

My colon was not convinced it was finished, but I knew it was and willed it to relax. My stomach felt beautiful and free. In came the dog's bark, the crickets' chirps, my elbow's throb. The cool night compelled me to cover myself. A screech owl hurled its alveolar trill into the woods, and another tossed it back in the dark.

By far the longest and most stressful day of my trip ended in the yard of people who knew me. They remembered, with disinterest, how and why I left this area, as they might remember a microburst in 1980 that had ravaged some fields and torn down a barn, but nobody was killed; everything was rebuilt better than before.

I would get on my horse in the morning and ride through my old hometown, not mother or wife. Not success or failure, but the original girl, hollow and light, who'd been calling me out here since she was ten.

Remembering Baby Colin

We rode away from the Deitzes on gusts of warm wind, the greens and browns and yellows and pinks of nature somehow clearer today. We would ride only a few hours before stopping to rest two nights, because, behold, when I had gone to the back porch to say goodbye the next morning, Mrs. Deitz had said, "Look who's in here, Lisa." It was my old friend John, horseman, rural mail route carrier, coon hunter, heavy equipment operator, farmer, and rancher—like many men in the county. I caught John up briefly on my life, and he did the same for me. Since he knew everyone in the country, I mentioned that I would be looking for some place to stay two nights in a row, I assumed somewhere south of Rich Hill, so Chief and I could have a full day off. John immediately said I could stay at his place a few miles away. At first, it seemed like cheating to ride only a few more miles—and to the home of a friend, so easy. "Yes!"

Though I was exhausted from last night's illness and lack of sleep, I departed the Deitz place feeling light, freer, knowing that by early afternoon, Chief and I would begin our first day of rest on this trip. We headed toward the café in Hume, through flatter pastureland and smaller tilled fields bordered densely by hardwood trees.

Within an hour, the Hume Cemetery gradually came into view. An ancient pine and equally massive cedar divided the cemetery's two halves along a center drive. The whole collection of old and new stones stood open to the sun, with their profusion of pink plastic flowers for mothers and babies, royal blue for the fathers, and yellow and purple for the beauty of it. *Ah! Memorial weekend*, I remembered. There was no rule to prevent the continued installation of big-shouldered monuments in this country cemetery, as most city cemeteries now forbid. The profusion of bright bouquets and sprays made the scene feel like a reception hall before the guests should arrive. We rode slowly past the sunlit adornments.

I looked ahead and the world seemed to be rising slightly higher, toward the Ozarks, invisible, sixty miles off. To our right, still-green wheat industriously converted its nitrogen and sunlight and water to fuller heads, and to our left, a two-story, wood-frame home where one of these days they'd clean up around the barn and maybe have a garage sale. That's when my eyes and nose began to burn. Tears spilled for the innocent souls beneath those stones—all of them innocent, at the end of the day—and for my mother-in-law who taught me to decorate graves each year, *before* Memorial Day, so the cemeteries would be pretty.

As a girl, I had moved five times before high school. My father kept his family of origin at arm's length. In the days when every long-distance call "cost money," my mother rarely phoned her parents and brother, whom I didn't know, in California. In this land, my mother-in-law, Blossom Brown, took me along to decorate her family's graves at Green Mound Cemetery near Harwood, Missouri, forty miles away, on the gravel road where she grew up. She spoke her memories with no silly over-emotion—and why should there be? She cared for her parents and grandparents in her own home until they died. She was hospice before anyone knew the word. People got old and died. Then we buried them. Then we visited and remembered them. What was there to be uncomfortable about?

I turned in my saddle to look at the cemetery and then ahead to the open fields and sky, and the burning sensation became tears for the baby I lost at term, December 28, 1989. I had reported at 6:00 AM to the hospital for my scheduled caesarean section, and nurses came into my room with stethoscopes and left. I thought nothing of it. One came in and told me they needed to bring in an ultrasound machine, because something wasn't working with their stethoscopes. I felt a dawning. Sometime later, a man came into my hospital room with a machine on casters. He had the doughy face of one who had been awakened for this moment. He asked me to watch the screen and said, "You see there? That's the heart." Yes, I did. Interesting. "There is no heartbeat," he said. Oh.

After the C-section, Collin was weighed like any other baby. Nine pounds, ten ounces. A nurse brought him to me tightly swaddled. His eyelids and lips were purple. He already had been gone a few days while still inside me. "He has my nose," I said. My best friend, RN, Lamaze coach, La Leche League instructor, and wife of the man who performed my section turned out of my room to cry. Collin would have been the only one of my three who would have looked like me. I didn't weep or wail. I didn't even feel numb. I felt confused.

I always have reveled in handling a challenge—taking charge while others fall apart. I cried little the first three weeks after the stillbirth. To this day, my former husband says I was changed. He said it enough I came to understand he meant "damaged." I couldn't see how. For an entire year after Collin was born, I felt him kick. Every night for a year, I dreamt that I had carelessly misplaced him.

Chief and I walked beyond the cemetery, imperceptibly higher in elevation, moving east through the fields of fluttering stalks and bending flowers and air split a thousand ways by the trees. I uttered a clear cry. There was nothing clamped or strangled or wracked about it; no one to hear it but me. Just open-mouthed, spontaneous, filling my ears with the sound of my wails. Chief pointed his ears at me. My mother never would cry like this. "I don't want to cry," she had said several times. "I'm afraid I'll never stop." I cried not caring if I never stopped, "I'm so sorry," I repeated dozens of times. "I love you," then, "thank you," dozens more.

After a mile of this, I was finished. A distinctly different sound filled my ears. A kind of tinnitus, as I had heard beneath the tree at Mark and Shari's when my mind went blank with fatigue and relief. The noise grew. It brought with it a feeling of protection. A presence.

Instinctively, I looked around for its source, and there it was: the wind, the sun, this gravel road, that field, the fences, the trees, the sky, enveloping me, like the gentling on of a comforter in chilled half-sleep, when someone thought to cover me. It wasn't an otherworldly force; it was the worldliest of forces. I had cried and asked forgiveness and expressed my love for a baby lost and had thanked him for the forty weeks he gave me. After riding a hundred miles, and exhausting myself, and cleansing my body with lilies, and trusting strangers, and staying in the middle of my frightened horse—I became aware, for the first time in my life, this world was here to protect me.

I would listen often in the coming miles for the high-pitched tinnitus. It was a million bells so far away they might have been chimes on a distant porch. It was the hum a farmer thinks at first is a bee, then realizes it is his neighbor's tractor a section away. For me, it was the sound of the world—a very busy Body. It came most clearly when the heat made my heart pound, and I had no idea where I would lay my head that night. I rode past this cemetery on Memorial Day, and I remembered my baby. With the sound of the world in my ears, I was beginning to perform simple acts on this trip without thinking that seemed directed by some internal knowledge new to me—turn here, knock there, cross the river at one particular moment—and each was the perfect thing to do.

A Girl for My Heart

Two hours later, I was riding across a belly-deep pasture and into John and Jan's yard. Ten-year-old Riley and her mother braced against the wind's early afternoon crescendo. Riley had sandy-blond hair, a slender, strong build, and a half-amused and half-amazed expression. A woman riding into the yard on a horse from Kansas City is a magnet for a girl who loves horses.

Jan and John's three-bedroom, white, one-story farmhouse fronted a gravel road just off Route V, two miles west of Hume. It had the kind of plains architecture that a violent spring storm could roll over without lifting an eve. Jan had planted flowers in beds near its footing. Wispy perennial asparagus waved like underwater fauna, three feet tall from its round bed. Jan showed me a 1960s sedan parked by the barn. She had tediously covered it with a net of string and planted ivy around it to create a car-shaped topiary by summer's end. There was a hitching post by a small barn that served as their tack room, and ancient trees shaded large swaths of the yard. A few coon dogs quietly wagged their tails and curved their long bodies with excitement beside their houses, on circles of bare ground the length of their chains. It would be easy to feel sorry for these chained dogs except for their happy faces and shiny coats and flesh strengthened by miles-long runs through the woods at night, chasing raccoon with John—pure joy. Jan and Riley watched me unload my saddlebags in the yard, where I would pitch my tent, then Jan followed me in the family Gator as I rode Chief across a hayfield to what looked to be a forty-acre pasture with pond and grass up to Chief's privates. We left Chief there and brought my saddle back to the barn.

When we returned, Riley said, "Do you want to see my mare?"

Behind the house was another large barn and surrounding it, a series of clean, weedless lots in shade. "She's a Quarter Horse-Paint cross," Riley said.

Riley's mare was copper-penny red, slightly shorter than Chief, and all-Quarter-Horse build, which meant bulky muscle (opposed to Chief's thin muscle), massive hindquarters, wide chest—practically a different species if the two were compared. People in this part of the world have raised and ridden beefy Quarter Horses all their lives. They must think my horse ugly, with his sharp lines and thin muscle.

"See, this blanket looks like a running rabbit." She pointed to a "blanket" of speckled white along the lower half of the mare's belly that indeed looked like a bounding rabbit.

"She has a heart-shaped blanket here." Sure enough, a heart-shaped blanket of white splashed across the side of the mare's neck. Her hooves had been regularly trimmed, my guess by John, and were in perfect shape. She was all shed out and gleaming. She respectfully sniffed her small master, too well-disciplined to be pushy or nibbly. Riley stroked the horse's neck as absently as a mother touches her child's head in passing.

By the time we returned to the shaded spot behind the house where I would pitch my tent, not far from the family picnic table, Jan emerged from the house with paper plates piled with cheese slices, grapes, apple slices, and sausage.

"This is Riley's sausage," Jan said. I thought perhaps the girl had helped grind, season, and stuff it.

"This is from the doe I killed last year," Riley said. (When she was nine.)

"Wow. I don't know many girls who can say they've made sausage from the deer they killed."

"The meat packer actually made the sausage," Riley said.

"Well, right."

We weighted our plates down with our drinks.

"You'll have to tell Lisa about the fish," Jan said.

I think Riley was too modest to mention it herself, but she seemed anxious to add, "I won a fishing contest with a bass I caught over eight pounds."

"You guys! A horsewoman, hunter, and fisherman?"

Riley tried to check a smile.

"Lisa, Riley has a softball game this afternoon. Why don't you come with us?"

I already was embarrassed to stay two nights instead of just stopping for one and moving on—doubly so to tag along to the game.

"And an athlete! I really don't want to mess up your night, though, Jan." Riley looked a little concerned, I think, that I might not come.

"I'm sure Riley would want you to be there." Already we two were bonding, probably because I already adored the girl.

"I wouldn't want to miss seeing you play," and then I pulled her under my arm as I would my daughter.

"I'll let you girls visit. We'll leave at five. You sure you want to sleep outside?"

"I have all my stuff here in one place out here. It's best." On so many levels, I thought. Less imposition (in my mind), more privacy for everyone. Riley and I nibbled our schoolgirl hors d'oeuvres, and I asked her questions about the life of a girl who grew up where I did, but unlike me (who arrived a freshman in high school) was born on this land, surrounded by generations of family who loved her and taught her how to work and hunt, ride and fish, drive a tractor, and hit a ball.

I had caught Riley on the crest of adolescence, all upswing and no downside. Her brown eyes were lit with a confidence undimmed, as yet, by heartbreak. She walked like all us country girls, sweeping over the clumps and dents in the turf in a smooth, ground-covering stride. She spoke like she walked, every sentence a series of quarter notes, no fancy inflection, staccato, or crescendo. Nothing nipped at her insides to make her giggle or jabber. No sharpness or quest for attention. She had a belly full of love and good food, thanks to her mother and father. Riley and I related. I felt ten, too, right then, and missed my own daughter, Natalie, at ten.

After the forty-five-minute drive to the Archie, Missouri, ballfield, Jan opened a folding chair for me and sat me beside her like we were old friends. By that, I mean Jan treated me with respectful rural manners, whose hallmark is not formality but familiarity. In fact, she had known my former husband when she worked at a trophy store that made engraved name plates for our saddles. We sat near the bleachers with a setting sun in our faces. By then, I'd had a "blessed shower" and wore my one pair of shorts, flip-flops, and a clean T-shirt.

Sunny Jan had a short blond haircut with a sassy, dark brown fringe at her nape. She wore sparkling clean acrylic nails, French-tipped toes, and a rhinestone-studded ball cap, which to me is an art. I wouldn't know where to shop for such a saucy look, and besides that, I couldn't pull it off. She sat in her chair and tightened the screws in her sunglasses with her pocketknife and lobbed barbs and self-effacing quips to the other girls' moms. Thirty cars and pickups parked around this ballfield on a flat prairie that some people would term desolate.

The girls' forms were shadows against the mile-wide footlight the sun became on the horizon. They pushed off with muscular thighs and threw with hard arms. Afterward, they posed for pictures, bellies down, heels up, arms over each other's backs, on a sandy bed by home plate—future West-Central Missouri Girls' Fastpitch Softball winners. Mothers and fathers with digital cameras and phones captured and posted their shots. We came home, and Jan insisted I join them for grilled ham and cheese sandwiches in front of the television.

The next day, my first full day off, I lazed and wrote in my journal in my tent while John made his daily mail-route run. Jan did laundry, moved a piece of equipment to a hayfield to help an aunt and uncle, and later helped John hay. I climbed as high as I could on their metal gate by the horses to get my phone call to catch and swing through the towers to my husband. AT&T was not the right carrier for this trip, I had learned. Verizon would have worked better this far between cities. My husband's son and wife had had their first baby that morning in Chicago—our first grandchild. How could I not be home to receive such news?

I brought in towels and underwear from the line and folded them on Jan's drier. Propped in the corner by the back door stood Riley's pink .22 rifle along with her mother's and father's rifles in stair-step lengths. Later, Jan took me to the pasture to fly-dope Chief where we had left him across the section. Chief stood nearly pressed to the gate, as near as he could get to me. Surely, he had looked for the pond. He was covered in biting flies, having no other horse to help him swat.

That afternoon, we all crowded into John's pickup and rode to their favorite spot in the county, where Jan hoped they someday would build a house. The sun nearly had set, and the three stood in the back of the pickup. All the better to see the land surrounding us from this highest spot in western Vernon County, arms around each other, smiling, tinted pink by the sky. We could see the Osage Cuestas out of which I had ridden a week before; the La Cygne, Kansas, coal power plant on the horizon; and fields and trees in the form of a rumpled blanket of green brocade around us. The dream they shared—the grilled sandwiches, the ballgame, the pasture, the feed, the place in their yard, the daughter they gave me for forty-eight hours called for a slumber party for us two horse-loving girls, who must say goodbye too soon.

The next morning, I lay under layers of homemade quilts in my tent. Just outside, on the grass and wrapped in quilts, lay ten-year-old Riley, a girl whom I took for my heart when I rode into her parents' yard the day before yesterday. Only her crown was exposed against the cold that piled on thicker as the night turned into morning. The sun now quietly lifted the blinds one ray at a time. This would be the only night I slept warm in my tent on this trip—under quilts Riley's grandmother made.

Dozens of sparrows peddled their squeaky wheels in the trees. I had left the screen door unzipped between us, because my tent barely slept one, and I didn't want Riley to feel alone. She lay perfectly still—growing. A stomp came from the lot where her horse stood behind the house. The flies already were biting.

At 8:00 AM Jan heaved Riley's saddle onto her mare at a hitching post under a massive tree behind the house. Riley and I mounted up and headed down the gravel road in front of their house, east, toward my next destination, Rich Hill, Missouri. Jan followed us in the Gator. After a mile, I looked back, and Jan was gone. She would not insult her daughter by hovering.

Chief had processed ten pounds of grain, I guessed, in the past two days, but he seemed calm, probably because he was with another horse. Riley's mare jigged a little—alert—but not jumpy.

Riley jounced gently on her mare to keep up with Chief's smooth, quick gait. She wore a carved, western belt whose elongated holes bore proof of her daily growth. She wore jeans and boots (better known as Ropers) with smile lines from walking. She was the real deal. John had taught his daughter to hold her riding crop out to the side so the mare could see it out of the corner of her eye and know Riley would use it. The wind spun up tiny twisters in the road.

Who knows what we ten-year-olds talked about? We arrived at the blacktop she was not to ride beyond. Jan was nowhere in sight. I worried the little paint might try to run home with Riley, but I pretended no such thing could happen. We dismounted and hugged. She mounted up and turned west for home. I turned east for Rich Hill. I wished I had a picture of us on that flat expanse from a half mile off—two entities having collided, altered by one degree, and on our respective paths around the globe. After a bit, I twisted in my saddle to check on her. Riley was holding the mare down to a walk, courage screwed up, and in control.

Chief Gets a Spanking, and
Mennonites Take Me In

C hief brought me the fourteen miles of gravel road to Rich Hill like a gentleman, through fields and woods from Riley's house to the edge of town. We entered on a quiet side street that gradually turned to asphalt, past houses even the Department of Housing and Urban Development wouldn't rent, and past others so pristine you felt worried they might catch the blight the neighbors had.

My chest felt heavy at the sight of ripped screens, a window propped open with a BB gun, dogs on chains, the screwed-together lives of people born to people born to parents who drank or drugged. The movie *Rich Hill* was filmed here, about three boys who lived in three of these houses. The documentary set the stage for what it might take for the boys to achieve anything better. At the conclusion of the film's screening in Kansas City, my daughter and I sat in silence, clamping down sobs.

My schoolmate in Hume, Curtis, didn't want me to come into his house nearby, because they kept chickens in the front room in winter. My best friend from junior high lost two front teeth in her thirties from drugs. My son's good friend died of an overdose at twenty. A young relative spent time in jail for the crime of being eighteen in his own house when police found his father's gallon bag of OxyContin.

Poverty isn't just about drugs. My children had seen their father and me lose everything after his wreck when our business went under. He lived in a small RV for a time, after having been one of the largest employers in our town. We'd done everything right, worked day and night to build a business, employed a hundred people, then watched it disappear, until I was selling pre-arranged funerals door-to-door to get through Christmas. My kids went on MC Plus, Medicaid health coverage for poor children, for three years, and I had no coverage at all. If it could happen to me, what chance did a kid have whose parents couldn't hold a job?

And still, these parents would have treated me with the same respect and care as did John and Jan. I know these people. They're lost, maybe chemically messed up, but not criminals, not any more than any cocaine-snorting mortgage broker who sells loan packages to people who can't afford them, then drives off in his Audi.

I was determined to stay on Chief's back through the asphalt side streets of Rich Hill and ride all the way to a convenience store, Mennonite café, and grocery store on the east side of town. I'd tie Chief there somewhere and maybe get a sandwich. We tapped down the quiet side street. I draped myself like silk around my horse and kept my eyes soft. I watched Chief's rigid ears and bunched neck, and rode his sports-car suspension so I'd be ready in case he shied. As if it had read my mind, a large, black Chow came from behind a house, stood its ground, and stared at us hard. Chief glimpsed the dog and planted all four hooves on the pavement. Both hind legs went out from under him. I grabbed for his mane. We nearly went all the way down. I dismounted. This slip was a good reminder for him to keep his act together. I should have stayed on. He had re-learned his lesson; he could handle pavement. But my nerve wasn't back, and all I could see was my head popping on the street.

The remainder of our trip through town proved that I never, ever should go into any town—ever again. By the time we reached the intersection near the 71 Highway overpass, clotted with a Swope's Drive-in hamburger joint, two convenience stores, café, grocery store, and continuous truck-stop traffic, I barely could lead Chief. He trotted in place beside me, shaking his head.

Grow UP! I said.

I can't help it, he seemed to return.

I spotted a short section of white plastic fence in a grassy area between the grocery store and convenience store parking lots and removed Chief's bit from between his teeth. I tied him there by his halter and then got permission from the convenience store to use its garden hose in the back. I carried buckets to Chief one hundred yards each way.

That done, I headed to the café across a parking lot and over a small side street. By the time I made it almost to the door, I turned to see my horse pulling down the fence by his lead rope. I ran back to him and worked five minutes to follow his head up and down to get him to unclench his jaw and take the bit. I lead him through the mess of traffic, which further electrified him.

My crowning mistake was misreading my map and leading my faunching, pulling, horse over the 71 Highway overpass, only to learn that the road I wanted was many blocks backtracking through town. I'd come all that way for a sandwich I never got.

After another forty-five minutes leading Chief through the streets of Rich Hill, we finally reached the road that would lead us south on gravel many miles. We nearly were clear of town when a different black Chow materialized at a dead run from its doghouse just behind us and rushed the fence—a fact I learned only after Chief slammed into me from behind with his chest. I flew forward but caught myself by his reins. I spun and started screaming. I backed the bastard a city block, jerking down on his reins over and over, screaming profanities. In my mind I screamed at myself, *I am a terrible rider, an inept trainer. I chose the wrong horse for this trip. I am babying him too much. He was a good horse until I got my hands on him. I can't even read a map.* I jerked him and backed him and abused his mouth, and I did—not—care.

"Sometimes a child needs a good spanking to clear the air," an older woman I admired once told me.

Now I had his attention. I kept leading him until his head began to lower, his eyes softened, and his body lengthened. There was grass beside the road for traction, so at last I felt it was safe to remount. When I hopped to mount, a knife-like pain stabbed my right thigh, and something seared inside my left knee. I had mounted too many times on Route V, and this was the knee I had dislocated in high school playing basketball. Something felt tattered and swollen inside it. Somehow, one more time, I managed to get back on.

We rode south out of Rich Hill on a narrow, paved track and watched the homes grow farther apart. Chief's lowering head and swinging walk began to soothe me, and gradually I abandoned my default self-concept: That I was an embarrassing failure. I reminded myself I know nobody whose horse could be trusted any better on such a trip, and the town's stimulation had torqued my grain-hyped horse, like dropping a dictionary behind a trooper with PTSD.

Out of town now, we came to a groomed yard, an oval of water, two screaming, white geese that terrified Chief anew, and a brick, ranch home in perfect repair. Across the road from it stood a mobile home with dirty, bent siding, toddlers' riding toys stained the color of earth, and two hoodless vehicles in a barren yard.

At the ranch home to our right, an older Mennonite couple sat on folding chairs inside their open garage. I knew they were Mennonite by the woman's black cap, calf-length cotton dress, and the man's trimmed beard. Before them was a pile of parts they clearly were trying to assemble into something drawn on the large instruction sheet the woman held. I turned into their driveway. The woman, some fifteen years younger than the man, came right outside in response to my large wave and smile. "Hi! I'm traveling, and I wondered if I might have a little water for my horse. I have a bucket."

Her blue eyes and full cheeks blossomed as I dismounted. "Of course!" A Mrs. Klein, I would learn, circled in front of her house and dragged over the hose that was unspooled there. She was gray-haired and plump and looked to be in her late sixties. She belonged to the Mennonite sect I grew up with in high school, like the Dirks family who farmed Dad's land. They use no radio or television but have modern homes and equipment. The ladies' dresses in this sect are cotton, all made from a similar pattern with small, feminine, floral prints, and hemmed just below the knee. Comfortable shoes and short, white socks completed the workaday dress. Chief drank two-and-a-half buckets. By now, Mrs. Klein's tall, slender husband had pushed himself from his chair and sauntered over. Mr. Klein looked to be near eighty. His blue eyes snapped with curiosity. I felt naked beside this couple in my skin-tight riding tights, but they seemed not to care what I looked like and were intensely curious about a woman riding alone.

"I wonder if you know someone down the road who might have a pasture or lot I could put Chief in for the night. I'd like to make about five more miles."

"You can stay right here," said Mr. Klein.

"Oh, I don't want to interrupt your afternoon."

"I have a lot right back here your horse can stay in."

Sure enough, behind the small back yard, and beside a small wood barn was a lot grown up in volunteer wheat and fescue.

"I'll pull the fence together. We'd like to have you," he said.

I should make a few more miles to justify the stress of the day, I thought. But I feared that if I refused, I might hurt their feelings deeply.

"I'd love to."

I unloaded Chief in the mowed grass and did my best to carry on a cheery conversation while I worked, which left me forgetting important parts of my routine. Mrs. Klein periodically glanced over her shoulder at Mr. Klein's glacial progress closing gaps in the fence for Chief. Chief's attention was riveted by the shrieking geese Mrs. Klein referred to as "Japanese fighting geese" at her little pond across the way. I reassured her I easily could hide behind the garage and take a good bath from my bucket, but she insisted I use their shower whenever I wished and begged me to use their spare bedroom. I managed to refuse the bed, telling her I would feel more comfortable next to my horse to keep an eye on him. She left me to pitch my tent, while Chief stood tied to a fence post, pawing a hole in the earth. He didn't need a readied room. He needed thirty more miles.

An hour later, I emerged from the back door of the Klein house with clean, wet hair and limped on my injured knee down a few concrete steps to their garage where the pair sat in their folding chairs. Again, I felt exposed in my short shorts and tight T-shirt, but that was all I had to wear. Mrs. Klein was gently directing a husband who seemed not to comprehend the value of written instructions. He already had installed the handle on the front of the lid to the barbeque grill and a wheel on a leg. I could see he'd taken the first obvious steps that were sure to gum up the assembly down the line.

"I'm good at putting things together. Would you like me to help you?"

Mrs. Klein's body seemed to sag with relief. "Would you?"

I sat cross-legged on the swatch of carpet on the garage floor surrounded by a seemingly irreconcilable pile of parts. We started over from step one. For the next hour, the three of us worked hand in glove, segregating the screws and nuts and washers and parts in reasonable order as we assembled our barbeque grill from the inside out rather than the ground up. We three were building our bond, one "Screw A into Hole B" at a time.

"My wife died when my boys were teenagers," Mr. Klein said. He walked quietly around the interior of the neat garage, now that I seemed to have taken over. He looked out the small window above his work bench with tears in his eyes. He gave no cause of his wife's death.

"We had been missionaries in Central America," he continued. Missionary trips for young Mennonite couples with small children are common. These commitments often spanned years, and to some non-Mennonite minds put small children at risk. The present Mrs. Klein continued reviewing the instructions as if she had heard the story before.

"That's where I met my present wife."

Mrs. Klein smiled. "I was a nurse. I loved the work. I never married. Until Mr. Klein."

"We became reacquainted after my wife died, and then we were married," he said. "She finished raising my boys as if they were her own."

"I love the boys."

"She did a good job with them," he said.

She released a sigh only I could hear, sitting so near.

"So, you're from over by Hume," he said.

"I graduated from high school there, but my dad's farm was over by Foster. You might know Wesley Dirks; he farmed my father's land."

"He's a deacon at our church!" said Mrs. Klein.

"One of his boys lives on that land now with his family," I said. "I don't know which one."

"Probably Bradford," she said. "I'm not sure, though."

The Kleins and I pressed through steps ten, eleven, and twelve with the patience only polite strangers can sustain. We backed out of step twelve, fixed my mistake, and found a missing wrench for the one and only nut that size. I learned where Mr. Klein had farmed and what he grew, that his people were from Germany, and that they dearly wanted me to see the beautiful church and school their congregation had built. We would go visit it as soon as we were finished, and then I would eat dinner with them when we returned. At last, we stood around the newly assembled barbeque grill whereupon I learned the couple and their family went through a grill every few years, they used them so much. This was not their first rodeo, building a grill.

Just as the sun was setting, we climbed into their van. Only a few miles away, the one-story, brick building stood in the fields like all Mennonite structures, well-built, high-end materials, unobtrusive, and attractive. Mrs. Klein unlocked the front door, and we walked reverently into the cool, muted light. The church contained at least a dozen spacious classrooms, a large activity room that could double as a carpeted gym, an open area for its cafeteria, and a vast, professional kitchen that could only be designed by Mennonite women who understand the requirements of rising bread and a pickup bed full of fresh sweetcorn to shuck, blanch, and freeze. We walked reverently through the building. Mrs. Klein flicked on and off the ceiling lights as we padded from room to room.

The land surrounding this church stretched flat and ribbed with crops, treed only where homes needed buffering or creeks made them a natural. Mrs. Klein beamed at the same time she matter-of-factly allowed that their enrollment was down. She openly expressed her concern over why it seemed hard to keep their grown children staying in the area. Mrs. Klein walked as the Mennonite women I have known, who've never balanced on high heels or learned to glide with their tummies tucked and their breasts pushed up. Such women said what they meant and laughed when appropriate, not nervously after every sentence.

That's how they had laughed in my best friend's kitchen in Nevada, Missouri, ten years before. My girlfriend, Julie, a fellow Lutheran, and her Mennonite friends sat and chatted during a lunch break from spring cleaning in her home. She always hired her Mennonite friends for spring and fall cleaning. Julie had grown up near a Mennonite community on her father's wheat farm in central Kansas. She attended summer vacation Bible school with Mennonites, because it was on a different week from her Lutheran vacation Bible school, so she could attend both. Her blond hair had been braided in the fashion of preadolescent Mennonite girls. She felt at home with them, and when she moved away from Kansas to Nevada, Missouri, she reached out to the Mennonite community there for spring and fall cleaning help.

One day, I remember her saying, they had sat at her table to rest and drink iced tea. The youngest among them was to be married soon. My friend began to ask how she was prepared for her wedding night, and the girl's older sister shushed Julie and asked the young bride-to-be to leave the room. Incredulous, Julie confirmed that the girl had been told nothing about sex. She was nineteen. "It is her husband's responsibility to teach her," the older sister explained. Their mother and sisters would purchase her trousseau, including sexy underthings. Anything goes in the Mennonite conjugal bed, she told my friend, who stood up in shock and walked to her sink. Julie was an RN, a breastfeeding coach, a Lamaze instructor; she believed in health education for women. She returned and sat down with her friends, the bride-to-be still absent. Referring to modern sex education for non-Mennonite girls, the bride's sister said, simply, "Do they look any happier than we are?"

I stood in Mrs. Klein's bright, neat kitchen as she prepared our dinner of lunchmeat sandwiches on homemade bread. Mr. Klein referenced, for a third time, the wife he had lost and the children who lost their mother. Mrs. Klein looked up to the ceiling and turned toward the counter. The late wife had been gone more than twenty years.

Mrs. Klein added to the table her homemade strawberry jam and homemade pickles. We sat to Mr. Klein's prayer. Dessert came out, cookies first. Then Mrs. Klein got up for pastry, in case cookies weren't enough. In a few minutes, she jumped up and apologized for having forgotten the ice cream bars from the freezer and set the box beside me on the table. The strawberry jam, real butter, and thick homemade bread had been dessert enough for me. Before this trip, I was eating no dairy, no sugar, and as little grain as possible. On the road, I ate only Kind bars made of nuts, seeds, and fruit for my breakfast. For lunch, nuts and dried fruit, jerky or maybe a can of smoked oysters. For supper, packets of tuna or salmon and crackers. I was afraid to eat anything else that would make me discouraged with my own food, but tonight, I ate it all.

That night, I lowered myself to my pad with my good elbow. I had been able to wash my wound again here, and it seemed to be healing with no infection. Yet the flesh over the elbow could not be touched. My left knee felt like it had been replaced with a plastic joint twice its normal size.

I lay on my back. I could see the evidence of my beating heart by the tent's minute movement. I pushed my ear plugs home and slid my eye mask over my eyes. Chief's pacing in the lot beside me slowed as the geese quieted with dark. A chained dog across the road barked his love-starved obsession, which penetrated my ear plugs. My mind would not accept that its work was done. I was shattered by the riding, and leading, and walking, and holding my revved horse away from my feet, and tying, untying, and bracing for Chief's next leap. I could not will myself to relax and instead, mentally cycled through every misstep I'd made that day. Tomorrow I would ride twenty miles to Nevada, Missouri, where I had returned in 1982 with my former husband from a horseback trek that had lasted nearly eight months. I had lived near Nevada for twenty-five years, built a company from an idea, while paying off my husband's excavation business debt, had given birth to three children and raised two. I attended church every Sunday, cared for my ailing father, watched over my failing mother, and finally lost it all. Bob would come tomorrow evening to find me, bring me what I needed, and take me to a motel with a bed and shower, if I found a safe place to leave Chief overnight. I lifted my eye mask and was startled by how dark it had grown. I watched the green hue of my tent grow deeper, which slowed the gentle nudge of my heart.

As cool air began to infiltrate my tent, car doors slammed at the trailer across the road. Eighties metal music popped speakers, and someone adjusted the volume to a steady blare. I could distinguish every chord. A motorcycle approached and downshifted. The rider revved the engine three times as he coasted into the drive. Show off. The motor wasn't about to die; I'd ridden my own motorcycles enough to know that. Despite the gentle euphoria of the last of ten hydrocodone tablets, and the calming effect of twilight, the heavy metal music and cars and shouts kept me awake. I unzipped the tent door and dragged my damp rain poncho over me to trap some body heat.

An hour later, a man and a woman carried the tail-end of a fight outside and screamed at each other in the driveway. Pickup doors slammed. One of the combatants started a vehicle with the gas pedal floored, and the engine said, "WOW," in a mechanically unhealthy way. They drove off. The music stopped. Now it was just the dog. *Gasp bark, gasp bark, gasp bark, gasp bark, gasp bark.*

I hugged to my chest four religious tracts Mr. Klein had given me after dinner. Four sheets of paper in different colors, each trimmed to the size that would fit into a man's shirt pocket. I had studied the Bible enough to know I didn't believe one particular tenant the tracts contained. I had faith in the rest, and I knew the intent with which they had been given to me. Not a moment today was I not aware that something was holding Chief and me together. It was pulling us another block, another mile, through the ditches, over the interstate, to this spot on the edge of Rich Hill, Missouri, fifty yards from drinking and fighting and drugging, to a little, brick ranch with darkened windows where a couple slept so resplendent with love, nothing could penetrate their peace.

Birthplace of
Ortho-Flex Saddle Company

On the morning of our tenth day, Chief lilted with curiosity rather than fear from my Mennonite friends' back yard, a behavior for which I decided to take credit and begin to regain my confidence. Again, the sky overhead flashed blue, the ground grew drier, and the heat confirmed the wisdom of setting my cell phone alarm to 5:30 AM to make our miles before the worst of the heat. By 2:30 we would have ridden eight hours. Ten miles ahead on this gravel road was a new Amish store, the Kleins had told me. Something to look forward to.

I felt a mixture of joy and urgency: for riding toward an oasis tonight (Bob, in his pickup) and for the pull toward ancient homesteads, new homes on ancient footprints, and the next former town absorbed into saplings and vines or cleared and tilled. By the end of today, I would cross four-lane Interstate 71 north of Nevada, Missouri. I would walk toward my former home of twenty-five years, where Len Brown and I had built our business, raised our children, and lost it all. Chief and I would ride up the two-lane paved road with grass growing in its middle crack—old 71—to the barn and garage where my former husband and I started our saddle company in 1984.

I would ride past the expanse of rolling pasture where my son built forts with his cousin by the deep pond that our horse Red Wing loved to swim, and where all the horses we took on our trip earned their rest. I had ridden, now, from Kansas City in a beeline—entirely unplanned—to the site of my most exquisite pain—where I filed for divorce and took their father out of the children's daily lives—and to the site of our most glorious accomplishment, building a company from nothing and improving an industry. I had set out to ride east, not south; away from this country, not into it; toward the future, not the past, which for thirty years I have tried to transform from its native pain into something I could accept. In my four-mile-per-hour, twenty-mile approach, I wondered who lived on my mother-in-law's property, now that dementia had sent her to a nursing home in the city, and in what repair they maintained it.

A black bulk brought me back to the present, south of Rich Hill. To our right, a few hundred yards away in the middle of a field, a foreign mass trundled. Chief spotted it and reacted in a way one would if she turned the corner to find a bulldozer parked on her lawn. It was a four-up team of black Percheron draft horses breaking up a field far enough away Chief could not make out what it was. *Horses, just horses, Chief,* I said and scratched his neck. I recognized them only because I had seen them in pictures. I explained it all—peppered Chief, as usual, with logic.

I'll take your word for it, he seemed to say by not changing his pace but walking with his head turned to make it out.

We rode on, between tilled fields and pastures, mostly flat and bounded by garishly leafed trees, and now and again large, two-story frame houses, sans shutters, trim work, or landscaping where Amish families lived. Beside them stretched truck gardens covered by black plastic to hold in moisture and prevent weeds around the cartoonishly large plants for May. We came upon occasional trails of horse poop, not piles, because Amish horses don't get to stop trotting to poop. Chief slowed for them, and I let him lower his nostrils, even sometimes to sniff so deeply in and out that his barrel swung my legs. He'd been ripped from his herd when we left his pasture, twelve days ago. I hadn't let him get his nose to other horses in that time. He was desperate for a horse hug, which came in the form of teeth gently massaging the crest of his mane or rump. The least I could do was let him sniff. Louis Rasmussen at NO-Bar Ranches in northwest Colorado told me once, "They work hard for you. You gotta' let them be horses."

I waved to Amish men in straw hats standing in gardens and women in bonnets on porches. They stared and waved as if they should know me. I must have looked like a young Amish man from a distance in my white, long-sleeved shirt, black pants, and large straw hat. Buggies were parked in shade and in sun, at this house and that, held in place by thin, dark horses with pointed shoulders and greyhound waists. They stood bored, being eaten alive by flies, some cooking in the sun. Chief passed them, confused by the dark contraptions behind them. I could feel him processing the carts into the equation—that if the carts were attached to the horses, they must be all right.

At one home, where three buggies and horses stood tied under trees, Chief slowed as he passed, and I was overwhelmed by his message, *"Mom, can we let them go, please?"* I have no way to justify this notion. It was something about the way his body felt under me and the expression on his face. *I know,* I told him.

Hours passed as we walked south, parallel to Interstate 71, just out of earshot and sight of it. The heat was beginning to feel damaging. I longed to reach the Amish store the Kleins had said was down this road. Then we would be only a mile from the garage and barn where my saddle company was birthed on Len's parents' property. Surely, I would find something to eat and drink at the Amish store that would make me feel better. I kept bumping Chief with my rounded spurs to remind him to keep up the pace—two lilts above a dog walk. At every crossroad, he slowed and tried to stop and look longingly to the right and to the left. Sometimes I let him, since I'd made him walk quickly the previous mile. I debated with angst whether I was riding him hard enough, letting him be horse enough, or babying him too much.

At last, I saw movement ahead on the flat expanse of farmland. A pretty, white-and-green metal building with divided, double-sash windows and cooling front porch came gradually into view. When I drew close, I could see a buggy and horse parked at a massive hitching post and rail. At last, a reasonable structure to which to tie my horse. The buggy horse curved its neck in a C to look past its blinkers at Chief. Chief walked with jerky legs as we approached the black buggy with its tall wheels. Chief's countenance expressed the same concern of earlier that day, as if this horse hitched to that thing needed help.

When I dismounted, Chief stood like a good Amish horse due to the heat, the miles, and nearness of his own kind. I took long gulps from my canteen and left him. Another buggy pulled in while I was in the store—the exposure Chief needed. *Be glad you didn't fall into Amish hands, Chief, or there'd be no spook left in you, and no initiative, or curiosity, or joy for that matter.*

Inside, the concrete floor and open windows felt cool. The store seemed brand new, unadorned, and barren. The growing season was so young, not many vegetables were available for sale. I could take nothing fresh and had no interest in glass jars of preserves but needed to talk to the blue-eyed girl behind the counter and youngsters fiddling around. I craved talking with people between the hours-long stretches of silence and one-sided conversation. Again, I felt naked among their full skirts, and, again, was reminded that these folks have seen it all, and worse, at Walmart to which they clop on the weekends and tie their horses beside the big block box. The Amish were regular people in a particular wardrobe, like my artist friends with their piercings and tattoos and mishmash attire.

After seven hours of riding, our day neared its end. We approached my mother-in-law's, Blossom Brown's, property, the place where I became a writer upon publication of my first magazine article at twenty-three; a business owner soon after; an employer; and seventeen years later, a seeming failure. Chief and I trudged up a ditch bank onto the two-acre lawn my father-in-law had mowed for twenty years. We strode toward the garage apartment and barn where we started our business. I once had thought it would sustain us all our lives.

I had dreamed as a girl of making my living with horses somehow. By following my dream of riding cross-country on horseback, I found the man with whom I could do both. He had enabled me to leave on the journey I wanted to take alone but did not have the courage. His entrepreneurship gave me an outlet from which to record our discovery—that saddles often damage horses' backs, and how to prevent that damage. My writing—more than one hundred articles published in equine magazines—launched into the world the saddles he so elegantly designed. The garage we had lived in now seemed lifeless but was bright with new white paint. The two-story barn behind it, in which our first dozen employees worked, stood the same as it had. When our company outgrew it, my mother-in-law had turned it into a dollhouse of a rental apartment.

In front of it, near the road, her former home wore fresh barn-red paint. All the windows had been replaced. The trees she kept trimmed and sprayed were as she left them. Blossom Brown had been the neatest housekeeper I ever knew. She taught me how to clean: *Take everything out; clean the space you left; clean what you moved; then bring it all back in. If you haven't moved it, you haven't cleaned it.*

On this lawn, I had posted smoothly to my Saddlebred, Lucky's, aerial trot, back and forth for catalog pictures of saddles we made. Brukamira, our Arabian mare, had reared with me here, and her loose girth let her saddle slide off her rump, spilling me onto the ground behind her towering, teetering frame.

I neared the sidewalk that we poured between the garage and house, whose twenty yards my son crawled from our little apartment to his grandma's back door. Her six-foot-tall potted oleanders were gone, but someone else's petunias and impatiens shook their red and white faces at me. Everything looked better than before.

There was a work pickup in the drive, and as Chief and I walked toward it, a man in his thirties appeared and met us on the freshly graveled drive. His face was serious with work and heat and a lifetime of adherence to the high road. He was a Balk. He had been a schoolboy when I lived here. His grandfather had owned the Balk family Allis-Chalmers equipment dealership where my first husband's family bought their tractors. Like the young Dirks son on my parents' farm, this fine man had replaced what needed replacing here.

Blossom would be thrilled her home was occupied by a good, young family. Anyone would understand young Balk tearing up the native grass pastures and drilling wheat to make money for his kids' college tuition, though it broke my heart to see it. When cattle prices came up, maybe he'd seed it back to pasture.

Blossom's mushroom cloud of a tree above us seemed to burst with wind. The lots behind the barn had all been torn out, so nowhere to put my horse for the night, which was fine. I didn't want to stay on this place. I was hot and tired and every mile I rode now was an endurance test. Young Balk told me it was ninety-five degrees outside. I instantly felt better. It really was hot; I wasn't a wimp. He pointed up the road I had ridden hundreds of times.

This young couple overwrote our story with their own early draft. The trees, lawn, buildings, the old, red-block silo persisted, played host to this generation as it had the previous one, and the ones before that, the Natives, and the buffalo, and millennia before, the sea of melted ice that rocked here in its basin. I rode through the yard and down the road, as if nothing happened to me here, which it hadn't, now that all was said and done, except my expansion, me bigger, moving out, spun off.

Robert Stewart

I have always been aroused by truck grills, or subtle dents in seats where the men I have loved had sat, or dual wheels that provided suspension to pull heavy things they owned, or the sight of a pickup coming home. Though my father wore white, pressed shirts to work, I had felt my first sexual urges toward horsemen, cowboys, farmers, mechanics. My adolescence was spent near men who owned land and had car lifts in their garages, and more dollars' worth of seldom-used equipment parked around their modest homes than most city lawyers had in their five-car garages. These men had swollen knuckles from slipped wrenches and fingernails that wouldn't come clean and eyes that flicked around when a buddy asked them to listen to his engine. They knew how to talk to another man without ever dishonoring him.

My husband, Bob, was a new species of man to me when I met him ten years earlier. He never questioned whether I should take this trip but asked only how he could help. To get my supplies, he would stop at five stores to make the right choice, then drive hours to find me. He knew I could write well and told me why. He came to me, taller, more slender, more well-read than my girlhood crushes and womanhood loves. He looked like the English professor he was, balding, in glasses that he took off to read. His back and shoulders had been fortified by high school sports, by digging ditches as a young man for the St. Louis Sewer District, and mechanicing in his working-class neighborhood in St. Louis. He came from pipefitter lineage.

He fit all of my bill and none of it. He was twelve years older and financially stable, but not rich. He studied English on the GI bill after serving in the Navy during the Vietnam War. He introduced me to new literature, better wine, to his mother's Sicilian food, and wept when he read me poems. He had not been married in more than twenty years; he lived alone in his bungalow in midtown Kansas City with his books, and nothing on the walls except one small painting of two olives. He had worked for the University of Missouri-Kansas City more than thirty years by that time, and he brought the world's most famous poets to town for readings in his Midwest Poet Series for as many years. Robert Stewart lived within his means, a poet first, an academic second. Bob had many friends, the same friends for decades. After twenty-seven years as managing editor, Bob was promoted to editor-in-chief of *New Letters* magazine, a literary journal founded in 1934. He won the 2008 National Magazine Award, the equivalent of an Academy Award for editors.

He obsessed if he thought he had slighted a colleague or friend. He wrote thank-you notes and sent them through the mail, bought greeting cards two weeks in advance, came home at the same time most evenings, thought everything through, and because of it, required forty acres to turn his mental rig around. He taught poetry writing, magazine writing, and editing, and created twelve-page-long syllabi because he felt obligated to save the world from sloppy writers. He was linear and expansive, and right-brained, and a lover of meaning expressed through words. He hated knickknacks and things on walls, and music with words, and loud music in restaurants, and blaring TVs at Costco, and barking dogs, and neighbors with drum sets. He loved contemplation.

While we dated, he drove two hundred miles, round trip, four years to see me, which satisfied both our needs to keep our families out of it and to put off talk of marriage. He scared me the day he hesitated to alight from his Bronco onto a parking lot covered with dead beetles. He made me laugh when he suggested he should roll his new pickup a few times before driving down to Vernon County to see me. He learned to lead a horse. He taught me how properly to use the words "that" and "which." When he visited me in Nevada before I moved to the city, he came and left too quickly, to return to his office where he worked seven days a week.

Though to this day he feels exotic in my bed, and as such, I sometimes wonder with psychic distance how I can be allowed to feel at one with a third husband, I understand. I got to have what I wanted—what I knew was best for me—and I am grateful I persisted to that end.

Hometown—Nevada, Missouri

Chief and I rode east from where Len and I started our saddle company, along Route M, near the place where the town of Compton Junction used to be, now a liquor store and nest of homes. We were riding away from 71 Highway, which we had crossed that afternoon. We would skirt east and south of my old hometown, Nevada. Surely Bob was getting close.

Two- and three-bedroom homes and farmhouses came and went on their acre plots of pasture, but everyone still was at work—no one answered the door. I needed to park my horse in a safe pasture and get into my husband's air-conditioned pickup and into town to a motel to shower, and to a restaurant to eat, and to tell Bob everything I'd seen and felt, and have him hold my hand. Chief seemed to melt into each step in the grassy two-lane right-of-way, and I did not bump him with my spurs but stroked his neck and searched ahead for a likely stop. Only the top of his rump still was dry. I dialed Bob from Chief's back.

"I am just getting ready to leave town," he said on the phone.

"You haven't even left Kansas City!" (Two hours away.) *How could he not know he should be here by now?*

"I've been making stops for the things you said you needed. Where are you staying?"

"I don't know yet. Talk to you later." I hung up.

He was supposed to be here when I was ready to stop. It took another eighth of a mile riding for me to process the fact I had not specifically told him that nine hours of riding would translate to

3:30 PM, the time it was now. As a result, I would be sitting on the ground two hours in the heat, waiting for him outside some pasture. Or, God forbid, still riding.

My feet were soaked with sweat in my boots. My scalp itched like fire, though I'd rinsed my hair in a garden hose twice that day. I felt sorry for hanging up on Bob, but it was too much trouble to dial him again from the back of my horse. I continued east under a hyperbolic sun, a buffoon of a sun, a bully. Chief's face was ashen with dried sweat. The grass gave off its own damp heat. The wind quickly dried our endless production of sweat and took our precious calories with it. The blacktop cupped thin, fake pools, and the horizon seemed to tilt occasionally.

Half an hour later we invested in a ride up a relatively long lane to an expansive, brown brick ranch home whose tall roof told me second-story windows gave a view of the pasture out back upon deer or wild turkey. The two-acre yard had been neatly mowed. I walked Chief to the etched-glass front door of the house and fastened his reins up out of the way of his hooves and rang the bell. Mrs. Wilson, in her forties, opened the door looking startlingly clean. Yes, yes, she was sure her husband would let me put my horse somewhere on their place, but exactly where, she couldn't say. The Wilsons owned a tire and auto repair company in Nevada, which my former husband and I often had patronized years ago.

I would have been like her, had my husband not come off his motorcycle at fifty miles per hour. Established, respected. Everyone in town had known us. What if our business had survived thirty years, rather than just seventeen? We would have kept up our pretty home in the country, put our children through college, maybe traveled. Would we have?

In the windy shade, I watered my horse with her hose, while I waited for her message to flow through the office of Wilson Tire, out in the store, back in the shop to find her husband to learn where to put my horse overnight.

Two hours later, I sat on the ground outside a pipe metal gate, behind which my horse stood in a sixty-acre pasture. Half a mile away, a silver club-cab pickup stiffly turned the corner at Route M onto this gravel road. My core warmed at the sight of my husband's grill in the distance, silent in its approach beyond the breeze and birdsong. Next, I could hear the gravel popping, and finally its quiet Chevy engine. Chief lingered on the other side of the gate, smelling of DEET, not wanting to go near the cattle in the Wilson's large pasture. Beside me in a pile was everything we carried.

I got up, and Bob stepped out of the truck, seeing me for the first time in four days. We hugged hard and swiveled back and forth. He was sweaty, preferring his window down to air conditioning—the lizard, he called himself—loving the heat. We loaded all my gear into the bed of his truck. We climbed in and immediately I wanted the air conditioner and motel. Instead, he pulled into a patch of shade an eighth of a mile up the road.

"Let's sit for a minute." I knew what he meant—get out and sit on the tailgate. Bob had been cooped up in his office for the past thirty years. I'd gotten him out. Far out. I didn't protest. We sat with our thighs tight together, a hand on each other's knee. He had proposed to me on this tailgate.

Bob pulled a blessed beer from a small cooler in the truck bed. In a moment, he reached into his pocket and pulled out a small package.

"I thought I'd give this to you now." The box was wrapped in craft paper with a bow of raffia ribbon. I unwrapped it with hands only recently cleaned with a succession of baby wipes. Inside I found a hand-carved and polished wood box, one-and-a-half inches square, with a Chinese symbol for "love" engraved on its sliding top. "I thought it was small enough you could carry it with you. Happy anniversary." He bent his neck and kissed me.

It was our fifth. I had forgotten.

Hay

Bob and I spent that night in a kind of cloud of bread and wine and cotton sheets at the Nevada Inn. Three days later, Chief and I had traversed sixty-seven miles of vast tables of wheat turning the color of buckskin. We stayed with friends of John and Jan, who arranged for us to spend this night on the farm of their friend, Bill Garrett.

Chief and I descended from the high plains into Clear Creek bottoms along creeks that wrinkled the terrain of extreme southeast Vernon and northeast Cedar Counties. Over the past three days, we rode beside woods and flat pools of pasture and crops abutting tributaries that flow northeast toward the lush, low, Schell-Osage wetlands and wildlife refuge twenty miles to the north. I felt fine—toughened. My elbow hurt only if I touched it to something. Today we climbed back into higher, open wheat country, riding twenty-seven miles, our longest day yet. I endured the midday heat by telling Chief the *real* story of why we had to ride on:

We have the fine lady's letter, Chief. We have to get it to the train station before the Colonel leaves. The lady has changed her mind. She wants to marry him. He has to get this letter before he boards the train, or he may fight too bravely in the war—having no one to come home to—and not live to return.

I bumped Chief with my spurs. Chief perked up his walk. *Good boy. To the train, Chief, to the train.* Thus, we passed a nine-hour ride through mid-nineties heat and uninterrupted sunshine in high spirits having a life-saving mission in our hands.

At 3:00 PM, we swung into Bill Garrett's driveway.

The Garrett's farmstead served as a launch pad for tractors, mowers, and balers. A fifty-by-seventy-foot "pole barn" (a one-sided structure whose so-called poles were not made of traditional wood but of half-ton, steel I-beams) provided the focal point for this farm scene that seemed to float like a raft on hundreds of acres of ripening wheat. A machine shed nearly the same size, nearby, had likely replaced the original wood prairie barn; a 1980s raised ranch, flanked by a wood shed with sliding doors, and a woman's attempt at local flowers, completed the plain-Jane agriculture base that didn't even have a dog.

The place felt empty at 3:00 PM. Farmhands surely had spun off like electrons to mow and bale hay. A "custom" haying operation means someone does the cutting and baling for others, paid per bale, like "custom" combining, where waves of men hauling combines sweep across the Midwest from south to north, harvesting wheat for farmers who choose not to own their own combines.

Near the driveway, a man in his mid-twenties, whom I would learn was Bill Garrett's son, stood beside a power-take-off brush hog that was held two feet off the ground by the hydraulics of its tractor. Another teenage boy stood on the mower deck and a third boy lay underneath it with a long-shank wrench trying to break loose a mower-blade nut. I hoped the hydraulics held for the boy underneath.

Young Garrett said his father was expecting me, and just then, Bill Garrett stormed up in a tall, red pickup with tread-plate flatbed. He told me I could camp wherever I wanted and make myself at home. He apologized for Chief's pasture being overgrown—a quarter acre with a small pond—but one of the mowers was broken. Imagine, a man who mows for a living having unmown pasture. Like a carpenter's unfinished house. Bill walked over at the speed of a trot to pull two long gates together and wire them in the middle for Chief, and before I knew it, Bill was gone.

In Bill's wake, I asked young Garrett if he thought his dad would mind if I stayed one more night, so I could let my horse rest tomorrow. We'd ridden six days in a row. He said, "Nah."

Soon, the boys dispersed into the fields again, as there were at least eight hours daylight left in which to bale hay before night made it too moist. Hay baled too moist could spontaneously combust once stacked in a hot barn.

I stood in the sun beside a small, weedy field without a tree, which now held my horse, who had come to accept that each night he must swallow his need for equine contact and settle for standing as close as he could to my tent. I reached through the pipe gate, and he let me graze the tips of my fingers against the hairs of his neck, but not make contact. He insisted on some dignity, having allowed me to dominate him the past nine hours.

I pitched my tent nearby in the lee of the two-sided hay barn between us and State Route 160, five miles north of Golden City, Missouri. Here was the only patch of shade I could find on the place, except for a few trees near the house. I liked being tucked behind a twenty-foot-high wall of big round bales of hay tucked under the eve. The only downside to my tent's placement behind the barn was the long hike for water each way.

Once I had pitched camp, I entered the barn's open west end, which faced the house. The floor of the Garrett's hay barn consisted of jaw rock (three-inch chunks of limestone gravel) dusted with hay and dried mud that had fallen off tractor and truck tires over the wet months. Four I-beams sunk and bolted into squares of concrete in the ground down the center of the barn held up its peak. Parked inside was a tractor, a large blade that was detached from its Hesston 1260, and a freshly washed, new semi tractor-trailer with a shining aluminum tread-plate flatbed made for hauling a load of hay bales over the road. Little did we know, the impending drought would send the Garretts' hay flying on trucks down to Texas at quadruple the normal price. The barn made the semi look small, and the truck's chrome stacks had plenty of headroom to the roof.

Bales like giant spools of gold embroidery floss surrounded the trucks and tractors three high, raised there by a tractor heavy enough to lift them over its head with bale spears without falling forward. Despite the number of bales, the barn held only a small amount of hay at the moment. I walked to an interior corner made in the northeast by two walls of hay that intersected in front of the semi—to what in youth would have seemed a secret hiding place. I felt a stillness in that corner, towered over by hay—a dense, earthly protection that only dried cellulose, Mother Nature's insulation, could provide. Straw and mud had protected humans tens of thousands of years—imagine the sanctity of huddling beside tons of cultivated, groomed, nutritious hay wrapped in dense circles of gold ribbon. If this barn were a Yankee Candle fragrance, I would name the fragrance "Honeyed Hay" (with a spritz of diesel from the truck).

I had played "fort" with Terrie Wahling in her dad's hay barn. I had played hide and seek in the loft of my father's barn with little nephews and nieces. Nothing felt more quiet, alive, secluded than a wall of hay, fifteen feet high and twenty feet thick in those days. Hay shed from bales had cushioned our bottoms on the barn's wood floor and poked through our socks and pricked our ankles.

People my age remember small round bales, revolutionary compared with loose stacks of hay that had to be pitch-forked. The newfangled, small round bales could be thrown into a hay wagon or pickup. Their curved surface of stems and leaves shed rain. Then came small, square bales, which were easier to stack in barns than round but were not as rainproof. It took special training and talent to stack either small square or small round bales inside a barn so they wouldn't cave and crush someone. Young men of my generation bought cars in high school from money made while working in hay fields in the summer. They got sick with fever from stacking hay in 120-degree barns, breathing dust from shattered clover, brome, lespedeza, fescue, alfalfa. Then came large round balers. Progressive farmers bought the big balers to pull with their tractors and spears to mount to their pickups. They could back into a bale with a spear, tilt it up with the hydraulics kit they had installed in their pickup, and drive out with a bale for cattle in a nearby field. Large bales are lined up and stored in long rows like

Jurassic centipedes across America. I often climbed on them with little nephews and nieces and my own little children, and we hopped from one to another to another. They eliminated a million summer jobs for teens.

By dusk, the sky had become a skylight to a world that had slipped its sun. I lay back at last with my good elbow on my thin, golden blow-up pad. Chief had dried from the shower I had given him when we first arrived. His coat gleamed with DEET. His head hung from its cantilever. Not an inch of skin stuttered. His tail hung straight; not a fly would come near. I pushed myself up on my good elbow and unzipped my screen. I crawled out on my hands and knees, past the rainfly staked to protect me. To the west, the heavens seemed to spill a dark blue ink into an absorbent sky, and it seeped toward us. Towering overhead was a white shaft of cloud unlike anything I had ever seen, like a hound's leg with a big foot planted against the vault above.

That night, I lay dead asleep when a thunder crash sat me up, gasping. The wind raked my lightweight rainfly and stretched its gold cords against thin stakes in the ground. Fat drops snapped the tent. Above, dark blue, smoky billows flashed to nature's Morse code, clearly visible, then disappeared. I searched for my Teva rubber sandals with their soft, sturdy crisscross straps, my headlamp, gathered all my clothes in my arms for a pillow, space bivy, rain poncho, the one phone I could find, and pushed through my now unzipped tent, on the run. I stretched the tent door, popped the stake out of the ground that held my rain fly, and ran, leaving the tent door whipping in the wind. I ran in rain now coming sideways. I ran down the seventy feet of hay bales and around the corner, into the open south end of the hay barn—the direction from which this storm bore down. In flashes of light I could see an upside-down question mark hanging from a blue-black wall of cloud. It dragged toward us through the watery sky like a giant fishhook. I ran up and down the length of the barn, slipping on my wet rubber sandals over the jagged rock, dropping pieces of clothing, finally to the interior corner of hay bales. I crouched there a few moments. Hay and dust whipped in circles inside the barn. The torrent pounded the metal roof like Niagara. Mist from the blowing rain reached fifty feet into the barn smelling of the sea. I squinted my eyes against a whirlwind of hay and dirt.

My friend John from Nevada had been caught in the Joplin tornado the year before, which had killed more than 350 people. Joplin was only an hour from Nevada, where I lived in high school, and a frequent shopping destination for us. My friend had been delivering medication to a nursing home in his job as a pharmacy driver. He had been standing near a center wall in the nursing home that was flattened, across the street from Freeman Hospital, which had been moved fifteen inches on its foundation. My friend survived by falling to the floor against the wall. When the tornado passed, he pushed debris off himself and began digging out the patients who were still alive. One week before that, my sister's good friend lost two grandchildren in a central-Oklahoma tornado two miles from her house. Those two storms had the same atmospheric genesis.

I had been made to run to root cellars as a girl under skies turned green, and where cold air from the Rockies had trapped hot air on these plains, to be relieved only by a violent upward spin. I'd often wondered as a girl what I would do if I were caught in a tornado on the plains on my horse. I would lie flat in a ditch. I would cinch myself inside my saddle with the girth around a fence post or bridge—or an I-beam of a hay barn. I ran to the semi and threw everything in my arms onto the flatbed behind the cab. I ran for my saddle and jerked it off the implement where I'd set it. Its cinch caught, but I worked it free and slipped and tripped with my twenty-five-pound saddle to a center I-beam. In the skinny, wiggling beam of my head lamp, I set my saddle nose down on the ground near the I-beam. I shimmied between the two and sat as close as I could on a corner of concrete with only silk between the concrete and my privates. I wrapped the cinch around the beam and threaded the latigo through the D-ring on the saddle and tightened it by feel until the cinch ring met the rigging ring on the saddle—tight as it would go. Which left three feet between me and the post. That was when it dawned on me that I am smaller around than my horse.

My mind's version of this scene had the saddle tight against me with my arms and legs wrapped around the beam or post.

Now, the fat, white question mark in the sky was upon us. I could see the trees around Mr. Garrett's home prostrate their ancient limbs to sky's bizarre punctuation, then invite it in by spinning their arms in circles. By the yard light, I could see leaflets and dead branches disappear into the night. The mist of rain and hay became needles.

I imagined my husband right now driving up to this scene to find his wife wearing her red silk pajamas, her sleeping mask around her neck (embroidered with the words, "Working on my novel") with her saddle loosely arranged around her and a steel beam. I burst into laughter, which I could not hear for the hail on the metal roof.

I took my time shimmying out of my saddle, because if this were a tornado, I'd be dead anyway. I scuttled to the bed of the semi where my clothes seemed all to have stayed put. I jumped and wiggled onto the bed (tall as my chest), slid into my space bivy, tucked my rain poncho all around me, gathered my clothes into a pillow, pulled my eye mask over my eyes and prepared to be sucked out of the barn by the hook cloud that soon would touch down. I listened to the percussion of rain and hail and felt the mist through every gap in my gear and mourned for the miles of hay and wheat that the wind and rain and hail surely must be laying flat and ruining.

I awoke many times through the night on my tread-plate metal bed. At last I awoke to bright light, soaked by my own condensation in the chrysalis of my space bivy. Three high schoolers, two boys and a girl, stood fifty yards away in the drive. They'd come late, 9:00 AM, as it would be too wet to bale earlier. Today's wind and sun soon would take care of that.

I eased off the truck bed and walked toward the high schoolers, trying not to limp on my swollen left knee. I wanted to know how many homes and acres of crops had been damaged. The girl, especially, looked at me the way Chief looked at his first buggy. Nonetheless, the youths treated me with respect, even before I explained why this puffy-faced, middle-aged woman had slept in the barn last night. The boys said heat records were set to break today. No fields were wrecked last night; no tornados turned trees into twist ties. One young man asked, did it rain last night?

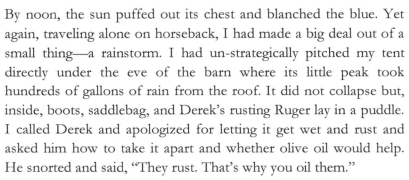

By noon, the sun puffed out its chest and blanched the blue. Yet again, traveling alone on horseback, I had made a big deal out of a small thing—a rainstorm. I had un-strategically pitched my tent directly under the eve of the barn where its little peak took hundreds of gallons of rain from the roof. It did not collapse but, inside, boots, saddlebag, and Derek's rusting Ruger lay in a puddle. I called Derek and apologized for letting it get wet and rust and asked him how to take it apart and whether olive oil would help. He snorted and said, "They rust. That's why you oil them."

I walked around my campsite and Chief's pasture picking up clothes and accoutrements scattered by the wind. I draped my tent over Chief's gate to dry. Soon it took big gulps of air. Before this trip, Chief had nearly jerked a fence post out of the ground the first time I'd popped it into shape near him. Now, it waved in his face, a symbol of home. I washed, dried, and folded my clothes into two colorful piles on the chrome tread plate of the flatbed trailer.

By late afternoon, I lay in my little green home glistening in my clean sweat (six feet farther away from the barn). Through the screen I watched an iridescent black bird land with a thump and scrape under the eve of the hay barn. Its voice was like a dry hinge. Chief blew his nose like an old chainsaw that wouldn't start. The farmstead outside my tent was vacant, proof of frenetic work elsewhere.

The one thing I didn't worry about is the one thing everyone else worried about for me—people. I wrote in my notebook: *How many people do you know? 200? How many murderers do you know? Are there really a lot of psychopaths out there? Almost everyone I meet tells me so. I just walked into your yard; are you one?* I always have chosen to believe that evil can have no actual, substantial effect on me, as long as I paid attention to the feeling I got from people and places around me.

Gradually the light faded outside my tent. I heard what seemed like ten thousand warriors in full battle cry, miles away—mosquitoes on the pond. I looked at the sky through the mesh door. The white pillars of Mount Olympus floated on a footing of lightning that processed silently toward us from the same direction as last night's storm.

I only have to ride tomorrow, I wrote in my notebook. *I can go easy and stop early if a place feels right. I can't live the whole trip tomorrow. I can only live tomorrow, tomorrow. I am so happy and grateful, God, that you have provided a beautiful, safe place for me to stay tomorrow night, wherever it is.*

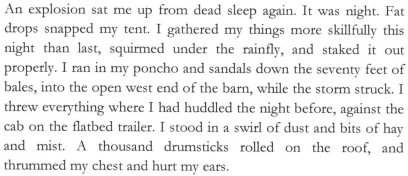

An explosion sat me up from dead sleep again. It was night. Fat drops snapped my tent. I gathered my things more skillfully this night than last, squirmed under the rainfly, and staked it out properly. I ran in my poncho and sandals down the seventy feet of bales, into the open west end of the barn, while the storm struck. I threw everything where I had huddled the night before, against the cab on the flatbed trailer. I stood in a swirl of dust and bits of hay and mist. A thousand drumsticks rolled on the roof, and thrummed my chest and hurt my ears.

It occurred to me to look at the semi cab. I climbed up and tried the door handle. It was unlocked. I shouldn't trespass. The skinny beam of my headlamp swept the two velour bucket seats sized for NFL players. From what I could see behind the seats was a velour, double-sized sofa bed laid out flat, a pillow and blanket. I climbed down, gathered from the truck bed my bivy, my silk sleeping cocoon, pillow of clothes, bag of toiletries so they wouldn't blow away, and Derek's pistol this time, to keep it dry. Leaving the driver door open, I slid past the steering wheel and between the bucket seats and crawled onto the plush bed in the cab's muggy air. I didn't require fresh air. I lay on the cloud of foam. In a moment, I found a pillow and pulled it under my head. It didn't smell like anybody. Against the thunderous roar, I pushed myself up, crawled across the driver's seat, and slammed the door.

Silence.

Stitches

It was time to take out the stitches. I still couldn't touch my left forearm to anything. But I trusted the doctor's advice to get the stitches out in ten days. I stood in line at Casey's General Store in Golden City, Missouri, at 7:00 A.M., after the five-mile ride from Bill Garrett's. My arms cradled packaged cheese and crackers, Lay's Kettle Cooked potato chips, two pieces of pizza, Advil, jerky, a can of Vienna sausages, a cup of excellent coffee, a handful of sugar packets, and—behold—tweezers.

This store was one of more than two thousand Casey's stores positioned in Midwest towns of five thousand or less and known for clean, hometown friendliness. Four people waited in line ahead of me, two behind, and my horse stood tied to a grain truck parked in a mowed side yard with a for-sale sign on the bumper. Chief was twisting and fretting when I left him. He'd only come far enough this morning to get his engine warm. The farther we rode on this trip, the more endurance he had. We had ridden under a sky that looked like the storm clouds had been ripped off all at once, and the blue beneath was inflamed. We rode beside three-foot walls of wheat, then clacked on the pavement, up and over dark culverts for creeks still full of last night's trauma. The day felt relatively cool from the advance of a fair, new weather system. Our ride to this air-conditioned riot of brand names that screamed *eat me, drink me* had only served to rev Chief's engine.

The Casey's throbbed with the heartbeat of every thirsting, sugar-craving, break-timing, babysitting, mothering, man and woman, boy and girl, each making urgent eye contact to keep from seeming rude, yet not too much—tossing jokes across the room to startle a friend. In Golden City, the Golden Rule.

Population eight hundred, Golden City sits on the ninety-degree bend of Missouri Route 160, which connects Lamar, Missouri, northwest, to more towns like it to the east. Its collection of homes tamps down two square miles of what had been Missouri tallgrass prairie. Three preservation areas now hum with grasses and flowers of past millennia within a few miles of Golden City, thanks to the Nature Conservancy and a small tax Missourian's agreed to years ago to fund wildlife refuges in the state. The word "golden" may have come from early nineteenth-century settlers who thought the mines they found were abandoned by Spaniards seeking gold but actually were excavated by prehistoric Indians for flint. A month from now, friends will be rolling friends down the main drag of this town in beds fitted with wheels for the Great American Bed Race and judging pets and babies in beauty contests in the annual Golden Harvest Days.

"How much you take for that horse?" said a man's voice behind me in line.

I swiveled on my heel and caught my breath. The questioner was handsome, six-foot-five, hard as a marine, forties, western hat, buckaroo boots on the outside of his pants, spurs, and dusty as me. Another horseman. A real one.

"Fifteen dollars and a ride home," I answered.

He wasn't expecting that and laughed. He wasn't a blowhard. He was the only person in this store who knew what I was up against, and I sensed his concern that he voiced as a joke. I'd have been embarrassed by my English attire if I didn't look so trail worn and my horse weren't so ripped. I'd ridden from Kansas City. Even if my horse were acting a fool outside, he'd gotten me this far. I let my compadre know what I was doing because he was curious, and everyone in front and behind me in line listened carefully.

"I'm just hoping he stays put until I can take my stitches out in the bathroom."

"You're going to do that yourself?"

"You're welcome to come in and help me," I said. I could see him take a mental step back, at which point I realized that sounded like a come-on.

After I checked out, I ducked into the ladies' room feeling like I'd left a toddler wandering the parking lot (Chief). I set my bags on the back of the toilet and thanked Providence I'd hurt my left arm so I could remove my stitches with my right hand. I had thought at first I would find the town clinic on Main Street that housed an osteopath, a gynecologist, and a nurse practitioner. Then I thought, *How hard can this be?* Besides, where would I park Chief while I waited in a doctor's office?

The scabbed wound covered an area about three-by-six inches, but the worst of it, where the doctor stitched it, was the elbow. I pulled the first three stitches almost painlessly, but the fourth was embedded. I dug for it, and made it bulge with blood that began to drip. I could hear voices of people needing the restroom. Someone said, "You okay in there?"

"Just a minute," I sang. I wrapped up my arm temporarily and left the bathroom to check on Chief. I threw my groceries on the step of the grain truck. Chief was twisting and turning and pawing and tossing his head like a pumpjack. He nearly had himself untied. I retied him and looked around for the real cowboy, gone, thank God, and told Chief to STAND. I trotted back inside with my roll of VetRap and waited in line for the bathroom. At last, back in front of the mirror, I dug in the blood until I finally pulled out the last stitch and its knot. Then someone banged on the door, "Hey, Lady, your horse is taking a walk!"

"Okay," I sang. I padded and wrapped my arm tightly, gathered my tweezers and gauze and rinsed the blood down the sink and opened the door. Four people stood staring at me. Chief was gone. I threw everything on the truck's running board. He was two blocks away down a paved side street and moving out. Fortunately, his lead rope was dragging, and every few strides he stepped on it and slowed himself down.

"Ho, Boy," I sang to him. "Ho buddy." I followed him at a minimally threatening pace and finally grabbed the trailing lead.

When I tied him to the truck, again, I could see by the look on his face that he got it, finally, for the first time: *This woman will never understand anything I want, ever.* I stowed the groceries in the moving target of his saddlebags, jerked his rope loose from its knot, and walked him past the pumps, tossed my full coffee into the trash, and lead him onto Highway 160. I walked instead of rode, so I could eat my pizza. Chief followed obediently.

A bearded man in a pickup with bare shoulders under his overall straps slowed and bent his fat arm out the window to ask me if everything was okay. (I was leading my horse and not riding him.) Yes, I'm just trying to eat, I told him. My stomach accepted nearly unmolested bites of meat, cheese, and crust, while the man told me about his own horse.

People are lonely. Those who love their horses like I loved Honey (and who don't have to earn a living on them every day) crave an interested third party, and here I walked, horse in hand, bearing the nectar that fed this man's affections. I had time for a lonely horse lover, no matter the beating sun, or my ill-masticated lunch. He stopped to see what I was doing by way of asking if I needed help. He was squeezing out of me the last of my workaholism.

At last, the tailings of the blessed gravel township road I would take for the next six miles scattered onto this high-speed two-lane that transmits my kind of people from their farms to town, to school, to the highway, to the City, and back in their cars. They fly like any Kansas City friends, wearing clothes they bought where city people do, all listening to the same music, knowing the best restaurants in the City, and knowing, also, how to pull out a tick, drive a tractor, butcher a deer, and load a gun.

The remainder of the day's ride on my handful of horse flowed as beautifully as Chief flowed beneath me, his neck round, head tucked, ears alert, coat glittering, rocks flinging behind us or skipping ahead to the sound of his striptease gait. His bags flopped gently against his sides, and I hoped nothing hard was sticking out and bruising him.

The land rose beneath us, then let us down into trees along creeks where gentle, pastured hills brought us to a shady, 1930s farmhouse close to the gravel road. Eighty-year-old, ornamental, double-loop fencing surrounding the shade-darkened lawn. Three small boys and a larger one played close to the road. I stopped and asked them if their mother might let me use their hose to give my horse a drink. A big boy, eleven or twelve, a ways off in the yard holding a shovel, looked at me out of the corner of his eye, not wanting to be associated with the little ones. According to a lisping sibling, the bigger boy was digging worms. My sweat cooled me in the shade.

"Our mother's not home."

"Is somebody else home?" I asked, becoming alarmed.

"Our cousin."

"Would you mind asking her?" They all ran away into the house.

Out the door with the three spilling ahead came a girl in early teens, dark brunette, styled hair, foundation smoothed superfluously over a flawless complexion, blue eye shadow masterfully applied. She was plump and so radiant I could see how she would look in her third trimester of pregnancy someday.

Chief stood still, a bead of sweat dripping down the back of one trembling knee. He sucked the water from his bucket, while the three little boys knelt around his face. Chief seemed to absorb the boys as much as the water. Their soft hands with dimpled knuckles caressed his cheeks, forehead, displaced the flies by cupping his eyes, and caressed the edges of his ears. This was when I realized a four-year-old's hand is smaller than a horse's ear. A five-year-old's torso is shorter than a horse's head is long.

After I stowed my bucket and hugged the children, I decided to practice mounting from the off side (the right side instead of the left) to save my left knee. These days, when I swung my leg forward as I walked, my knee stabbed me with pain. I was sure I had tattered my meniscus, mounting so many times along Route V. I asked the teenager to hold my horse. My first attempt had me falling over Chief's neck. Chief stiffened and watched me with his ears. I tried again and straightened my back and held it firm, swung my creaky left groin as high as I could over the bags and settled on top. The way Chief walked off, I imagined he did a Jim Carrey impression—*O-KAY-dee-then*.

A hundred feet up the road was an eighteenth-century cemetery, shady around its edges and neatly groomed. I let Chief walk into it and begin to graze. I sat astride in the breeze and called my oldest sister on the phone. My hips did a subtle hula to Chief's three-inch steps and jerky bites. My eyes moistened over the long talk with a sister I imagined I had disappointed over the years with my two divorces and their various dramas. She had thought my motorcycle riding in my twenties was foolish and dangerous, all true. Our words softened my focus. How dangerous this trip must seem to her. She said she loved me, which I shouldn't crave but did, even at fifty-four. I shoved my phone back into its holster. I pulled up Chief's head, and we slalomed through the scary stone pillars at the cemetery's entrance, and Chief continued to slalom a few paces down the road until I straightened him up with the coordinated gigs of my spurs and tugs on the reins. He must glide the straight rail between my hands and hips and heels. I felt, somehow, I finally was on my trip.

If This Be Blasphemy

We walked in high, full-out row-crop country that reminded me of central Kansas with its calm surface and massive sky. Rows of beans and corn flowed up to ladies' flower beds and driveways. A person could breathe out here. I was so far between cities, a car or truck passed only once every hour or so. The houses seemed to repel each other with green terraces flowing in ripples outward, some fed by long lanes up to their knolls, others smack on the road, ignored by 1930s surveyors. The red paint on the west side of a large, wood barn ahead had been scrubbed to a fashionable patina by hail and rain. It stood straight, like buildings that have a sense of belonging from ongoing use, making it a possible stop for us, now about 3:30 PM. There must be a hydrant somewhere. I would not open the gate and go in. The one driver who might see us would get to his destination and make a call: "Dan, who's that at your barn with a tent and a horse?"

Six days ago, in the Deitzes' kitchen, we heard a tractor in the distance, growing louder on the road. Mr. Deitz had sat up and yelled to his daughter, "Carol, go see who that is!" She leapt from her chair to the front window, just in time to see whose tractor was bouncing toward its field at twenty-five miles per hour, implement nodding behind it. Carol called the name. Mr. Deitz nodded, knowing the field his friend ought to be in this morning, and what he was doing to it.

Before I got to the barn, I ducked into a rare hedgerow to go to the bathroom. As I was pulling up my pants and gathering my phone holster from around my ankle, I heard something coming (the first sound is always some metal part clanging, followed by tires on rock like peanuts in a food processor). I mounted and kicked Chief back to the road just as a dually pickup passed, pulling a six-axel flatbed trailer hauling eight bales of hay (or 6,400 pounds) in a confusion of dust. I waved my arm, but the handsome young man was focused on "geoplaning" (a cousin of hydroplaning) at just-under-fishtailing speed. Thank goodness he braked and pulled into a field road ahead. I kicked Chief, and we fox trotted as fast as we could the half mile, bags and canteen bouncing, to catch the driver before he unloaded and left us. He might know who owned that barn.

He was just pulling back to the road when I neared, waving my arm in big circles. He waited, and I could see his face stretch forward under the shade of his bill trying to categorize the sight of me. He was dark blond, mid-twenties, open faced, and handsome. My son, Derek, seemingly came to me everywhere on this trip, in other people's bodies. I wanted to wrap my arms around his shoulders and tell him he was doing a good job, not to worry, and write him a check. My son, and probably this boy, too, could strip a Camaro down to its frame, remove all the wiring, the computer, replace the engine with another two sizes bigger—drive train, cam shaft, new wiring harness, appropriate computer—and actually get it to run. Too fast. My son's first job, at fourteen, was working (illegally because of his age) at a mechanic shop in Nevada, Missouri, replacing water pumps. He could skateboard, shoot guns, throw knives, was a fifth-degree black belt in Kenpo Karate, could see energy auras around trees and people, rebuild wood duplicators, had a CNC operator's certificate, and was adept at learning languages. Handsome, capable, young men were everywhere in this country.

This young man thought he knew the owner of the barn I was casing, and he'd be happy to try to call him. He looked at my business card. His open truck window created an eerie vortex of heat and cold. Shards of hay stuck to the skin on his neck and arms. "My boss has a little cabin he might let you use. They have it to keep rustlers from stealing their cattle."

"Okay, now that's something I'd never heard of in this part of the world," I said. "How far is it?" I couldn't bear the thought of ten more miles. Or even five.

"It's just down here a mile."

"Great!"

He called, and they said yes.

"You just take this road to the next corner and turn down that way." He pointed west. "It'll be the first barn you come to. You'll see the little cabin. Somebody will unlock the gate for you."

When I reached my turn, I could see the hired hand's pickup and a large SUV a half mile off, conferring in the middle of the road, while a third pickup pulled up, then turned around. The sight of $90,000 worth of vehicles driven by businessmen who deal in millions of dollars' worth of dirt and grain, convening to make a place for a woman on a horse to stay the night, melted me in a way no hot June afternoon ever could.

I met the Knuteson men and their hand in a semicircle driveway in front of an eight-by-twelve-foot cabin with three windows, a diminutive porch, railings, and pulled-back curtains. Adjacent was a large wood prairie barn with two open doors that led to a wide, horseshoe aisle in the center. Wood-board corrals surrounded it. The father wore jeans and a well-washed dress-shirt-turned-work-shirt; the son, in his early forties, wore jeans and an Eddie Bauer-type polo that had been worn enough it now could be used for work. A grandson home from college stood quietly, the apparent pride of his elders. I could picture the college student as a small boy, barely able to see over the dash, listening to his father and grandfather work the puzzle of how to get all the tractors and pickups home from the field with just two of them. This young man would be tapped, by eleven, to drive a truck home. He stood here in quiet respect and anticipation, like back then, I imagined.

"I'm Warren," the eldest Knuteson said. He extended his hand. "I've called my wife. She's on her way back from Jasper."

Jasper is just north of Joplin where this family likely did their shopping.

"She can't wait to meet you," he said. "She loves her horses."

"We do, don't we," I said. "I'd love to meet her, too. Thank you so much for letting me stop over here. What luxury not to have to sleep on the ground tonight!"

"We're glad to have you."

The afternoon breeze caught in the trees surrounding this old home place that no longer had its house. Ancient cedars and elms shaded the little cabin and the footing of the absent homestead beside it.

"Mennonites built the cabin," said Mr. Knuteson. "We put it here two springs ago. We had mothers and babies up here for weaning, and yearlings. Rustlers came up with stock trailers and horses in the night. They loaded all the yearlings and left the babies and mothers," he said. "Different family members take turns staying in the cabin at night when the cattle are up, now. We're not the only ones they hit."

"It seems crazy someone doesn't know who's doing it," I said. "Everybody knows what everyone else is doing around here, if it's anything like Vernon County."

Mr. Knuteson chuckled, "Oh, I think the sheriff knows who it is."

Hence, why the rustler isn't caught.

Soon the men went back to work, and I watered Chief and unsaddled him, sprayed him down, and grazed him an hour in the tall grass surrounding the cabin, while I waited for Mrs. Knuteson to arrive with some things she thought the cabin needed.

Just as my laundry had dried enough to take flight from the porch rails, Nancy, my hostess, buzzed up on her Arctic Cat four-wheeled all-terrain vehicle, bearing for me what she called creature comforts. On the front rack of the four-wheeler she had stacked an electric fan, rugs, an electric pot for boiling water, paper toweling, a box of teabags and sweetener. A twenty-year beautician, she wore a sassy, blond haircut, a farm-girl's tan, makeup, and manicure.

As with all middle-aged women who were born beauties, the years melted from her face when she talked about her children and grandchildren, and in Nancy's case, especially when she talked about horses she'd owned. She grew up loving and riding them, and she told me their names, makes and models—mostly Quarter Horses and Paints in this country.

"I'd love to do what you're doing," she said.

"I highly recommend it."

"We're busy. With farming, my business. I raise Alaskan huskies and Australian shepherds. I send them all over the world."

"Really! How do people find out about you?" (Even I can forget country people are as connected as anyone.)

"I use a broker. The lines are pretty well known."

Country humility. No telling how "well-known" this woman's dogs were in the show world.

"How did you wind up in this gorgeous country; did both your parents farm here?"

"Warren and I met in high school in Lockwood. We've been married fifty years. Warren's people came from Germany, two brothers, who settled in Indiana in the 1840s. His father was born in southeast Missouri. He was sickly, and that climate didn't help. The family discovered these tallgrass prairies and settled here to farm. My people came from Ireland and Scotland by way of France."

"Are your children in this area," I asked.

"They are. All three of the boys and their wives are college educated. We have eight grandchildren. The oldest is twenty. He's in his first year of architecture school."

"I met him earlier with the men, I think."

"You probably did."

We stood at the fence that surrounded the barn and watched Chief.

"I can still ride, but it's not comfortable. Turns out I have a bony growth in my spine giving me grief. I broke my back in a horse fall just before my son Jeff was born."

"Holy cow."

"Jeff was fine, but I didn't know it at the time I fractured a vertebra. I'm going to ride my granddaughter's abandoned horse in the Christmas parade, all sparkled up."

Daughters and granddaughters abandon their horses when they go to college, leaving behind these unsellable, animated symbols of the financial lengths parents will go to keep their girls happy and out of trouble.

"I want to come back and ride in that parade with you," I said. I meant it and believed it, despite the fact I didn't own a trailer, and to rent one would cost two hundred dollars, plus another hundred for gas. Still, if I could take this trip, I surely could figure out how to get back down to Lockwood for a parade and ride with a "sister."

Nancy opened the cabin for me. It contained a double bed with plastic-covered mattress, a pillow, a blanket, two folding chairs, two tiny side tables and a lamp. She arranged "my" pot and tea and showed me the outlet where I could charge my phone and asked me to forgive the dust. By the time Nancy left to start her husband's supper, the sky began to tarnish, and the trees along the horizon seemed burned into it. She wished me luck and Godspeed and disappeared down the road on her ATV. Her motor faded, then all I heard was gravel popping.

The sun reached its conclusion. The wind ceased. I stood in my shorts and sandals in grass and tall weeds and grazed my horse another hour. The lot where he was to stay the night was bereft of forage, except for weeds that grow fast in the powdered manure of barn lots, between tramplings by dozens of cattle, scared, literally, shitless at weaning time.

I held my four-by-eight spiral notebook, my pen, and my horse's lead rope. The grass bent over in blond waves. I stepped my bare legs and feet high with only the rubber soles of my sandals for protection and dreaded the microscopic slices on my ankles that would itch. I watched for hidden scrap metal or, God forbid, an open well that easily could be hidden beneath these tresses.

Under a hedge tree so ribbed and old it would take two men to wrap their arms around it, my horse snatched his dinner.

As if overcome by an urgent need, Chief lifted his head and, in an oddly familiar manner, pulled me by the lead rope south of the cabin into wheat stubble from a crop that had been removed only days ago. He bent his front legs and lightly touched down, first a shoulder, then his side. I held his lead in the air so he wouldn't catch a hoof. He lay his head down and rubbed the side of his neck back and forth against the stubble and fine dirt, making one side of an angel wing on the ground. He rocked up to a half-seated position with his legs curled beside him, then threw himself onto his back. He ground his spine into the dirt, twisting and grunting. He threw himself over again, this time hard enough that he tee-tered upside down, twisting until he flipped all the way over, then made the other half of his dirt-angel with his neck. He sat up, facing away from me, then he threw himself to his back a third time and rolled toward me again. Chief sat couchant a moment. I stood over him. A horse would never lie down with a predator near. They don't often let people approach when they're down. He rubbed his chin on his knee and rested. Then he stretched out first one front leg then the other in a V. I retreated to the end of the lead to give him space. He shifted the cantilevered weight of his head over his back, then threw it all forward and pushed himself onto his feet. With all fours spread, he shook a horse-shaped cloud of dust into the air. A shake like that can vibrate a rider right off her seat.

Daily, Chief and I used the restroom together. We ate together. Tonight, he lay down beside me and rolled. I had stood on the sidelines for 250 miles, wanting to be on Chief's team like his friends in the pasture back home. Sitting on top of him, tugging his mouth, poking him with spurs, disqualified me. By prostrating him-self while I held his lead, Chief treated me the same as Dreamer, his best friend back home, the tall, black Missouri Fox Trotter he spent all his time with. This act of trust made me weep.

A storm front swept in while the sky was still light. The clouds were fluorescent green and fluffy in the way of wool still attached to its animal. There was a long, prone S imprinted on the front, as if it'd been keyed. For an hour, jagged, bright currents of electricity joined the sky to the earth and replenished the nitrogen we all were farming out of it. I wrote in my notebook, *What are the chances I would be lying on a soft bed with a pillow and blanket in a tiny Mennonite-made cabin during the third tempest of our trip?* That night, the earth would get its last soak for the next three months in what would become the hottest summer here on record. In a flash of lightning through my window, I could see Chief standing at the outermost edge of the scary black opening at the front of the barn.

I had been gone fifteen days, roughly 250 miles, with two days off, and the first three days, short ones, to leg-up my horse. My ink pen lines traveled off one and onto another of four topographic maps of Missouri and Kansas. I wrote the name of my benefactors beside a circle for each camp. I missed my husband. He would come day after tomorrow, and, for this, I would ride all day tomorrow—to get to the next day to ride all day to see him that night. Tomorrow would be an adventure, but not scary like before, when I didn't know how to ride alone. I was free now to witness the unfolding of the Earth and meet its caregivers, its creatures, and breathe its perfume, while calming my horse in the face of bulls, and ducking the firing line of pickup grills.

Like the first astronaut to see one humanity in a distant, blue globe, I did, too, by feel—one rock and tree at a time. If the Bible said I were not supposed to be of this world, I certainly was in it. If the God of my Lutheran upbringing were in, with, and under the sacraments of bread and wine, I was in, with, and under this Earth, identifying blasphemously closely with the essence of God.

Ticks

The low-pressure system that generated storms the past three nights would produce today a record low for a high—sixty-five degrees. When we departed the Knuteson's cabin this sixteenth morning of our trip, I was wearing a sweatshirt and windbreaker for the first time. We left the open cropland and entered the tailings of the Ozark Mountains, scruffy breaks, short, steep hills sprouting scrub oak and rotund cedars, indicating poorer soil. We rode past fallen rock walls around fields cleared in the 1800s and houses that looked like smokers who'd been toking so long, no doctor would give them a facelift. I began to feel uneasy. My husband's and my friend Daniel Woodrell wrote the novel *Winter's Bone* about violent drug cookers and dealers in the Ozarks, which later was made into a movie. Daniel has lived in the southern Missouri mountains most of his life. I, too, had friends in the Ozarks. I had ridden its rocky hills in endurance races with Ozark natives who never saw a schedule-one narcotic in their lives; I'd bought horses there; Chief was raised there. Among drug users and cookers, the Ozarks also crawled with hard-right Pentecostals and Southern Baptists, for better or worse—often better.

Pastures scrolled by among walls of trees, up and down hills. It was so cool, I made Chief quick-step uphill and gait downhill. I tried to remember what I had written in my notebook that morning: *No separation between us (people), no danger, no lack.* I would take the world at face value: six large box turtles, a brown striped snake. I spotted five wild turkeys in the road ahead, dark brown against the shade, unseen by Chief. They stealthily slid into a tall pasture one-eighth of a mile away and, after running like fat men, took ponderous, flapping flight. After riding four hours at a quick pace with only short breaks, I stopped Chief in the shade to let him graze, and I wrote while astride:

I had started to write "fat women" when describing the turkeys and wondered why the first thing that came to my mind was to compare the awkward turkeys to fat women and demean them. Then I chose to demean men. I don't want to criticize anyone ever again. Or judge anyone. Or make assumptions. The impact of my horse's every step is tenderizing me.

We walked on. Chief needed water. Not a car had passed us on this gravel road for two hours. Now, a fifteen-year-old red pickup eased around us and turned into a field road ahead that became dirt tracks beside a parade line of corn almost as tall as the cab. When I reached the drive and peered down it, I could see the man was headed toward cattle in a field behind a barn. Chief automatically turned into the drive, all stiff legged and high-headed at what might be hiding around the tree line. He turned despite his apprehension, because turning, to him, might mean stopping. I rode up to the man's window. He stepped from his truck into the cool June day. He had dark hair, was in his late thirties, and carried an honestly earned extra fifteen pounds. Who resists buttered starch after leaving his sweat and calories all over his ancestors' section of land? I introduced myself. As seems to happen with folks out here, I soon learned about his people.

"My wife's family settled in Hermann, Missouri, over close to St. Louis. My dad's people came here from Kentucky. We have cattle and hogs and row crops."

"One must diversify," I said.

"One goes up when the other goes down," he said. Meaning prices.

I noticed the pitch of his voice and expression on his face never changed during our conversation. He wasn't a charmer. The kind of confidence and determination required to keep a family farm profitable makes a person quiet. He was a custodian of land and probably a pathological gambler—as all farmers are.

"I wonder where I could find water that would be easy to get to."

"There's a hydrant over there." He pointed to a half-fallen-down house on the other side of the road so bearded with vines and tucked into ancient trees, I hadn't noticed it. He owned that, too.

I thanked him, and we said fond goodbyes, each of us needing to get back to work. I seemed to bond with everyone I met. Chief and I must inspire a caregiver's impulse in them, I thought.

I led Chief into the arm-pit-high grass by the old house. After a few retches, the drain-back faucet erupted with cold, fresh water. Chief drank it nearly as fast as it spewed into his bucket, surrounding his nose with foam and roaring next to his ear. Like me, so many things that scared him once, now redeemed him.

I mounted again and rode between this man's fields another mile. Soon, he drove up cautiously behind us and matched our speed. I stopped along his driver's side. "I wanted to give you this," he said. He handed me a torn corner of notebook paper with his name and phone number on it.

"The bridge up here two miles is bad. I don't want him to fall through it. You can take the next gravel road east around the section to get around it."

"Is the whole thing out?"

"There are lots of holes in the planks. You don't want him sticking a foot through that."

"No I don't, thank you."

"Call if you need anything."

After another mile, I decided to keep to our plan. If the bridge were dangerous, maybe we could slide down into the creek beside it and climb back out onto the road. Or we could backtrack around the section. I just didn't want to go out of my way a single mile if I didn't have to.

We fox trotted deeper into the land where the Missouri Fox Trotting horse breed was developed to cover long distances smoothly. The breed came from gaited horses brought into this part of the world before Missouri's statehood in 1821. The breeding stock was descended from Arabians, Morgans, American Saddlebreds, Tennessee Walking Horses, and Standardbreds. Many foundation Fox Trotter studs were the offspring of Tennessee Walkers, refined years earlier for covering vast plantations comfortably. To be registered a Missouri Fox Trotter back then, the horse must do an ambling, four-beat broken diagonal gait, in which the front foot of the diagonal pair lands before the hind, eliminating the moment of suspension, and giving a smooth ride, according to the Missouri Fox Trotting Horse Breed Association. The trot is "broken," making it more comfortable for the rider to sit.

We descended a hill toward Crackerneck Branch and the rusted steel suspension bridge I had been warned about. It had a pair of wood tire paths running the forty-foot length of it. Supporting these, and running horizontally, were more wood boards resting on the steel trusses. Many of the horizontal boards were missing. By now, Chief had slowed at the sight of the looming arches. *Cool it*, I said. *You know what these are.* I dismounted. If Chief were to drop a foot through one of those holes, he would tear himself up trying to get out. Chief must walk directly behind me on one of the wood tire paths if we were to make it.

I tried to breathe normally and held Chief's reins aligned with the center of my back and walked confidently and quickly onto the bridge. Chief held his head low and rattled deep breaths, smelling his way across and did not hesitate to follow directly behind me on the tire path.

After big hugs and pats on the other side, and the treat of an individually wrapped prune for Chief, I mounted up. We rode up another rough hill and cleared the top. I stopped, stunned. We looked out over a chimerical scene, as if someone had plucked us out of one movie and deposited us into another. Before us, spread the real-life valley of the Grant Wood painting *Young Corn*, or so it seemed. Steep, rounded hills seemed to *dance like little lambs* into the distance, as the psalmist described. They were covered in green plush and dotted with fat cattle and fringed with deciduous trees. I had driven through the Ozarks many times, but never had I seen such tall, perfectly groomed hills, graced by neat, old farmhouses and new homes. I would not have been surprised to see round hobbit doors in these hills.

We rode hills another hour under clear skies in a cool breeze. How far I felt from Mr. Garrett's high, flat seas of hay and wheat. I finally could breathe, having left the meth-looking country. That's when my ease ended. The nonskid gravel road turned into chipseal pavement. It wasn't as slick as concrete but slippery enough with steel shoes. The pavement also gave drivers permission, they thought, to treat it like a highway.

We clopped along—the road barely wide enough for two cars to pass, and bowling-lane gutters for ditches abutting each side. There was no room to ride in the ditch. The hills were roller-coaster short and steep. I felt fragile in my saddle knowing how quickly Chief could slip and fall (a possibility only if he shied—which was a distinct possibility). When cars came, we seemed always to be safely at the bottom of a hill where drivers had time to see us and slow down. Instead of relaxing into the scenery, I now rode like a tennis player waiting for a serve, listening for cars in front and behind. What if all the fine blue lines through the Ozarks on my map were not gravel but were paved like this? This was not the ride I had planned.

The next road I crossed didn't match my map, which unnerved me. I went south when I should have gone east and had to back-track. I needed to camp. I tried two nice homes that sported new metal roofs and outbuildings, but no one was home, and who would be at three in the afternoon? We clopped on the pavement east for miles and at last, to our left, appeared a cedar home with stained glass windows, green metal roof, professional landscaping, and matching outbuildings.

Just beyond it, to our right, was a 1920s farmhouse sans shutters, eves, or architectural interest—a serviceable two-story box with period beveled siding, three bedrooms up, and likely one bathroom, added later, and a concrete summer porch on the front. The house sat close to the road, surrounded by trees. In the driveway beside it, I could make out an older woman and two children. We all caught sight of each other at once. The driveway to the stained-glass house was right there and led to a nicer place, but the children, ahead, drew me with stares, then jumps, then smiles. My diaphragm unstitched when Chief and I left the pavement and crunched up their gravel drive. The little boy hopped about. Until this trip, I never had noticed how many strange and sudden bursts of noise children produce, and sudden flaps of arms and spins. Chief jounced his head up in time with each one.

I dismounted and scooped up the woman's offered hand.

"I'm Lisa Stewart. I'm riding around Missouri—from Kansas City."

"I'm Nathalene. These are my grandchildren J.J., he's six, and Allissa. What are you?" Nathalene asked Allissa, then said, "You're nine."

The woman looked about sixty. She wore hair long enough to pull back, and loosely fitting, stretch denim pants, and a blouse.

"I've got them while their mother works."

"I couldn't resist stopping when I saw you kids," I said to them. "I'm really just looking for a little water for my horse."

"Kansas City!" Nathalene said. "Settle down around the horse," she said to J.J. in a tone that knew its strength and trusted good results, and therefore was quiet.

"You'd be welcome to stay here the night," Nathalene said. "Our pasture is leased, but your horse can help me by eating down the side yard."

I surveyed it: a 150-by-100-foot grassy rectangle bordered by the road. Fencing bounded it on only two sides, which meant Chief would not be contained. He would have to stand in one spot, picketed all night.

"I could certainly try farther down the road."

"You'd be most welcome if you want to stay."

I slid into the arms of two country children and their grandmother.

I watered Chief while the little boy jumped like the first kernels in a pan to pop. I bent at the waist and looked into his feisty eyes and whispered, "We have to be very gentle and quiet around Chief. He gets scared." J.J. simmered down. I hated to discourage him. I was not concerned for Chief, but that the horse might crush a little foot. "Stay far away from his behind. Come right over here by his shoulder where he can see you," and the truth is, all Chief wanted was his saddle off, and to tear at the yard with his teeth, and look and smell around for what might be prowling. Allissa did her best to reason with her brother. I reassured her that he was just perfect.

Nathalene returned to the house. My feet felt glued to the earth as they always did when I dismounted at the end of the day. The children chatted and wiggled, while I strategized my order of duties—each one, I realized, to include them.

Later, I grazed my horse in sandals and shorts. Nathalene returned with thick slices of watermelon for everyone on doubled paper plates that soon went limp. She had been keeping the watermelon in a deep spot in a creek. It tasted like icy cotton candy.

When we finished, Nathalene led me to the cold, spring-fed creek she clearly treasured. The land sloped steeply downward from her small backyard, and we took small steps to keep the round rocks from slipping our feet out from under us.

"This old creek carries three, year-round springs," she said.

The water flowed from a narrow hole in the hill we just descended and drained off into an ancient cut in the woods. From the creek behind the house, the land rose into lush meadows interrupted by puddles of trees.

"When we were young, my husband had set a metal pipe here in this outcrop. He died ten years ago."

"That's too young."

"I would agree with that." She spoke about the creek as one who tells the story of a favorite novel she has read a dozen times.

Icy water flowed from the pipe her husband had set, a faucet that never turned off. The little creek was only a few feet wide, perfect for wading to the ankles. Wild watercress waggled in the steady flow, and minnows flashed their bodies every time they turned around. The creek curved out of sight into the trees.

"It's beautiful."

"We had a dairy in the early days. We stored our milk here."

Nathalene pointed to a giant old cottonwood tree about twenty yards down the creek. "When we first cleared this area for our home, we killed eighteen copperheads under that double tree over there. That was thirty-three years ago."

"Wow. I guess they're all gone," I said looking around with my eyebrows raised.

"Oh they're still around. Not as many. It's too bad. I feel bad about that. There's so much development there aren't many snakes anymore."

We inadvertently gave the diminished snake population a moment of silence. As the wildlife goes, so go we—we both knew this. Every farmer can name species of birds and animals they hadn't seen since they were children, and not a one didn't know humans could be next if we weren't careful. Hunters are some of the best custodians of wildlife—Ducks Unlimited a case in point.

"I love watercress," I said. "I might come back and pick some for a salad tonight."

"If you're not used to it, you might be a little careful with it. It can work on you."

"I actually had an encounter with too many wild lilies two weeks ago."

"Ha. You'll only let that happen once!" she said.

"I think I'll leave the watercress alone."

Nathalene chuckled.

On our way back to the house, Nathalene stopped and pointed to a spot in the grass on the gentle slope. I could see the faintest path.

"I meet a big scorpion here almost every day. He comes and goes to and from the pasture like he's clocking in for work." Just then I was struck by sadness for the millions, billions of people who would never meet Nathalene, or anyone like her. They would fly to Paris or to New York for enrichment, when Nathalene lives right here with her scorpion and her spring in a peace that could inspire any striving soul. How many Nathalenes must be within driving distance of us all if we would just get out of the car and ask for a drink of water.

The children had not yet caught up with us.

"Their father died last year," Nathalene said to me quietly. "My son."

"I'm so sorry."

"Allissa has a lot on her shoulders."

"I'm sorry."

"Life goes on."

I grazed Chief an hour after our trip to the creek. Then I strung his picket line in the far corner of her side yard between a tree and a fence post. I carried a satiny, double-braided nylon rope for the purpose—only the second time I needed it this trip, the first time at Jerry and Sharon's. It went slack, no matter how tightly I tied it. Once tied, Chief pawed and twisted his frustration at not being free to graze.

From time to time, Nathalene checked to be sure the children weren't bothering me. I gave up any hope of rest in order to play with the children. What could be more important than putting my hands on my knees, looking into these eyes, and listening? J.J. proposed a wide variety of scenarios and asked me whether Chief would bite him in each one. Allissa had been preening Maggie, the dog from the stained-glass home across the road that stayed over here for loneliness. She was marked just like my Sparky at home. Black body and black head; white stripe between her eyes and down the center of her nose; white collar and legs with black spots.

"Look," Allissa said. "These are the three kinds of ticks we have." She held them out on her flat hand, three distinctly different ticks, one quite full of Maggie's blood, its legs waving around, and the big one, unfortunately, wearing a collar of Maggie's skin around its needlelike head.

"I guess I never looked at them closely before," I said. "I just pull them out and try not to look."

"Two of these get on both dogs and people." She pointed as she explained. "This is the dogs-only type." She was referring to the fullish one.

"I'm sorry," she told Maggie (for pulling her skin with the tick). Absently, Allissa tried to pull the dog's skin off the tick's head and popped the tick. Black ooze squirted up the side of her thumb. She skipped away to wash her hands.

I grazed Chief, again, in the last of the light. In a few minutes, J.J. and I heard the sound of an ATV coming up the road. A man stood on the foot pegs howling, "Harold! Haaa-roooold!" The man, in his fifties, looked all around, calling for what must be his dog. He wore a camouflage hat, camo hunting pants, and a full roan beard, clearly grown for protection. J.J. looked at him as if it weren't unusual to see this man coming down the hill on a four-wheeler. He put-putted into the drive, turned off the ignition, and sat back. I pulled Chief over to the driveway, to talk to him.

"Looking for my new dog. Hasn't learned to stay home yet."

"Yah, he went by," J.J. said. "Big gold dog?"

"Yes."

J.J. pointed up the road the way the man was going.

The man was in fit shape, a neighbor who knew Nathalene and her family.

He turned his attention to me and asked for my story. I could see his own story building within him as I gave him my synopsis.

"I used to explore all these rivers around here and down into Arkansas," he said.

"In a canoe?"

"Yes. This country is webbed with streams. I'd be gone a month at a time—when I was younger. I can relate to what you're doing. I'd like to do it again. Probably won't. I have maps that cover the whole country you're riding into, if you think they'll be of any help. I don't have any use for them."

When I charted my route last night, I had drawn a line off section fifty-one of my maps, going south. I would have to start a new section of map day after tomorrow.

"Do they show the little roads? I'm trying to stay on gravel as much as I can."

"They show roads that aren't even roads anymore."

"That would be cool." I didn't need one more ounce to carry, but this man yearned to pass some torch to me.

"I need to ask you something. Are all these roads chipsealed around here? I was planning to stay on gravel most of my trip. They're not too slick, but if my horse shies—"

"I know. They're pretty much all paved."

"That's a big problem for me. On my map, it doesn't distinguish between gravel roads and these chipsealed ones."

"They started paving these roads about fifteen years go," he said. "You've got a lot of development. Springfield, Silver Dollar City, Branson, Bentonville [Arkansas, home of Walmart]. Probably there's more gravel when you get out farther east and south."

"People drive on these like they're highways," I said.

"I know; it's dangerous."

"It might take me weeks of riding southeast to run out of it, right?"

"Maybe not that long," he said, "but it won't be fun until you do."

Won't be fun was his euphemism for "spine-chillingly dangerous."

This country wasn't as isolated as it felt. Chief and I had circled south of, and within paving distance of Springfield, Missouri, population 164,000.

That night, in moonless black, I lay in many layers: clean riding clothes, long johns, windbreaker, inside my bivy, and under my plastic poncho. I felt and heard, through my ear plugs, Chief's front hoof pound and scrape at the picket line. *Every minute I ride you, I have to brace for your spins and stops,* I thought. *You can't even stand picketed. You're getting worse instead of better.* In a few seconds, Chief stopped pawing. I lay still, listening. I did not hear him the rest of the night. I would wake and turn often when my hands and hips went numb from being curled in a ball on the ground.

Nearly a pound of maps lay beside me in my tent, one as big as a dining table when unfolded; one an antique work of art. The man on the ATV had putt-putted back into the drive at dark with the bundle bungeed to the rack on the front of his four-wheeler. "I won't do anything with these; maybe you can use them," he said. Like the Mennonite tracts Mr. Klein had given me, I clasped this man's maps in my arms as I drifted toward sleep. I would carry his explorations forward, in my way, picking up gifts like stick-tights— maps from him, zip ties and rivets from Jerry, fly dope and fuel from Jan and John.

Desmodium cuspidatum, the stick-tight plant, produces seed pods covered with deceptively soft Velcro, which inspired the product's inventor. Stick-tight pods grow in strips that look like strings of paper I pulled from my notebook spirals in school. On this trip they ride on my tights, Chief's fetlocks, his tail, my shirt cuffs, to go where we go. They bring the past to the future, to land and sprout, little brown stars moving away from their source, like Arkansas maps and Mennonite tracts.

Turning Home

"**I**'m headed home."

Through the phone, I could hear Bob lean back in his chair. "Okay."

I could picture him surrounded by stacks of paper-clipped, double-spaced manuscripts from unknown, master-of-fine-arts writing students and some of the nation's most celebrated authors. Sunlight would dapple his desk this time of morning in the 1930s, three-story, Stick Style house, reminiscent of Gothic England, on the university campus. He would leave midday to begin the three-and-a-half-hour drive to find me and bring me supplies. He knew I didn't mean for him to come get me. I was turning to ride back home. Five hundred miles would be my total.

On the day I confessed my desire to take this trip, I had convinced Bob I would not change; I would want to come home. Bob takes people at face value. When I am sure what I want, and it makes some degree of sense, he delivers, either with acceptance or physical support, as needed.

Bob always has been clear about himself and his work. There is something about his presence, tall, with the vigor of willow, able to sustain the shifting force of politics, religion, society, literature, even university bureaucracy, without becoming boorishly opinionated or self-centered. One of his most common phrases in conversation is, "I don't know anything, but..." which may be the quality I love in him most, because he *does* know a lot, and he never presumes. He takes time to formulate his thoughts into words, or crack a joke, which makes him late in the flow of conversation. At dinner parties, I have seen his mouth open with a joke in the pipeline, when two other people toss in their quips ahead of him. I watch in discouragement as his mouth slowly closes, and he takes another sip of wine. His joke would have been funnier than theirs. At least twice per night, however, he will tuck one in, and the table will explode with laughter, because Bob's quiet demeanor makes his humor a shock. You have to get to know him.

Bob won't repeat himself, won't explain himself, and rarely apologizes, which is why he is deliberate, to avoid the need for inefficient mistakes. On this trip, he used his reserve to reserve judgement. Everything that I had said would come to pass, had, so far. He trusted me. When I told him I was turning back for home, he may already have guessed it, from my call last night, when, after I excitedly described Nathalene and her spring, I worried over the pavement. I no longer would be gone ninety days, and I would see only the western side of the state. That was never mentioned.

My husband was learning what I had discovered thirty years ago in my first journey on horseback: Making X number of miles or arriving at a particular destination along the way was almost always irrelevant to the trip—and inconvenient.

This trip wasn't about trying to impress anyone; it was about me. Chief and me. Without Bob, none of this would be happening, but it wasn't about Bob. This strange person I had become, this neutral observer, this feeler of heat and light and energy, was a being outside of the Lisa Bob had married. This was okay, because, for the time being, he had become my neutral helper. For the first time in my life, I had no man to take care of. I had let Bob go in order to ride, to greet, to observe, to record. He listened to my morning raptures and my evening relief. He brought me things.

"I feel myself for the first time in my life," I had told him on the phone during one of my morning gushes about the beauty of the land. I felt like a man. That was the only way I knew to describe this feeling of mastery and calm, having no such female role models.

There were moments, in the past, when I had felt powerful and capable—as when I rode my motorcycle alone to Washington, D.C., and to Houston on business with a .38 revolver in my breast pocket. Like when I crafted feasibility studies, marketing studies, and business plans for entrepreneurs. I've had no powerful female role models to demonstrate how it is a capable woman feels. Emergency has always made me calm and clear-headed. I could lead soldiers into battle, I believe, with the right training. I could drive a bulldozer. I nursed my son twenty-four months and my daughter thirty-three months and felt exactly that powerful and comfortable in doing so, despite modern belief that letting children nurse until they are ready to stop (as most ancients did) is weird. I followed my heart, just as I did when I rode Chief away from his pasture.

Now there was nothing but pavement ahead instead of safe gravel roads, which provided traction and repulsed fast cars. It was one thing to ride on high alert on gravel roads and highway shoulders; but to ride on narrow pavement with nowhere to go when a car popped over a hill was a level of drama I couldn't justify, even if fourteen days from now I'd be on gravel again. I didn't come out here to get myself killed.

"I want to see more of this cropland," I told Bob on the phone. "I haven't filled up on it yet. I was too busy to see it when I lived here."

"That's just great."

"I'll call later to let you know a little better where I am. Don't get here too late."

"Have fun," he said.

I had trained him to stop saying *be careful.*

Vision on the Plains

When I began my trip, the days were dry and temperatures in the eighties and nineties. Today, June first,
I was on the verge of chills in three layers plus a
windbreaker. I had curled in a ball last night against the cold in
Nathalene's yard. Each time I twisted inside my foil blanket, I
found myself smiling. *I'm going home.* Last night's cold would be
swept away today by dry breezes, under skies the color of blue
sailors (chicory blooms) lining the roadside.

Now I proceeded again on the slippery pavement from
Nathalene's. The verbal directions she had given me the night
before included descriptions of houses, hills, fence posts, and not
the name of a single road. Her words evaporated with my first
wrong turn. We stopped often to check our maps, and Chief ate
ravenously each time, which freed my hands from holding him. By
the second hour, the road names finally matched our map. We
arrived on a sixty-mile-per-hour, two-lane county route with sharp
ditches, heading north from Lawrence County. I gave Chief his
head on the pavement to gait as fast as he could to get us to
patches of gravel, miles ahead.

When I finally arrived at my planned dirt road, I could breathe.
Open fields surrounded us, and we followed miles of sandy chat. I
stopped two times to ask for water, but no one was home. On a
rise before us was a neat, white farmhouse surrounded by hayfields
and wheat stubble whose borders were groomed like a golf course.
The house had no shrubs around it and only a few fruit trees to

block the wind. Imagine my joy when, in the distance, I saw a car pull into the drive. It took fifteen minutes to get there, and just as we neared, a ten-year-old pickup pulled into the drive as well. A man in his seventies stepped out. *Look how handsome he is, Chief.*

He was slender, quick, serious. I gave my windmill wave. He was in a hurry. I have a bucket, I told him. Of course, we could use the hydrant near his small, white-painted well house. This land was his, but he did not stay to tell me about it, because it was noon, and his wife was waiting inside with his dinner—the largest meal of the day, always served at noon.

After stowing my bucket, I led Chief back to the road and its mowed, grassy right of way to let him graze as long as he liked. Imagine a chicory bloom as a parasol—that was our sky. Chicory grows wild and tough in ditches in the Midwest this time of year. The sunflower-styled florets create a lavender/blue haze against the grass. Its roots can be dried and ground to season coffee, to make insulin, and the leaves can be eaten like endive.

It was at that moment, grazing my horse on the top of the world, I had a vision: I saw blackness, like a moonless night, miles away from the nearest yard light. I saw a thin, bright outline of the United States' map. Within the map were millions of specks of light. Each was a home. People. Here and there, were small areas without light, voids, as if waiting to be lit, easily avoided, easily illumined.

In my vision, I saw the United States of America arrayed with stars—generators of goodwill. Points of kindness in the form of people. My people. In my country.

Harold and Martha Adopt Me

Chief and I had left Nathalene's hills this morning, but it felt like days ago. How could I predict I would encounter a rare geological artifact that only could be discovered on this road, on a horse? We seemed to be climbing a plateau. I could see our gravel road turn ahead and trail along a wide gunnel between low ridges of pasture and working farms. We rode toward the ninety-degree bend and a cottage there, cooled by mature shade trees, blocked off with a flower garden, and, in waiting, a clean, small tractor that told me this place was a retirement plot.

A woman in her late sixties must have been looking out her kitchen window and came out of her door and strode to meet me before I even reached the drive. Her husband came shuffling behind her, not old enough to need to shuffle, but his hands, I could see, were distorted by what appeared to be rheumatoid arthritis. Despite his clouded eyes, the vitality in his smile defied any sense to me that he was handicapped. From a distance, I saw the woman dip her head toward her husband, as if narrating the scene.

"I'm wondering if I might bother you for a bucket of water," I called across the yard. "I have my own bucket," I said, dismounting. "I'm Lisa Stewart, riding cross country, headed home to Kansas City.

"I'm Marilyn, and this is my husband, Wayne."

My encounters with people took on the form of speed dating, and before I knew it, they had summed up their lives.

"I drove a bulldozer for forty-two years," Wayne was saying. By then, Chief had finished two buckets of water, and I was rolling it up and tying it to the saddlebag.

"I have something I want to show you," Wayne said. "It's around behind the house."

I pulled up Chief's head from the lawn, and we followed Wayne to a sight that would have made me shy sideways, if I were a horse. Resting under a wide shade tree adjacent the back steps was a round rock that I guessed measured four feet in diameter.

"I was digging a pond, and I hit something solid, which isn't unusual around here," Wayne quipped. "I'm pretty careful with my equipment, so I didn't force it. It had a different feel to it, so I just started easing it up a little at a time out of the ground. I could see it was round, and I knew what I had. I've never seen a bigger one." Marilyn stood with her arms crossed, looking tenderly at her husband and his four-foot-diameter geode, recorded as the largest ever found in Missouri.

"I wonder if there are giant crystals in there!" I said.

"I don't know," he said, "but I'm not going to crack it open."

"No, I wouldn't either."

How else might one chance to stumble upon the largest geode in Missouri, except by happenstance on a horse?

After some time, I mentioned my need to find a place to put my horse overnight.

"My husband comes every Friday to bring me supplies. If I find a safe place to keep Chief tonight, Bob can take me to a motel for a shower and a meal out."

Marilyn turned to Wayne. "I would think Harold and Martha would have a place, wouldn't you?"

"Call Harold," Wayne said to his wife. "They and their kids own all this land between these hills. One daughter is about a mile up the road, and then Harold is on the far hill over there." I looked toward the half-mile-wide swale between rises.

Marilyn returned in minutes to tell us, yes, her neighbors would be expecting me.

"It will be the second home place you come to up this road, past the T intersection that goes east." Marilyn pointed. "Let me go get you a little something to take with you." She hurried into the house and returned with a Ziploc bag stuffed with apricot leather she'd just made and cooled for her grandchildren.

She handed it up to me sitting on Chief, while Chief grazed. As if to buy time she asked if I would like an apricot for the road, and, of course, I said yes.

She soon came back with a translucent, freshly picked apricot. It appeared to be a velvet balloon filled with liquid gold. I cupped it in my palm—too fragile to save for later. It had come from a pile on her counter awaiting transformation into jam and leather within twenty-four hours of picking. Its tree shaded the front lawn nearby with a treasury of fruit, like gold coins. Marilyn seemed disturbed to see me leave so quickly, so she stopped me from walking on and trotted into the house, retrieved scissors, and snipped me some fresh lavender from the bush out front.

"There!"

I sniffed it. "This will perfume me for miles, Marilyn. Thank you so much." I tied it to the front of my saddle and rode away, waving.

Soon, I saw a compact pickup in the distance. By now on my trip, I often could tell something about a driver, or house, from a ways off. A man slowed to a stop fifty feet in front of us, turned off his engine, and let Chief walk up to his driver's side window.

"I came to get you," he said. It was a closely shaven, gray-haired elderly man in a clean shirt and a high-quality straw hat with sweat stains around the brow band. He greeted me with something more affectionate than a smile: He gave me the familiar indifference of an old friend.

"Are you Harold?"

"That's what people keep saying."

"Thank you so much for letting me put my horse on your place tonight."

"You think he can make it the rest of the way?" This obviously was a joke, because Chief was nodding his head up and down and marching in place beside Harold's truck. He'd just gotten a whiff of a literal herd of hogs that had gotten loose and run in a pack behind a row of bales a sixteenth of a mile away. Chief hadn't seen them, and I was dreading their tearing back into sight.

"I don't know; he's about dead," I said.

Harold lifted his hand in mock annoyance and rolled past us, turned around, and idled behind us the two miles home.

It was quitting time, 3:00 PM, by the time Harold and I and Chief reached his house to find his wife, Martha, awaiting us under an old elm swishing its thousands of small leaves against the sky. Harold and Martha's raised-ranch home sat on a knoll, shaded by purposefully retained trees and backed by the gentle upward slope of pasture adorned with a straight wood barn and lots. Horses first: Harold left Martha and me to visit while he drove ahead of me to open the gate to a small pasture, check the fences, and run water into a tank.

"My husband is coming to bring me supplies, which he does every Friday. I like for him to take me to a motel when he comes if Chief has a safe pasture. Do you think that would be all right if we left him overnight?"

"Oh, I'm sure that would be fine," she said.

"I hate to impose."

"You're fine."

Soon, I released Chief into a large, grassy lot behind the house that contained a thirty-foot-long, three-sided tin shed, a trough for feeding cattle, and a drain-back faucet in the corner. The land flowed treelessly away, bounded by the typical, impenetrable belt of assorted hardwoods. I slid off Chief's headstall and turned my back. He crumpled to his knees to roll in tall grass. He would have shade, water, and grain given him, I was to learn, by a lifelong horseman and cattleman.

Now, Harold was bringing me back to the house in his air-conditioned truck. "He'll find the water," he commented to no one. Through the window, I watched Chief stand and shake and stride toward the water tank in the far corner. My head turned as we rolled away, the way a truck driver looks back at his rig as he walks toward a café.

Harold was five-foot-ten, pulled down like a "using horse." He stopped his pickup beside a tall thistle with a purple-puff bloom, bigger than a golf ball on top. He snarled at it. He looked over his shoulder into the bed of the pickup and snarled about not having his shovel and asked me if I wanted to wait here while he drove back and got his spade to dig it up. (I would have to get out and stand there in the heat while he fetched it, which I made noises about being happy to do.) Then he caught himself and said, "I'll get it later." We jostled through the field as on choppy waves. We rolled past a straight, paintless wood barn the size to store a winter's worth of small, round hay bales (which was the only kind that existed when the barn was built). It was surrounded by a corral with posts made of cracked, eighty-year-old hedge trunks the density of concrete, and oak boards bowed by decades of rain and heat, and I'd dare anyone to tear one off. The nails were better back then. It's been said that metal fence posts are superior to old hedge because they're easier to drive a nail into. Harold told me about building that barn and the lots, where, for decades, he'd sorted, vaccinated, and castrated calves before taking them to the sale barn.

He looked at the barn with the unguarded sentimentality of one who'd forgotten present company. "The ground was hard as rock, digging those post holes. I built it with two friends. The sweat was just pouring off us." He might have been talking about last week. Folks like Harold and Martha reclaimed miles of rolling woods for cattle pastures and crops and, in my experience, remember every rock they pried out of the earth.

"My dad was no-account," he said, and jerked his hand in front of his face like swatting a wasp. "Mother was the best woman there ever was. She raised us four boys on her own."

Harold pointed to a hill in the distance. "Two miles over there was where my grandparents lived. I walked there every day when I was a boy. They helped raise me." Harold pointed west. "Lockwood is that way a few miles," and he swiveled and pointed east, "and that way a few miles is South Greenfield. Those were our towns. I did a lot of walking."

"Did your grandparents farm here, or how did you get your start?"

"I bought my first forty acres for $1,500 when I was in high school, from money I earned milking cows. I bought a little every year. Worked for people. I had a good bulldozer driver. I'd have him clear forty acres a year."

You, too, would take personal issue with thistles that had to be dug by the roots from pasture you'd cleared yourself, and planted, and tended for sixty-seven years.

"I own a section of land, minus one eighty-acre piece," he said. "I've given a big patch to my son, and I gave my daughter a patch. You met her on the way here," he said, which I had. When I first rode in, she had been standing close to the road at the front of the large lawn on which sat a ranch home I supposed measured about 3,200 square feet, and with a twenty-five-foot travel trailer out back, and barns and equipment and nice vehicles. She'd been trying to figure out how to get the escaped hogs back, which belonged to her and her husband.

I couldn't help fixating on the fact that he said he gave the daughter less land than the son, but in Harold's mind, I'm sure, he figured she had a husband, so she wouldn't need as much.

"I worked for the sale barn twenty-four years. We weighed cattle." The "we" included the friends who had helped him build his barn; and though he didn't say, I was sure he'd helped them build their own as well. "I've worked hard all my life."

Most city people think farmers just farm. That has been rare for generations and is especially rare, now. They drive to the city and work alongside city people. My own sister's father-in-law and her husband farmed more than a thousand acres of wheat and ran cattle in central Oklahoma. Mr. Simmons wore a white shirt and slacks as an executive at Aero Commander in Oklahoma City, thirty-five miles away. His son, my brother-in-law, was a school-teacher, then ran a computer hardware business, while farming with his father. A real-estate agent I knew grew up on a 1,500-acre farm in Iowa. They had cattle and row crops and hogs. His father drove to Brown Engineering in Des Moines every day and worked the fields at night—a lit-up ball of dust rolling across the fields. He rose at 3:00 AM to do chores. Got off at 3:30 PM. Got home at 4:30, started farming, and did that for decades. Nobody's families are fat cats on farms. These folks can get annoyed when they hear people whine about not having a job.

"I've had horses all my life," he said, over the steering wheel. We eased into the driveway. "Raised cattle all my life. All I've ever done."

I told him my dad had a small cow-calf operation. He nodded his head. "How many cattle do you run?" I asked.

"A hundred and twenty-six head of cows." Not about a hundred, or a hundred and twenty-five. One hundred and twenty-six, and each one counted every day.

My dad always figured four acres per cow on good pasture in Missouri. It sounded to me like Harold was a conservative pasture husband, too, which is a ridiculous statement, because he had been ranching more than sixty years, and the family's all still here on the farm—a miracle.

When I asked what kind of cows, he said, "The ones that give a lot of milk and have fat calves." That was his way of saying he could tell by looking at a crossed cow whether she would do just that. "Never had registered cattle, except the bulls."

We debarked the truck behind the house, and Harold had me store my saddle on the bench seat of an older, second pickup parked in the shed—no mice. A town person might not give my saddle a second thought, like propping a bike against a tree over-night. Harold knew a saddle represented survival when you lived on horseback, and it deserved as much consideration as the animal to which it was cinched.

Martha met us in the shade behind the house.

Harold turned away. "I'll go grain him."

His offer to grain Chief surprised me, given Chief was in knee-high grass.

"Oh. Let me help," I said.

Martha touched my arm. "It'll be good for him," she whispered. The occasional gaps I had begun noticing in Harold's short-term memory seemed to close when he had a job to do. "He misses the horses," she said.

We entered Martha's kitchen through the back door. Having just come in from the field with the man who owned this land mitigated my discomfort for inconveniencing them. I felt uneasy just the same, in my dust and drying perspiration, to sit for what might be two hours before Bob arrived. I pulled off my boots at the door.

Tall, willowy Martha led me into the living room and insisted I wasn't too dusty to sit on her couch. She left to fetch me sweet iced tea, and I took in the living room, decorated with clusters of picture frames containing the faces of children and grandchildren. There were no expensive antiques, but furniture that had been chosen for its history and good taste with a few treasures adorning it that might have been made by familiar little hands in vacation Bible school. The expanse of the room, and the light pouring through the sheers, relaxed me. I sat. After my week in the saddle, the couch seemed to absorb me in a way that felt, for a moment, inappropriately comfortable. Martha found her seat in the smaller of two recliners, and she crossed her thin arms and touched the front of her blouse at the neck as she talked and rocked minutely. She told me about their children and grandchildren, the facts of which entered my subconscious directly, because my conscious mind was numbed by wind. I was supposed to be out in the heat, working. It took time to adjust to comfort and conversation.

"Our daughter's husband runs a café in Golden City," she said. "I guess it's popular. It's full every night. Cooky's Café. That's his nickname."

"Really! I'll have to have Bob take me there tonight."

Harold returned and took his seat in his recliner.

"Are you sure you don't mind if I leave Chief alone here tonight? I'm happy to camp out back if that would be better."

"You go right on and get to town and get your shower," said Martha. "I wonder where you'll stay. There aren't any motels around here, unless you drive to Lamar."

"That's what I was thinking."

"Cooky has a very nice travel trailer. I'll give them a call. It has a shower and beds."

"Oh, I don't want them to have to worry about that." In truth, I wanted to be in a real motel, with a real shower. I'd been looking forward to a king-sized bed all week, and I couldn't bear the thought of anything less.

I heard a second and third time Harold's stories that had captivated me so much at first. Each telling brought forth from me even greater expressions of surprise and delight, which relieved Martha, who rocked a bit harder with each retelling, and finally she began interrupting her husband, which seemed to surprise and annoy him. Two hours became one as we waited for Bob.

"I left my job at the outset of the recession," I said, when asked what I did at home. "I have a freelance business helping other businesses with grants and business plans and marketing studies. Even though it would seem the wrong time to quit my job and go out on my own in 2007, I thought, if there are seven billion people on this planet, and I can't find two hundred who need my work, I'm not trying very hard."

Martha lowered her lids and nodded.

"The stock market is nearly to fourteen thousand. NASDAQ," she said.

I had no idea what that meant, precisely, though I often heard such totals on the news.

"It's not that high," Harold barked.

"It lost another two percent last week, but I see this morning it's soaring—as they say—up more than five percent. The European banks came to an agreement in Brussels yesterday, and it bounced."

We all let that piece of information float in the dustless living room, with the afternoon light filtering through lace, and the central air-conditioning, which blocked the clicking of grass-hoppers and the brushing of leaves upon leaves outside.

Harold shook his head, annoyed.

People who don't have money don't follow the stock market.

Sensing enough time had been spent sitting in one place, Martha invited me back into the kitchen for a refill of my tea. She disap-peared down a hallway and, in a few minutes, returned leading a young woman by her thin, white arm, like a sacrament, in her own slender hands.

"This is our daughter, Betty. She's forty-three."

I took Betty's hand and bent slightly at the waist, as I would when touching a horse for the first time. "I am very happy to meet you, Betty," I said. She had Down syndrome. Betty wore white cotton pajamas with tiny pastel florets spaced over the fabric, so the overall impression was that of morning mist—and a matching, untied cotton robe. She held out her arm and pointed to a dark, red scar running more than half the length of her forearm.

"Betty had to have surgery for carpal tunnel syndrome. She had to quit her job at a sheltered workshop," Martha said. (Sheltered workshops are non-profit light manufacturing companies that employ people who have physical or mental handicaps.) "She misses it." Betty was quiet, fair, sweet-eyed, and slender. She looked twenty-five.

Finally, to the relief of all, Bob arrived. We four stood in shade beside the house. Bob bonded instantly with every family that cared for me. Harold put his arm around me and said to Bob, "Don't need to expect her to come home. She'll want to stay with us here in God's country."

Bob took pictures of me with my adopted family. In the photo, my short waist was lost in my blousy shirt, and my legs looked cartoonishly straight and thin. My hat was misshapen, and my eyes and face looked puffed, considering how little I weighed. I could have been their daughter.

I later learned that Harold didn't sleep all night worrying something might happen to Chief while I was gone.

When Bob returned me to them the next morning at 11:00—after dinner of pork tenderloins and fries at bursting Cooky's Café in Golden City, after my long shower at the Blue Top Inn, and after two beers that evening, which were two beers too many—Harold called me Daughter. He hugged me goodbye and told Bob, "You don't need to come back. She's going to stay right here with us."

It was 1:00 PM before I was packed and ready to go. That blistering day, a few miles north of Harold and Martha's, I watched my car top a hill a mile ahead of me. I saw the brake lights come on. Bob was dragging his feet on his way back to Kansas City. He was keeping pace, a white rectangle hovering on the plain. Chief and I were nearing a farmhouse close to the road when we shocked a dog by our silent approach, and he rushed my horse from the porch. Then came another dog, then another, until they numbered five, circling Chief and barking and trying to bite his legs. I saw my brake lights flash in the distance and Bob turn the car. I kept turning Chief and yelling at the dogs. Then more dogs rushed out. I tried to chase some, and the others swarmed in behind us. In a moment, Bob came tearing up the road, slipped past us and into the pack. I gaited Chief away while Bob broke up the party and sent the majority back to their yard with our car. Chief and I chased the stragglers away and gaited onward an eighth of a mile. Bob caught up with us and got out.

"I knew you could handle it," he said. "I just couldn't drive away while you were being attacked by a pack of dogs."

He reached up and patted my leg. Here was my new Bob, who had not changed at all, but from my view five feet above on a thousand-pound horse, after three weeks riding, he was illumined in a way that I could only behold from on high. His big hand squeezed my thigh. My knight returns to court, while I continue to survey my realm. That touch—a man pats his queen on the thigh before she rides away eighty thousand Scottish falls (or 250 American miles)—was more arousing to me than anything else he might do.

Hansson Cattle Company

There are two types of "junky" when it comes to houses where I might camp: 1) happy/busy/homey junky, and 2) alcohol/drug-soothed/hopeless junky. By midafternoon two days after I left Harold and Martha's, I had passed up three of the latter.

We rode along fields whose green hides draped over a muscular earth and beside others so flat I wondered how they drained. Despite our more than ninety-degree afternoon, the breeze pressed my wet shirt against me like a cool hand. This past hour, as every last hour of a day, I strained toward a safe place to camp, fretting that tonight I might finally be forced to tie my horse in a hedgerow at dark with no water. We seemed to creep, and I forced myself to focus on the next utility pole, and the next, and pat Chief for reaching each one.

In the distance, I caught sight of a chocolate wave in the field, flowing toward us in a great sweep—young, beautifully uniform cattle driven to a trot by their curiosity about us—clearly never having seen a rider and horse. They stopped at a safe distance from us, heads up, aristocratically. Beyond these milk-chocolate cattle was a beautifully manicured, bricked and rocked home with an addition on the back that provided banks of windows for viewing its green fields. It was a country cottage, likely eighty years old, whose charm had been elevated by the need to stay current—a modern kitchen, no doubt, and bathrooms, closets, perhaps master with en suite, all the things our great-grandmothers would want but couldn't imagine. As I approached, I could see in the lots three horses and more of the pedigreed cattle I couldn't identify.

There are two types of "neat" when it comes to homes: 1) happy/industrious neat, and 2) sad/lifeless neat. "Happy-neat" creates landscape with symmetry, but not too much; a mailbox made like a barbeque grill or some other sculptural joke; dusty trucks and all-terrain vehicles parked around; and the place mowed and sporadically festooned with hardy flowers. "Lifeless-neat" has few or no bushes at the home's foundation; is mowed down to the ground; and no toys, no swing sets, garden, flowers. The home of the milk-chocolate cattle was happy/industrious neat.

A man's shriek cut across the field. At first, I thought there might be a fight. Then I heard a big-throated cackle and whoop followed by daintier cheers, *happy birthday, happy birthday*. I pushed up my sunglasses. I could see small children jumping up and down in the backyard.

I felt joy at finding a possible camp and irreconcilable dread, because I imposed on people, and here I might interrupt a party. When I reached the driveway, I dismounted and peeked around the side of the house. On a raised, concrete patio arranged in the shade were cushioned chairs and chaises and a handful of adults and a school of young children mingling among balloons and bubbles, a speck on this western Missouri plain.

I always have assumed people in the city didn't understand that life in the country is virtually the same as life in the city. What really is the difference between birthday parties in the city or country that all come with cards made by Hallmark or plates and napkins and balloons from China? Our gifts in the country come via FedEx trucks that billow their vapor trails of dust down these roads as readily as their twins stop in front of my niece's home near D.C.

I bent at the waist and peeked a bit farther when the man I heard shriek jerked up his head, and placed his hands on the arms of his chair, and pushed himself up. The children flitted. Their pale arms gleamed in the sun. The man worked out his kinks as he walked toward me. He struck me as a mirthful monarch over these green fields filled with bovine princes and princesses. In his essence, he might have been my former auto mechanic, all cleaned up, or the owner of a thousand acres I knew by Walker, Missouri. He wore a polo shirt stretched across World Wrestling Council-sized shoulders. How could I tell at a glance a man could be trusted, that he'd stop if he saw my car broken down on the road? I just could. We introduced ourselves in his driveway.

"I am *so* sorry to interrupt."

"Oh, we're just having a little birthday party for my granddaughters." He held out his hand, "Leo Hansson."

"Just keep right on," I said. "I don't want to stop you; I just thought I'd ask—I'm riding through on my way back to Kansas City, and in the next hour or so, I'll be needing to stop for the night. Do you think someone down the road might have a place I could toss my horse out overnight?"

He tilted his head toward his back yard, "This is winding down. I'm sure we can find a place for your horse." A slender, beautiful blonde with remarkably blue eyes walked up beside him, and she *was* the queen of this realm—Nora Hansson, Leo's wife. Both seemed near my age, a bit younger. I shaped a brick in the air with my hands to demonstrate how much space I needed for my tent. "I have everything I need except a few buckets of water."

"Let me get this wrapped up," he said, "and I'll get you in one of these lots." By you, he meant my horse, which as any horseman knows, meant me. I retreated as far back in the yard as I could, past young fruit trees, against a fence without a swatch of shade. I felt a momentary disorientation about where to put what, what to do first, whether to look for a hydrant and help myself, or wait, and how long? I began stripping my horse and slapping horse flies to death on his hide. I hoped to blend into the yard so they could forget me and get on with their Sunday lives.

Too soon, sons and daughters and grandchildren were leaving, and Leo came over and led me to the hydrant where I sprayed off my horse. He walked off and opened a pipe pen next to his own horses. He offered to drive to another farm for a small bale of hay for my horse, but I objected. I could pull hay from the big round bale in his horses' pen and toss it in to Chief. He wouldn't eat hay, anyway, I thought. Nora joined us as I was putting Chief away, "You can stay in our spare bedroom," she stated.

I protested from several angles. There would be no moving her. "We have company all the time from out of state on cattle business. I have three spare bedrooms," she said. "We were about to go check the cattle. Would you like to see our Beefmaster herds? You can come in and have a shower and dinner after that." The sovereign had spoken. My obeisance came in the form of un-corseting my diaphragm. The test of whether I agreed to stay inside always was to discern whether I would be more of a burden outside or in. For Nora, allowing me to sleep outside was insane.

"I would love to see your cattle. I miss checking cattle with Dad."

"Come to the house when you're ready."

The way she turned lightly on her heel said there was nothing I could do wrong on her farm.

I rode in the back seat of a Honda CR-V (a juvenile sport-utility vehicle). No big-truck ego for this massive man but a handy-dandy hatchback that would hold two small, square bales of hay or five, five-gallon buckets of grain. Leo sustained a baby-talk patter that both humored and pestered his wife. Nora ran a business they owned in a nearby town; Leo worked mainly from home, managing and promoting their registered Beefmaster breeding herd across the nation. I had no idea how many acres they ranched, or whether they also farmed, but I knew that Leo and his father, and at least one other family member, all owned the breed. How many cattle on how many acres, I never would ask. That's like asking to see someone's pay stub.

The Honda was remarkably clean for a work truck, aside from the dust that sifted between window brushes and door seals. Nora pointed the dash vents back toward me. When the cold air brushed my face, I was stunned by the change—an hour earlier, I was wishing utility poles closer as proof of my progress; now I was zipping along with new friends in an air-conditioned car. How needlessly I crawled across the planet in the heat and wind on a horse that teleported himself nearly out from under me at least twice a day. It would be easy to stop this trip. One phone call. The only call I wished to make now was for Bob to come see this himself. Not take me home—not yet.

Nora didn't say *I'll get it* when we pulled up to a field gate by the road. She just got out, unclipped a chain, and swung the gate open, and Leo drove through and paused while she closed the gate behind us and slid back into the truck. The Honda murmured through a pasture whose fescue had been cut once for hay and grown up belly high again.

We drove toward five flesh-and-blood trucks, Beefmaster bulls, which lifted their sixty-pound heads to watch our approach. There was no living weight more compact than these massive bulls whose eyes brightened at the sight of the CR-V. I remembered the sight of cows flipping up their heads to lift off in a lope at the sight of Dad's three-quarter-ton pickup waggling over the pasture with their hay. The Hanssons' bulls rocked their heads up and down as they swung around on their wide, split hooves. One bull was black, the others, varying shades of sorrel red. One filled the window beside me. Leo cut the engine, and we rolled down the windows. He got out and walked among his bulls, laying the flat of his hand on their backs as they passed. They had cuddlesome, tall foreheads and meaty eyebrows from their Brahman lineage, which made them look wiser than Dad's Herefords and Angus. Their hindquarters were full and round to the hock, and their forequarters bulged with chuck roasts and briskets and shanks.

Their backs were so flat they could pool water, and the meat draped like a cylinder around their ribs for rows of porterhouse, T-bone, club, and rib steaks, culminating under their bellies in a flap of flesh that drooped down in the middle where a shaft would descend to pee or mate. On several of these bulls, ample flesh gathered around their necks to give them dark collars. On these, extra hide dangled from their chins and flowed like a leather ruffle between their front legs. This flesh flapped side to side when they walked.

I felt tense, watching Leo among his bulls, whose toplines reached nearly to his shoulder. Dad's bulls never could be trusted not to charge a person, but Dad's were not pampered from birth or led with a halter and rope in shows like these had been. If I walked through our pastures in breeding season, I stayed within running distance of a fence. My mother's great uncle was trampled to death by his bull. Dad usually had two: one shorthorn and either an Angus or Hereford.

"I've never been around registered cattle. Do you show them often?"

"You pretty much have to be at all the major shows," Leo said.

"We won the Houston International Show. That's our advertising," said Nora.

Winning a grand championship at the Houston International Show could make a bull's semen worth $1,500 per ounce. For the purpose of artificial insemination (AI—impregnating cows), bull semen typically is sold in one-half milliliter doses in "straws." The bull generously offers up his "collection" in a fake vagina several times a week, or as often as the breeder deems prudent—up to a greedy ten times per week. (Leo didn't stress his bulls like that.) Some breeders collect a total of 80,000 to 110,000 straws per year from one bull (that's one billion sperm per offering, diluted with an extender made of milk or egg yolk and stored in straws for freezing). Prior to freezing, the semen is checked for "abnormalities of forward movement." In other words, if the sperm were a car, it should be zipping around at forty miles per hour. If not, it gets culled. The straws then are stored or transported in canisters of liquid nitrogen. One distributor of the "secret sauce" handles more than 1,900 gallons of genetically tested bull semen from all breeds each year.

Nora reached into a bag of cattle cubes on the floorboard—compacted protein, fat, fiber, minerals and vitamins.

"Here you go." Nora handed a cube out the window, one at a time slipping the cube under a muzzle and releasing at just the right moment. "Cow candy." She smiled. "They would crawl in my lap for these," she said.

That night I sat at the granite bar in Nora's kitchen and ate Beefmaster steak, homegrown sautéed zucchini, and salad. Leo showed me pictures of his 1956 Corvette with only forty-two thousand miles on it and pictures from his car-racing days. He was a big name in this region. I had been married to a car dealer, myself— my children's father—who also built motorcycles from a basket of parts, then cars, then ran his father's Ford-Lincoln-Mercury dealership before and after our horseback trip. To men like Len and Leo, there is something spiritual about the roar of a 265-cubic-inch, 225-horsepower engine opening up its two, four-barrel carburetors—metal parts shimmying up and down to hurdle their cargo the weight of a Beefmaster bull down a Dade County road that might as easily be Highway 1 in view of a green sea of pasture.

We slid into their leather couch and chairs to watch the Miss USA pageant that happened to be on that night. Leo kept up his gruff, baby-talk jokes, predicting who would make the next cut, and the next. We joked and chatted, and it never came up what *I* might do for a living. How do you ask someone who blew in on a horse what her other, real life is like? Might she be out of work? Out of options? Out of her mind? Because of the birthday party, I knew they had children, so I felt safe asking about them.

"Ah," said Nora. I saw pain in her eyes. I panicked thinking she had a child on drugs or in prison. "I lost my only son sixteen years ago in a car accident, when he was sixteen."

I glanced at Leo. His eyes were wet. Nora added, "Leo lost a son two years ago to cancer. He left the children and their mother."

Leo kept his voice soft, perhaps so it wouldn't break. "That's what my life is all about now, looking after them," he said. "That was their house I pointed to when we went to look at the open heifers this afternoon." The children had been playing outside in the shade not a mile from their grandparents'—the best that could be hoped for.

The uncurtained windows that looked onto the backyard trees and field beyond had grown black and reflected the indoor scene against a motionless night. I was swept with the feeling I'd left my own child somewhere. Instantly, I remembered Chief was safe in a lot with hay. I hadn't thought about him for hours.

In front of the television, Leo's banter was unceasing with every winnowing down of contestants, which Leo picked correctly, as he does regularly at stock shows, and the correlation was lost on none of us.

"Have you thought of installing a wind generator out here?" I asked.

"I've thought of it," Leo said. "I haven't taken the time to figure out what it takes."

"The US Department of Agriculture has a program for operators like you. It's not that difficult," I said. "I've gotten USDA money for a pecan grower, a pork producer, and a food seasoning processor. The wind program pays for the turbine and installation, and then you get the energy, and you can feed it back to the electric company and get the credit."

Leo looked at me as if for the first time.

I believed I saw everyone at their most genuine on this ride, because I didn't have an identity. I was a vulnerable traveler. What can a person say to that? It pricked me that the brain in my head wasn't immediately obvious, except that I must at least have sounded like a reasonable person, or they wouldn't have invited me to stay. Perhaps people could see me for who I was—not a business consultant but a traveler living inexplicably at this present place, among the things I loved most: my horse, this land, and you, Mr. and Mrs. Host.

The king-sized bed in a long dormer room the color of a hazy sun could not be described in terms of its comfort. Nor could the angel-food cheesecake I had just eaten. Disoriented again, by not being in my tent, I lay in the quiet: no strident mockingbird or whippoorwill using its outside voice, no barking dogs at dusk—just the reverberation in my limbs of my horse's thousand steps.

A Truce with Chief

J ust after daylight, I rode Chief out the Hanssons' drive, he, having received three days' worth of grain in one night from my generous host. Chief went sideways at a flowerbed, a swing, a fence, then the mailbox. *Don't start. You've been looking at this stuff all night!* But he couldn't see any of this from where he stood last night, and though we rode past it yesterday, he'd slept since then.

We walked onto the road and past the house. Chief pounced to an adrenalin-injecting stop twice at *objets d'ag* (big black gate, disk implement). Riding Chief was like being a passenger with an old person flooring the gas pedal right before dropping it into drive. I sunk my heels into the stirrups and softened my eyes. *It'll all be good when we get past this stuff.* A tall fertilizer truck had stopped in the road a short distance away. The driver could tell what I had on my hands, and he didn't want to make it worse. On cue, Chief spun 180 degrees and took three leaps the way we came. I lost my near-side stirrup but managed to find it and jerk him down and swing him around, *goddam.* I kicked Chief into a fast gait and kept straightening and gigging him and cursing him for the next mile.

We continued gaiting toward Kansas City, and before long, we came upon the field of Beefmaster bulls I had visited the day before—Chief's biggest fear, except that these had no horns. They stood near the fence. *Okay, my horse who never remembers and never forgets—we need to wear you out by making some miles, but we will stop, and you will graze beside bulls.* Chief froze when he saw what I could only describe as burnished Sherman tanks. I nudged Chief forward until we were within thirty feet of them. When I was convinced he was completely set, I dismounted. To my advantage, Chief had eaten no green grass all night, and he was desperate for it, so I lead him into the ditch, close to the bulls, to eat.

The big, frank inquisitors rocked one step toward us, then another, stretching their noses closer to the fence, puffing. Chief stretched his neck, too, and flared his nostrils and widened his eyes. Air rattled through his sinuses. Chief lowered his head to grab a bite, then looked up and stared at the bulls while he chewed, now only a few feet away. I drew Chief closer to the fence and closer, still. The outsized Curious Georges hove to. They lowered their heads and wrapped their alien-length tongues around grass stems before tearing them with gentle jerks, like Chief. Their rhythm of tearing and chewing and smacking seemed to comfort Chief. Air breezed through their pipes like massive snorkels. Their black, hairless muzzles glistened, freshly licked. Chief raised his head again and looked at his fellows a minute. Then, he lowered his head and released a long breath and ate peacefully in their company.

I reached through the fence and, by inches, one bull met my finger with its wet nose.

Midafternoon I sat in a ditch, again, writing in my spiral pad on my knee, while my horse grazed beside me. We had kept up a quick pace for most of five hours with stops every couple of miles to check my map. Chief had traveled the whole time as if we'd penetrated enemy lines.

Dried sweat paled his face. He tore at the grass methodically. A headache was building at the base of my skull, as it always does when I look down at my pad too long. I looked up and turned my chin from side to side, which produced a sound in my neck like boots on gravel. I searched for a description of the magnetism I felt from Chief—his hooves inches away from my legs, his heart cradled above my head in the thoracic sling of his ribs. I sat in his shade. He invaded my space as he would that of his friend

Dreamer at home in the pasture. I ran my knuckle down his satiny foreleg from knee to hoof. By now, he probably was down to nine hundred pounds. I couldn't see any ribs—that was good. I just had massaged fly dope into his coat. He loved me for that—if a horse could love.

Then he exploded sideways, over me. One moment he was a few inches to my left; the next, he was to my right. Nothing touched me, just an explosion of saddle leather and bags, and my canteen smacking, and his hooves landing with two thousand pounds of force. He spun and clattered into the middle of tranquil, paved Route O and stood. A hound from some house down the road had trotted into Chief's periphery.

I sat in the ditch looking at my horse in the middle of the road. His reins hung in front of his feet, not caught through one of his legs, not stepped on. His eyes bulged. One knee trembled. His ears were back, and his teeth were clenched. He looked like he just came out of a seizure. I set my pad and pen in the grass and climbed out of the ditch. I stood beside him a minute. Then I wrapped both of my arms around his neck, the way I'd gather a toddler, lightly, so not to tip him over. I rested my head on his neck. My arms stuck to his wet coat. We stood like this several minutes. This whole thing was a lot to ask of a horse.

A New Kin

Three days after leaving the Hanssons' farm at noon, we reached Cedar County Road 541. It became nothing more than two tracks in tall weeds sheltered by dense woods on both sides that smelled like merlot wine, and I was beginning to panic that I was lost. Why would the line on my map dissolve into densely forested bottom land? We arrived at the remains of a small bridge, not more than fifteen-feet long, rotted down to two steel beams close enough together for a silly kid on a four-wheeler to try to gun it across. I could see the evidence of their tire tracks. How would we get across—and should we? The so-called road beyond the bridge disappeared into tall grass and weeds with nothing beyond it but a straight gap in the trees leading up a hill. If we kept riding, would we be expending precious hours only to learn the road didn't go through?

I tied Chief to a tree and slid on foot down into the ditch beside the bridge and walked up the trickle-of-a creek to find a place to cross. I looked out for half-buried barbed-wire fence on Chief's behalf. Some horses will stand still if they get caught in wire. Some will tear themselves up before they let you get them unhooked. Chief is the stand-still kind, but I didn't want to test him. I found a deer path a few dozen yards from the bridge and climbed it up the bank on the other side. After pulling through the brush and briars, I reached the remnants of a road beyond the bridge. I stood and looked up the hill where the road had been.

Then I returned for Chief, having made up my mind to see if the road would go through to civilization. He stepped like a gentleman behind me down the creek, conscious of not catching my heels with his hooves. We dug up the steep bank and pulled ourselves through sapling branches, cobwebs, and blackberries and climbed back into the old roadbed on the opposite side of the bridge. We stood in tall grass on two faint impressions made a century ago by teams pulling four-wheeled wagons, then Model Ts, then Ford F-250s, kids on ATVs, and now a rider and horse. I had never felt more isolated. It would take me nearly two weeks to reach a symphony at Kauffman Center for the Performing Arts in Kansas City; then where would I tie my horse?

I stood beside Chief and studied my *Atlas & Gazetteer*. The breeze was faint. I looked ahead. The tracks gradually grew more distinct. I tightened the saddle cinch one hole and mounted from the off side. We rode on, and the deer path we followed became a real gravel road, and ahead, a stop sign and an intersection. Never before had a sign that read "STOP" felt so welcoming. As we came close enough to read the street sign, I could see it did not say what it should. I turned north anyway, praying that my map was wrong.

Over two miles we steadily rose. The trees gave way to emerald pastures, weeded and mowed and grown up thick. The sky expanded, cleared of any moisture by gusts of wind from the direction of Oklahoma. Gradually, a brick ranch house set off the road grew near. It seemed quiet, a farm place, but with little equipment, one barn—retired looking. Kitty-corner across the road appeared a smaller, white wood-frame house that must be the grandparents'. That's how you know if land has been occupied by one family a while: homes grouped in two or three stages of sophistication around a section of land. The grandparents' small frame home across the road from the children's expanded ranch, and finally, the grandchildren's McMansion with which some of them say God has blessed them, and which, in my opinion, resulted mostly from their ancestors' hard work.

In this case, we approached just two homes and with them my supposition that they were related. In front of the smaller, turn-of-the-century farmhouse stood three mature trees, and under them, a picnic table with party favors and a flashing plastic tablecloth taped down on the edges against a steady wind. There was the grandmother and grandfather, the birthday girl in her thirties, I would learn (in from Chicago), a grandniece from Kansas City, and three stair-step great-grandchildren. They looked of Swedish or German ancestry. I had arrived with entertainment for the children, on cue.

Unlike a local, who would wave and ride by, I rode toward their party, surrounded by thirty pounds of packs on my saddle. I swung my leg high to clear them and removed the barrier of my glasses and hat and apologized for the interruption.

"I was wondering if you could help. This road doesn't match my map, and I want to be sure I'm on the right road."

The group gathered around my swatch of map.

"Oh, I can't seem to see where we . . . " said the grandmother.

"I know; it's hard to orient yourself, because everything is blown up so large. Here's Pacetown."

"Oh," said the granddaughter, "so here's where we should be."

"That's what I was hoping; it's just that this name doesn't match the road sign."

The grandfather had taken a glance at my map and had shaken his head and walked off to his pickup for a regular map. He spread it on the table next to mine.

"This is what you need," he said.

I looked at it and could see that the road I was standing on did not even appear on his map. We all ignored him and clucked and murmured over my map.

"We're right here," Laura, the granddaughter said to him.

"So up here is a T intersection?" I asked.

"Yes. Look here," their grandfather said, which I respectfully did, and I pretended to get my information from him. He would have steered me right without my detailed map, in any case, but I depended on the fine lines more then he could ever know.

"Whose birthday have I just interrupted?" I asked.

"It's for my granddaughter," said Grandmother. "Laura lives in Chicago now. She's a meteorologist for the Environmental Protection Agency."

The woman speaking was of the generation of women whose granddaughters live in frighteningly large cities they will never visit.

Laura stood at least five feet, nine inches, slender, beautiful, sandy-haired with light eyes.

I still am stunned when a young woman who looks like a model and was born in the country is a doctor or meteorologist in "the city." What if my mother had said, "You can be a veterinarian, Lisa," when I was sixteen? What might I have done if just one person had encouraged me?

"Jennifer, here, is from Kansas City," said Grandmother, touching her arm.

"Oh! I'm in Prairie Village," I said.

"That's funny. I live in North Kansas City," Jennifer said.

I wasn't lost; these folks could have driven me home that afternoon, if I had wished, when they returned Laura to the Kansas City International Airport.

The family's apparent delight with my arrival was exceeded only by the children's joy at riding Chief. I led them around and around on his back in their front yard. "Good buooy," they said. He did not shy a whit but made his circles like a good Amish horse. The wind swept our hair free, and the tall trees in the distance dusted the edges of the sky. In time, I asked if I might use the restroom. "Of course," said Grandmother.

I sat on the cool, clean seat in silence. I always was stunned by how quiet it was inside a house. I was surrounded by pink-and-blue wallpaper that probably had been hung thirty years before. There was a half-used Kleenex box, half a bar of soap offering its spring-like Irish scent, cleaning supplies tucked behind the stool, the magnification mirror for Grandmother's pores or Grandfather's splinters, towels that almost matched, a gown on the back of the door, and me, like a daughter, welcomed to sit on this seat on this green hill.

When I came out, Grandmother sent me back into the quiet kitchen for a filled donut from the Krispy Kreme box on the metal-and-Formica table. The Chicago granddaughter, Laura, had bought the donuts on the way down from the airport, a treat not otherwise available within a hundred miles. I wrapped my donut in a paper towel I ripped from a roll I found on the counter. Grandmother insisted I also take a piece of birthday cake for the road from the table out front. While I prepared Chief to leave, I ate the donut with my DEET-drenched gloves. I felt ashamed for taking such large bites. Cake in hand, I turned west when I reached the T intersection. That road matched my map.

House of Spirits

I rode along paved County Road HH in deep grass beside a fence, and I was happy. We rode in and out of gangs of horseflies guarding their sectors with dull, large-gauge needles. The shimmering black road with faint center stripes flowed past at the speed of a walk, and Chief grasped a fescue head, which squeaked and popped, and he bobbed his head to get it around the bit in his mouth to chew it.

The next moment, Chief exploded straight up. I hung midair, no saddle, no stirrups, no horse. He came straight back down in a crouch. I rejoined him with a jolt. An eruption of brown feathers, four feet in diameter descended, too, and streaked away, barely shuddering the tall grass. Chief's low head pointed the way the creature went. We had walked directly over a wild turkey nest, and she'd flushed straight up under his belly.

With a breath of yogic proportion, Chief gathered himself and strode on. I gave him a lay-down hug around his neck and pats for such a sensible response to the mother of all spooks.

Through the trees ahead I could see an ample, split-level home on the top of a rise. Its lawn sloped toward HH. Parallel to the grade, a man and woman on two riding lawn mowers groomed the acre lawn, as if they were late for something—apparently a husband and wife in their thirties. A living-quarters horse trailer and toned Quarter Horses standing nearby were not lost on me. I rode into the drive. As if performing synchronized mowing, the couple turned their lawn tractors toward us from opposite directions, and we all dismounted together. We gravitated into the shade.

"Hi, I'm Lisa Stewart. I'm riding cross country . . ."

"Doing that again?"

That startled me. The man looked familiar.

"You're Lisa Brown."

"Yes! I'm dying here. You're . . ."

"Paul Acres. I shod horses for you and Lenny right after I got out of horseshoeing school."

"Oh, Paul, I'm sorry."

"This is my wife, Susan."

I'd ridden back into home country, approaching Nevada, Missouri, without realizing it. Again, I was struck by how foreign this planet felt because of my slowness. What everyone else could achieve in fifteen minutes was unreachable on my horse in a day, thus unattainable, unknowable to me.

"What are you doing?" he asked.

"I wanted to ride around Missouri. I'd always wanted to take a horseback trip—alone."

"We're getting ready to leave tomorrow for Eminence."

The word "Eminence" eliminated the need for several sentences and explained why I found them mowing like banshees to get things buttoned up before they left. In southeast Missouri, Eminence is a landing pad for one of the nation's largest organized trail rides, attracting more than ten thousand trailers full of horses to the rugged Mark Twain National Forest each year. Three major trail-riding businesses buttress the forest and three hundred miles of horse trails. More than thirty-thousand horses and riders splash through the cold, clear Current and Jacks Fork rivers. Seven major and fifty-one smaller springs provide pristine water from the depths of the Swiss-cheese-like Ozark and St. Francois aquifers on the 134-mile-long Ozark National Scenic Riverways. Cross Country Trail Ride, LLC, feeds two thousand horse-campers at a time and provides music and dancing every night. Paul and Susan would be there by this time tomorrow.

By the end of our talk, Paul handed me a key on a ring.

"Here's the key to the house."

"That is so nice of you. A real house and a real bed!"

"That'll feel better than the ground," Susan said.

They understood the symbolism of handing a virtual stranger the key to their deceased parents' home a section away. I zipped it into my breast pocket.

"All us kids own the property now," Paul said.

I later would find his parents' home, sitting on a mowed lawn, like a farm dog, waiting for its children to get off the bus. Paul drew me a detailed map that directed me back the way I had come on the blacktop and around a section on gravel. I could take a warm shower and sleep in a bed. As horse people, Paul and Susan were well aware of the magnitude of their gift to us—a safe pasture, water, a house, and solitude.

Chief and I turned and backtracked through the deep grass in the ditch along HH, through which we just had ridden, toward a gravel road that would lead us around a section to our home for the night. Chief pumped his head with tall, labored steps through thick weeds, when BOOM, he exploded straight up, and under him, a fracas of feathers. I hovered an instant midair, then slammed back down in the saddle. I'd brilliantly managed to walk Chief over the same wild turkey on her nest. She streaked away through the tall grass as before.

Good Buoooy! Chief had jumped only half as high that time.

I took a cold sponge bath in a dusty sink in a downstairs powder room of the five-bedroom, two-story house, tucked into trees off a T intersection in gravel—the former home of Bernadette and James E. Acres. It was a cold sink bath because Paul had forgotten the water heater had been turned off. I would have preferred bathing in the sunshine out back, but I was clean, in any case, and soon sat out front on folding chairs with Paul and Susan, who arrived at dusk. Beyond their chairs in the apricot light, the circle drive, once busy with a family of sixteen, plus grandparents, was filling in with grass.

The clothes I had worn today were clean and drying on the back fence with Chief's washed saddle pad. He stood still under a sky pink as a conch shell lip, or horse's lip. I ate a thick slice of warm banana bread Susan had just pulled from the oven before coming to visit me—part of their food for the week at Eminence. Between my legs was a quart Ziploc bag of venison jerky made by Paul. We sat and talked on this home place a quick drive from Montevallo, Virgil City, and El Dorado Springs. Only one mile away, I learned, lived Rosie and Larry Turner, long-time employees of my saddle company, whom I hadn't seen in years. They still worked with Len and our son, Derek, in Len's latest iteration of our saddle business. Larry and Rosie made saddle pads and tack on contract for Len. Everyone around here knew someone who worked for us once.

Paul reminisced about his Catholic family, the fourteen children raised here, who by now had spun off in all directions, most catching on towns nearby and some swirling into the vortex of cities "back east," or Texas, or Chicago. Paul offered me a beer, the only beer I would be given on this trip. He said at least five times that his mother was a saint.

Later, I sat at the kitchen table eating Paul's jerky. The evening was a blue-tinted skylight. In the large kitchen and eating area beside picture windows looking out over the back pasture were three tables and fourteen chairs. The dining room, beyond, had two large, oblong tables and another fourteen chairs. In the living room was a stack of mattresses and bedding for distribution around the room at night during family gatherings. Upstairs, each of the bedrooms had as many beds as could fit in them comfortably, topped with folded bedding. Paul had told me which room to use.

His mother, Bernadette Acres, long ago had positioned statues and pictures of Jesus and the Virgin Mary on shelves and bookcases around the house. Statues of Jesus stood in a garden beside the front porch and out back in line of sight from the sink.

Dozens of framed photos of children and grandchildren hung on the kitchen and dining room walls. A plaque in the kitchen declared, "Mom's Rules":

I cook it . . . you eat it.
I buy it . . . you wear it.
I wash it . . . you put it away.
I say bedtime . . . you say good night.
I say get off the phone . . . you hang up.
I say no . . . you don't ask why.
'Cause I'm The Mom.

Another plaque said, "Home—where each cares for the other, and all live for God." A framed cartoon from the syndicated newspaper cartoon series "Family Circus" said, "Lord, pick up my spirits, and I could use some help with this house, too!"

A certificate on the wall in the living room signed by Pope John Paul II proclaimed his blessing of Bernadette and James's wedding anniversary. Bernadette, the saint, had been a nurse at the Nevada City Hospital, Paul told me earlier. She died of complications from Alzheimer's disease, at seventy-two. James E. died several years prior, at seventy-three. Paul told how his mother had walked out of a procedure at the Nevada City Hospital. "I think that's why she lost her job," he said. "I have never seen her so upset in my life. She didn't ever talk about it, but what I've been able to piece together, Mom believed doctors were going to perform an abortion. She gathered the other nurses and informed them. She and several others refused to participate."

I turned on the ceiling fan in the upstairs bedroom that night. I propped myself on my good elbow and wrote: "I feel strange and delicious. It almost is scarier to sleep in an empty house than in my tent where I might hear something coming."

I would later learn, my son, Derek, was at Larry and Rosie Turner's, picking up saddle pads at the moment I laid my head down—one mile away. Within two hours, Derek was back home again in the city.

My Baby's Grave

Two days after we left the Acres' home place, Chief and I stood on what seemed the highest point in the world, officially clear of the Ozarks and entering row-crop country again. We braced against unimpeded westerly wind beneath a wrinkled veil of cirrus clouds. Green pastures and brown wheat stubble draped away on all sides. This midday I had stopped Chief at Lefler Cemetery, which we happened upon at the top of this hill. I'd heard of it but never visited before now. It cradled my children's father's family. My stillborn baby, Collin, lay only two sections away in Green Mound Cemetery, one-half mile from my former mother-in-law Blossom's birthplace and her family's now-forgotten truck farm. I nudged Chief into shade under a lone tree beside Lefler Cemetery. It felt about ninety degrees.

Chief stood beside me, grazing closer and closer to my feet, the intimacy of which warmed my heart, though I knew surely I must be standing on some forage he especially liked. I leaned against him here where my children's ancestors lay. The wind had been trying to pry off my hat, so I removed it to give my neck a break. I took gulps of canteen water, while my My-Sweet-Person-Horse grazed. He braced me—a small, two-legger who slaps his flies, and pats him a thousand times a day, and tells him he's not nuts, things really are scary.

I considered riding to Baby Collin's grave and pictured my ride east, the wrong direction, then north then west, to see the small rose-quartz incline of a gravestone with a kneeling-toddler angel

engraved beside the name Collin Brown. What a great name. I'd
visited Collin's grave at Green Mound Cemetery every Memorial
Day. The sky almost always looks like this, the wind unrestrained,
nobody within sight, except the Amish man training a mule in a
wood-rail round pen half a mile off. If we rode there, Chief would
wait for me while I stared at the stone, at the stones of Blossom's
family, no sound but birds and wind. Chief would graze in direct
sun around the monuments, while it wicked his precious stores. I
should go see Collin's grave.

I looked across an expanse of pasture northeast toward a
perfectly mowed half section and an enormous white and navy
barn with fields flowing in all directions dotted with black-and-
white Holstein cows. A wide, gleaming white gravel drive led to it.
I would learn that this massive corporate dairy operation was
owned by a company based in New Zealand. Tons of poop were
created here in what technically is called a CAFO (concentrated
animal feeding operation) and what I call a CAPO (concentrated
animal pooping operation). Like thousands of Tyson poultry
confinement barns and massive Murphy Farms' hog barns, the
state of Missouri welcomes all mega-poopers. These corporations
import Somalis and Mexicans—whoever is most desperate—for
temporary labor. While these agricultural behemoths hold locally
contracted farmers down to razor-thin profit margins, the state
boasts about new jobs. Meanwhile, the state now joins twenty-
seven others trying to weaken unions with its perennially proposed
right-to-work law. In Missouri, you might not have strong unions
any more, but you do have the lowest tax on cigarettes in the
United States, the lowest fuel tax, only one place in the state to get
an abortion, and one of the highest number of nonpoint-source
polluters in the country, covered in a blanket of green grass such as
I gazed upon this day.

I decided against riding Chief out of his way for a few moments
at my baby's grave. This living horse needed to be home in his pasture, and our mission was to get him there as quickly, pleasantly,
and responsibly as possible.

Cactus Kleinschmidt

Two days later, pickups powered down and tilted through the curve beside us on paved Route M, north of Schell City in Vernon County—thirty-five miles closer to home. We rode in the right of way. A swarm of green-headed flies clung to Chief's neck and shoulders. I leaned forward, slapping the flies and smearing Chief's blood, then dismounted and massaged every inch of his coat with DEET while he grazed. When I mounted, my horse walked on, a machine of flesh, of nodding neck, shifting shoulders, rocking rump, and swinging barrel between my legs. He was my legs, my heart, my gas, my breath, my obedient boy, the young man who, at night, placed the length of his face to my breast, while I rubbed his eyes and cheeks. His striding on without question or protest, day after day, warmed my core. I stroked his neck, *goood buooy*. It was all I could offer.

From my vantage, I could see cattle and horses and deer before Chief could. When we neared cattle now, I touched my friend on the side of his neck on which they would appear and said, "Cows, just cows." For horses, I said, "Horseys, Chief. Horseys." He had enough to worry about. I often didn't alert him to deer, hoping they'd hop away before he saw them, and anyway, deer rarely spooked him. In his former life in the Ozark Mountains, he saw more deer than people. No one could hear us. I could baby talk. My voice went high and soft, which seemed to calm him.

Our goal for the day was to skirt the Schell-Osage Conservation Area past Schell City. Around every bend, I looked for the stretch of guard-rail-narrowed road that would mark our achievement of the Bates County Drainage Ditch, Osage River (whose Bagnell Dam forms The Lake of the Ozarks). Its swollen tributaries converged to form the refuge. Bald eagles overwinter in this low land of rivers and creeks, attracting tourists from around the Midwest. "Schell," as the locals call the Schell-Osage Conservation Area, comprises nineteen hundred acres of bottomland and upland forest, eighteen hundred acres of cropland, seventeen hundred acres of old fields, and more than nine hundred acres of lakes and ponds. Five little patches make up more than forty acres of remnant native prairie. The Missouri Department of Conservation augmented an additional 170 acres of restored grasslands, and the whole affair includes eighteen hundred acres of seasonally flooded wetlands with waterfowl, shore birds, and long-legged species year-round. There are deer-hunting rules, bird-hunting bylaws, and frog-gigging guidelines. Beating hearts and wiggling things would teem on both sides of our Route M in shallow waters by midday if we kept up this pace.

The sky seemed proud of itself after a storm last night—the only storm this part of drought-singed Vernon County would see this whole summer. The cerulean sphere above was strewn with white nosegays for clouds. My horse and I stuck together with sweat caused by the sauna of evaporating rain in ninety-two degree heat.

We rode in tall grass, past new McMansions, cedar lodges, turn-of-the-century Victorians in various states of renovation or decay, and a 1920s Montgomery Ward kit home as attractive as a wart. At last, we entered a curve and spotted the high, straight levy and long guardrail in the distance. This levy was luxurious compared with dangerous Route V the first week of our trip. This one had ample paved shoulder. Chief and I paused before getting there, so Chief could graze in a triangle beside the curve. I drank water and peed. The grass was so tall, I had only to squat to be hidden. This ride could rightly be called "the trail of tissues."

The afternoon half spent, we climbed onto the blacktop levy. Chief always mistrusted guardrails and lowered and canted his head at the start and finish of each, which he did this time without shying, but with a nice side pass (a horse's pretty crabwalk).

I dismounted, thinking I didn't want to be trapped on the road should two cars meet beside us. I fed Chief a prune as we walked, *because guardrails are good, they bring prunes, right Chiefie?* He followed me, ears wagging, grateful to let me lead and do the thinking. I fed him another prune. He bobbed his head to get it between his teeth with a tongue designed for guiding grass, not small, round things.

Backwaters passed on either side, spiked with dead trees. There were no wet marks on their trunks. This proved the water was up. I saw a little hip of water bulge, surrounded by thick rings. Carp came to feed in the flooded field. Turtles clung in pairs and threes to exposed logs. A snake carved a wakeless S across the liquid silt. The heat made me climb back in the saddle. Usually, a trip going home feels faster than the trip leaving, I thought. Not a trip on a horse.

Two hours later we plied a dusty road west and north through flat, deep-soiled land, where turtles sat and watched us pass like bored travelers in an airport. We flushed more than one snake into wet undergrowth with our vibration. Expanses of woods took up hundreds of acres too low and wet to clear. We came upon a brick and block bungalow whose driveway Chief insisted on turning into. Its deep, dark porch gave it the solid look of a Lutheran lady sitting at the center of her orbiting grandchildren at a church potluck. This home sat among a forty-foot-by-fifty-foot machine shed across the driveway and a new four-wheel-drive John Deere tractor, a smaller Massey Ferguson, a disk and a planter, and two neat piles of metal fence posts. I dropped Chief's reins in the yard and climbed the porch steps to ring the bell. Then I knocked, because I couldn't hear the bell. I stepped well back.

After a few minutes, a blond boy of about eleven jerked on the inside door twice to get it open. He was wrapped in a Navajo-print plush throw and emerged slowly, as if someone had just yelled,

"Police warrant!" His face assessed the scene with the countenance of a capable young man and the artless eyes of a child who wouldn't wager against anything an adult might do. I asked if I might fill my bucket with water and told him I was traveling. He pulled a portable phone from under his blanket and said, "She just wants water for her horse."

"And I'm looking for a place to camp overnight."

He added that into the phone.

"I'll be right out," he said and went inside. In a few minutes he returned, having put on pants and a shirt, and handed me the phone. I introduced myself to his mother and explained what I needed, as usual, couched in the question whether she *knew someone* who might let me camp. The young woman said they could find a place for my horse and that she would be home in thirty minutes. I handed him back the phone.

"My name is Lisa Stewart."

"I'm Cactus Kleinschmidt," he said.

Cactus Kleinschmidt put the phone away and led me behind the house to the hydrant. He ran toward a utility pole, then checked his speed to appear not too exuberant. He flipped a switch on a box to turn on the well pump. I pulled everything off Chief in the shade of a wide, old apple tree, watered him, and sprayed him off, then tied him to the fence between the house and an empty lot of half an acre that contained two old grain bins and grass and weeds like the final crop on a bald man's head. In an adjacent lot were three clearly pedigreed Quarter Horses. Judging from this young man and those horses, the lady on the phone was solid as this house. I was sure this farmstead was some farm family's grandparents' place turned rental. This served as nerve center to some farming operation, and I guessed this boy's dad wasn't the farmer.

"Wanna see my baby deer?"

I paused, as if he'd just popped off with something in Portuguese. "Sure!"

Cactus went around the corner of the house and returned, dodging back and forth with his hand on the back of a trotting, spotted fawn no taller than my knee.

"Can you watch her for me?" and he disappeared into the back porch.

"Yah!" I'd never "watched" a baby deer before. I wrapped my arms loosely around her to keep her from feeling trapped or getting away. She bumped upward with her head against my chest and arms, looking for a teat. I looked into her navy-blue eyes and petted her coat, which felt like a German shorthair's and smelled of pollen. In a few minutes, Cactus returned with a bottle of milk replacer like we fed our calves on the farm.

"Her mother got scared out of our yard, and she never came back for her," Cactus said. "The Conservation Department said we should leave her alone and let her starve like any other abandoned fawn in the woods. I decided not to."

The baby sucked down its milk in minutes, after which Cactus petted her a sensible length of time, then put her in an enclosure originally built for chickens.

Cactus told me about running his traps and the two deer he shot. One was a six-point buck that didn't go down right away, and they never found it. The one last year (when he was ten) did go down. He told me, also, where he fished and the size and species he caught.

"I've caught every kind of fish there is in that pond. I ride bareback broncs. I broke my radius and ulna last summer. My uncle is a pro bull rider."

Cactus came from a line of rodeo professionals. Like most rodeo families, I'd wager some were pros and others gypsies, chasing points all over the country. His uncle made five appearances in the Pro Bull Riding World Championships, I would learn. That takes continuous travel over most of the United States to earn enough points to qualify each year.

"It is a job and a profession," his uncle told a reporter for the Pittsburg, Kansas, *Morning Sun,* which I later found in an article online. He said, "You treat it like a job and a profession, and you get out of it what you put into it. It's not so much physical as it is mental, and if that is right, you can ride through the injuries."

"My mother barrel races," Cactus said. "She has more horses in pastures in town."

Soon his mother pulled up. Bobbi Kleinschmidt was petite, pretty, wearing tight, expensive western jeans, and a perfectly fitted woman's ball cap with rhinestones. Most horsewomen of the twenty-first century wear ball caps every day, rather than cowboy hats. Bobbi radiated warmth in the way of horsewomen who offer respect and don't make their faces stupid with smiles. Her blond daughter, Shanda, who appeared to be a pregnancy cycle younger than Cactus, climbed out of the back seat. Both kids had their mother's narrow build and someone else's height. Bobbi stood respectfully in the presence of me and my horse. She instinctively glanced at his muscle, head, and feet. The horse looks good, she seemed to calculate; maybe the lady's not insane.

To prepare Chief's bedroom, we entered a human-width gate comprised of two rubber bungie cords crisscrossed and hooked, and a five-gallon bucket containing a ten-pound rock and some rainwater, positioned to keep livestock from finagling their way through the gate.

"We've only lived here six months," Bobbi said. "The landlord just started letting me put horses out here. I haven't had time to make it horseworthy." This lot adjoined another lot where three horses foraged a large round bale of hay. I liked that Bobbi would let our horses have only a few strands of wire between them. She was regular.

A scant five-feet-four, I guessed, Bobbi strode across the lots ahead of me. I had to trot to catch up. She stopped at an empty stainless-steel water trough and flipped it onto its side. She grabbed the hose that was strung across this lot to her horses' trough in the next pen and began spraying away the iron deposits that had dried into rusty potato chips. She dumped it out and curled three feet of the hose into the trough so the pressure wouldn't flip it out. She moved with the efficiency of a farm worker who has ten other things to do before starting supper. Her children moved the same way.

Bobbi insisted I come in for a shower whenever I wanted. Inside, the house felt substantial as a courthouse. The owner, or succession of renters, had chipped away at updates, including refinished hardwood floors and new, painted sheetrock, except one wall that still showed its tape and mud. A massive, rock fireplace with thick wood mantle brought the built-to-last exterior inside. Someone's pre-divorce (I surmised) leather furniture had been brought from a den three times this size. I could see from pictures, Bobbi had committed herself to an older man. Cactus and his sister plopped in front of the flat-screen television between two windows. Piled beside them was the Navajo throw Cactus had worn when I arrived. Bobbi's interior design didn't reflect a superficial hand with a high-limit credit card. No Chinese-made Western star sconces. Creators of cowboy kitsch pattern their fakes on Bobbi's reality: real buckaroo boots and spurs in the corner, a new calf rope, an extra bit, chaps hanging from a coat rack, and framed prints of the woman of the house, barrel racing.

"Want to see my knife collection?" Cactus asked.

"Let's let her get her shower," Bobbi said.

I missed my kids. "Show me your knives a little later," I told Cactus. The children had shadowed us from the time Bobbi arrived. They looked at their mother with unwavering interest and attention—the same way she looked at them.

"I have a pretty good horse," Bobbi said, touching one of the photos. "I started him, so I'm proud of him." That was the closest she would come to bragging. No telling how much that horse won. Grown women like her dreamed of starting the next world champion on their patch of ground in the Midwest.

A shower stall clung to one corner of the laundry room, which didn't have a door. "I'll make sure the kids stay in the living room," Bobbi had said. "The hot water's not too hot, so you probably won't have to turn on the cold." I did, actually.

Before she left me to a stream of well water on the land where tall, light-skinned Osage Indians once bathed in clear, undammed streams, she told me her girlfriend and kids were moving in with them for a while—that night. "I'm making hamburgers. You're welcome to join us." I assured her I had everything I needed to eat, and I was pretty tired. I'd be going to bed early, but *thank you.*

After my shower, Cactus led me to a built-in bookcase and drawers in the corner of the living room beside a wide, leather chair. He picked up each knife with two fingers so not to disturb the others and precisely returned each one to its position. At one point, Shanda slid between us to go to the kitchen. "Excuse me," she said. Of the 142 knives in his collection, Cactus described thirty-five of them as to their make, use, and origin of procurement, at which Bobbi finally looked into the room and suggested to Cactus that I might have other things to do. True, my stomach was yipping and whining for food.

After dinner in my tent, and before dark, Shanda and Cactus came outside, not to talk as much as be near. The two seemed to sense when I needed privacy and when I might like company. Shanda begged Cactus to play with her.

"I'll play with you if you climb up to the crotch of that tree," he told her, pointing to the tree above my tent in the corner of the front yard.

"I don't want to," she said.

He walked under the tree. "Then I'm not playing with you."

"I'm scared to."

"Get in here; I'll help you." Cactus held open a loop of a retired calf rope in which she was to sit. The rope was looped around one of the tree's thick biceps. All afternoon, Shanda had proven herself clear-eyed, direct, and mature as an eighteen-year-old, much less a girl of eight. "Oh, all right," she said.

She stepped through the loop. She pulled on the free end of the rope while we also pulled the rope and pushed her bottom, and somehow, between us, we hauled her ten feet off the ground. She hung level with the crotch and two feet away from it. She was high enough to break a bone. Clearly, Cactus had done this before, but I realized this was Shanda's first time. Perhaps she did it on my account.

"You can do it, Shanda," Cactus said. "Let go." Shanda had to let go of the rope and grasp the tree with both hands to haul herself onto the crotch. She panicked and cried for her mother. She was too high for me to help.

"Let's let her down," I implored. I was begging an eleven-year-old boy to please let us do the sensible thing, and I felt just as helpless as I had when I had implored other men in my life to please let us do the sensible thing.

Shanda finally let go of the rope with one hand and caught a narrow branch. She was able to pull herself close enough to get first one foot, then the next into the crotch of the tree, suspended three terrifying seconds before hoisting herself onto her feet in the crotch.

"That's it!" Cactus called.

She stood up with a face full of tears and both arms around the main trunk.

I could hear her breathing.

She scraped her arms and legs on the bark and slid away from the tree into the rope again and swung. He and I both were holding the free end of the rope. We let her down slowly.

Shanda stood up and wiped her face.

"See? Now how do you feel about yourself?" Cactus said.

Shanda lingered a minute more, then went to the house.

At dusk, I lay on my back with my head on a wad of clean clothes and my saddlebags for a bolster under my knees. I ceded my mind to the opioid effect of fading light. Chief and I drifted toward sleep along the edge of thousands of acres of refuge for awakening nocturnals. I heard a car pull into the drive—its hum, its chirping fan belt like a cricket in the kitchen. I heard doors slam and imagined children's stuffed backpacks and My Little Pony and Teenage Mutant Ninja Turtle suitcases inherited from cousins. Why did they have to come live with a friend? Another mother and

259

254259254254259254259254259254259254259254259254259254259254259254259254259254254254254254254254254254

254259254259254259254259254259254259254259259254254259254259254259254259

254254254254254254254254254254254259254259254259254259254259254

children on the wing. Perhaps this mother also climbed too high in a tree not of her choosing, wrong as it felt, and now swung on a rope in the night.

I drifted. I was awakened by the growl of a diesel pickup, likely Bobbi's husband. I peeked through the screen. The truck was worth more than this house.

Throughout the night, I rolled over when the earthbound hip felt like fire and ice. I placed my hand in front of me when I lay on my side, because these days my elbow was too sharp to let it touch my sharp hip. I had left the last of my fat along the road. I turned each time I got cold, adding a layer, until I finally succumbed to the breathless space bivy and slept in a sea of my own condensation. I gave thanks at every turn for Bobbi, her husband, Cactus, and Shanda, and for this spot of earth.

Cactus's baby deer would not have starved had he not taken it in. This summer, Bobbi had seen a cougar lying in the tilled field over the fence fifty yards from my tent. She said, "That was the only time I've seen him."

Guns and Grace

Now, eighty miles from home, I couldn't imagine my trip ending in only four days, for all the people I would not meet; but I did not know how many more times I could force myself to impose on strangers.

Southwest of Appleton City, Missouri, at noon, we plied a straight road between fields of corn and beans that felt like a giant's garden with hedgerows only a giant's horse could jump. I pulled Chief up to a metal field gate where Simmental cattle grazed in their big, red chassis. I needed to use the restroom, and out in the field stood a broad hedge tree crowded with saplings behind which I could hide. Near it grazed a massive bull whose low-slung scrotum swiveled when he stepped a hind leg forward. Several in his harem walked in a line toward a small rise. I presumed they were stepping away for a drink at a pond I couldn't see. I waited, because I was afraid of the bull. As I suspected he would, he soon took hoof-dragging steps to turn and swagger, pimp-like, toward the crest of the rise behind his cows. I would climb the fence and jog to the tree, but first, I heard the sound of surf, a new black pickup on this gravel road, blasting toward us at fifty-five. Saplings in the ditch (not thick enough to provide a bathroom) obscured the driver's view of us. I waited to climb the gate. The pickup tore past, abruptly let off the gas, then kept going. With the bull out of sight, I made my dash behind the tree in the field.

Soon, we were heading north when the same driver returned behind us, eased off the throttle, and rolled to a crawl beside us.

He called over the air-conditioner and past his son, "I'm sorry I blew by you so fast."

"No problem. I saw you coming."

He asked after my packs and trail-worn face and heard my tale of riding cross country. He was handsome with a few flecks of gray beneath his ball cap.

"Do you need anything? I live right up the road."

"I think I'm good." Then I thought, "Except I didn't get to charge my phones last night. By the way, I'm Lisa."

"Don. My son, John. We'll meet you at the two-story white house, a mile and a half," he pointed. "We'll be leaving to hay in a bit, but we can get you charged." He didn't have time, but he was making it.

I gaited Chief quickly to a straight, square home that stood among oak trees. The place had an air of dignity, and I soon learned why. This man—who might have been a businessman stepping out of a Starbucks in the city, for his gracious demeanor and the distressed business-casual clothes in which he farmed— had refurbished this former home of Missouri Senator John Baldwin, who served the sixteenth district from 1910 to 1914. The home wore new paint and roof and now a twenty-first century kitchen. He rolled his eyes at the house. "We've been wondering how we got ourselves into this [renovation]."

We stood in the shade near my phone, which was sitting on an electric meter and plugged into an outdoor receptacle on the back of his house.

"We needed a break," Don said toward my phone. "John comes home and helps me in the summer," he said of his slender, light-haired son.

"Where are you going to school?" I asked.

"Rolla." That was shorthand for the University of Missouri-Rolla, known lately as Missouri University of Science and Technology, where you can learn all you need, up to the doctorate level and beyond, about mining, geology, every discipline of engineering, and pyrotechnics.

"Engineering?" I guessed.

"Yah. Mechanical."

He was the kind of son who inspired in a man the exhalation-of-a-lifetime. He's going to do all right.

"I manage the United Parcel Service Customer Center in Appleton City," Don said. From the depot Don managed, regional folks received their UPS deliveries in a handful of counties.

"How far are we from Appleton?" I asked. (Around here, locals drop the word "city" in town names, but never from the town of Kansas City. Which is why it is jarring to Kansas Citians when New Yorkers come and refer to our city as "Kansas.")

"It's ten minutes to the northeast," he said. Again, I was stunned by the relative nearness of things in my twenty-first century consciousness, and the enormous distance on horseback.

"I get to work at 4:00 AM," he said, "and I'm home in time to farm and work on our project." He made air quotes when he said the word project. "This house has become the equivalent of another kid in college," he said, then put his hand on his son's shoulder and waggled it, which prompted the young man to widen his eyes and waggle his head dramatically.

Every day, this man had his hand on the tiller of a regional UPS hub. At night on the steering wheel of a tractor. In his heart, he kept a hand on a son's shoulder. I hoped this wind, fluffing thousands of pounds of tree limbs above, helped him breathe.

Half an hour later, Chief and I were riding 14963 Road. I saw two things ahead: the stop sign that signaled a blacktop (a scintillating milestone of progress I'd invented to keep up my spirits), and one-fourth mile this side of it, a man built like a crack-head standing beside a car with its hood up. We rode toward the broken-down vehicle.

Not often did I approach a person from three hundred yards at such a slow speed. This wasn't like whisking by in a car, stripped of manners by speed. I never rode past people within grabbing distance; I rode into yards knowing I was supposed to be there, though I never knew why I knew this. I told myself this young man was a child of God. Chief and I grew nearer at an awkwardly slow pace.

Behind me, I heard a pickup. It was Don and John. They rolled past me with lifted hands, on their way to hay. Fifty yards ahead, their brake lights went on near the young man and car for a quick word, then they continued to the stop sign and paused, blinker on, brake lights lit, two hundred yards beyond. Chief lilted toward the car and the young man.

I waved when I thought the young man had glanced up to us, but he didn't wave back, so I believed he didn't see us. I kicked Chief to eat up the space. My new friends in the pickup did not turn onto the blacktop. Chief and I neared the broken-down car like Midwesterners converging on a city street: One person glances up until the other person starts to glance up, then the first one glances down, then up, just as the other is glancing down until both parties pass, smiling at the ground.

No traffic passed on the blacktop ahead, and still, Don and John sat at the stop sign with their blinker flashing.

I rode beside the young man and purposed to make firm eye contact and speak confidently. "How ya' doing?" I said.

"Okay," the young man said, brushing off my gaze.

"You have someone coming?"

"Yah."

"Okay." I pointed to his engine. "Sorry about that."

"It's okay," he said, as if nothing ever went right—that day, or any other day in his whole, entire life.

"Take it easy," I said and gigged Chief.

When I was fifty yards past the young man and his car, Don and John pulled onto the blacktop, opened the throttle, and headed east.

An hour later, we rode into a low slumberland of tributaries that, twenty-seven miles to the southeast, combined to fill Truman Lake. Tall trees shaded our road. The gravel formed a T intersection I had been expecting, which comforted me. I was on track. To our right came an acre lot that contained a lone horse with ribs I could count, hip bones like coat hangers, and a dent in its nose, evidence that a halter once had been left on its head when it was young, so the bone grew out around it. We approached the house beside this horse.

The house seemed too close to the road for its two-story, country-Georgian style and its new siding and roof. Parts and implements had washed up around it like seashells. How could a three thousand-square-foot house with new siding and roof lack any effort toward landscaping? No surprise. Anyone who would starve a horse wouldn't take care of his home. Except, perhaps a man and woman with two hard jobs? Too many kids? A handicapped child? Lost their jobs? Who puts a halter on a horse before it's grown and forgets it like bound Chinese feet? I wanted nothing to do with this place.

Chief carried me beyond it. I reached forward and smoothed Chief's mane all to one side of his neck as I did hundreds of times a day. The sun sparkled in it. I never was too hot and tired to admire my horse's arched neck and red waves. One-half mile down the road, Chief saw his first Bobcat (with a man driving it) two hundred yards away in a field. Chief's shocks grew stiff, and he shortened his neck. We came nearly even with it. I halted Chief so he could look and perhaps get used to it. It ran forward and back at angles as if an invisible child's hand worked it in the field.

The driver was cleaning up the orange and tan roots of trees and chunks of sandstone after a dozer had pushed tall, old-growth trees into a two-story brush pile that would be burned, then buried by a dozer. Because I had stopped and was watching him, the driver thought I wanted to talk, so he turned his Bobcat toward us and came halfway, then turned it off (so not to scare my horse). *Oh, Honey, you don't have to stop*, I thought. He took big steps toward me over the rough ground.

Anyone who drives these off-track roads must know someone we know, have some reason to be here, which automatically involves us, we think. That's why when rural dwellers come to the city, we often employ direct eye contact, which we assume is good manners, but may come off goofy.

A second, handsome man in his fifties today. Was the universe trying to pleasure me with the sight of intelligent men of means who knew how to do things and wanted to help me? We made the usual leap from who we were to where our grandparents came from and what we do now.

"I own a concrete contracting company," he said.

Though I had ridden through rain on my trip, this land also had seen none of it since early May and this was mid-June. "We've been able to pour all summer," he said. "I've got two crews. We've been putting in fourteen-hour days." That's how you say you've made a lot of money in rural-speak.

I soon learned it was this man's place I just had equine-profiled (which is similar to racial profiling but judging him by his horse). He lived in the non-landscaped house with the starving horse. His wife worked, too, which accounted for the no landscaping. They were busy. The large metal barn held his collection of antique cars, he told me. "It's pretty-well full," he said. He wasn't bragging about his investments. He was happy.

"Would you mind looking at my map and telling me if you think my route makes sense?"

"Sure." He started patting his shirt pockets.

"Here." I pulled my reading glasses out of my pommel bag and handed them to him.

While he oriented himself, I couldn't help admiring not just his bulky, contractor's shoulders, but his softening midriff that stood for meals bolted behind the steering wheel most days, as he built cash reserves needed for months when weather was bad and the economy soft. After he confirmed my route was wise, he forgot he was wearing my sparkly-framed glasses. He put them in his shirt pocket. "I'd go the way you planned," he said and handed up my map.

"I'm thinking of leaving those glasses with you," I told him. "They're pretty cute on you."

He cocked his head. "They are, aren't they?"

He handed up my glasses and patted Chief on the neck. "Your horse looks good. I've only got one horse now," he said. "I rescued him from an old farmer who was abusing and starving him. Took me two years and a lot of money to get him to where he is now."

"Oh," I said.

"I know. Sad."

Hours passed with the swing of Chief's gait and his odd squirt forward at whatever he thought he saw in the corner of his eye. At a turn in gently rolling farmland northwest of Appleton City, Chief suddenly walked off the road, jerked the reins out of my hands, and put his head down to eat. The blue sky floated only a few white splayed feathers. I stepped out of the saddle and dropped Chief's bit so he could chew better. After a few snatches, he lifted his head so it hung in front of him, and he dropped off to sleep. I pulled out my pad with its pen poked through the spiral and began to write. The grass here was too high to sit in. I stood quietly near him.

I had been writing for twenty minutes when I lifted my eyes for some good reason. I spotted a pickup half a mile away.

Shit.

I didn't know the truck—couldn't identify it from such distance—but my sensor, which had been tuned by the miles to guide my steps, caused me to see this truck surrounded by a virtual black fog. I couldn't stop its coming, and I wasn't afraid, per-se, but I knew in moments, I would face a man who could hurt me.

The small, red Nissan pickup slowed and stopped. The driver was in his forties and had dark hair and deep-set eyes. His tanned arms contrasted with his white T-shirt, specked with bits of wheat chaff. He grinned at me as if he'd been expecting me. I looked at him the same way.

"How you doing?" he said.

"Good."

"You traveling?"

"Yup. About a month. Almost home now."

"Where you from?"

"Kansas City." *Why'd I say that?*

"Do you need anything?"

"No, I just got water. I'm letting my horse take a nap."

"I'm combining just up the road. You'll be riding right by me. My house isn't too far, if you'd like to eat."

"Thank you. I appreciate that. I'm trying to get in some miles today. My husband is meeting me in a little bit." He knew I was lying.

He said goodbye and drove on. Soon he drove past me again on his way back to the field. I mounted up and continued down the road the way I planned toward the field he was combining.

I hoped he would be on the far side of the field at the moment we rode by. Instead, he was closing in on the fence near us at a standard, wheat-eating seven miles per hour. We were going four. There was no way for me to kick Chief and trot by without looking like I was running from him. The cropland lay wide open and tree-less along this mile. His factory on wheels ate and chewed its wheat and spewed its chaff. He let off the throttle. The engine dropped from soprano to alto, and the combine rolled to a halt in the soft dirt. He set the brake and disengaged the wheat header, which slowed its turning like a ceiling fan turned off. The man climbed the barbed wires near a fence post, careful not to catch his jeans or rip out the staples that held the wire.

He walked up to Chief and me. After a few moments of nervous small talk (mine), I pulled my map from my pocket, and, dumbly, I showed him where I was riding and asked his opinion, like I did with everyone. He took the side of my map and pressed his forearm across my thigh in the saddle, the only man who ever came close to touching me on this trip. We held the map together five, six, seven, eight, nine, ten seconds, and I said, "Okay! That's going to work. Hey, I need to go. I'm meeting my husband soon," and I gave Chief a little spur between me and the man, so Chief stepped to the side out from under his arm.

He smiled like he knew what I was doing and what he was doing. I told him to take it easy and kicked Chief, and we took up a quick gait for the next half mile to my turn at the next gravel road.

We gaited another half mile north, exposed by uninterrupted miles of shorn wheat until we cleared a small rise. I stopped my horse. Chief dropped his head to graze, which was fortunate, because the only thing to tie him to out here was me. I no longer could see dust rising from the man's combine in the middle of the section. I looked behind me. The little pickup didn't appear. I unclipped the large bag behind my saddle, something I never did in the middle of the day, because it took all my strength to reinstall it over my head. But this was important. On the ground, I felt among my clothes and tent for my son's Ruger. I had long ago quit carrying it conveniently in my pommel bag at the front of my saddle.

I removed the holster, stood, and pointed the pistol at the ground in front of my feet. I pulled back the slide on the top of the barrel to chamber a load. I unzipped the right pommel bag at the front of my saddle, and slipped the pistol in, handle up, leaving the pocket unzipped. I reassembled my rig and rested a moment with my hand on my horse's hip, watching down the road. Nobody. I gathered Chief's reins, stepped him deep into the ditch so I wouldn't have so far to reach up my foot, mounted, and fox-trotted away, only four days away from home.

Board President

On the only day I felt threatened by someone other than Chief, the land lay higher and flatter, covered in pasture and golden wheat stretching to the horizons. This late afternoon, the sun was preposterous. I needed to douse my head, and I thought Chief would drink. A neat, large ranch home sat back off the road in such a way that I felt sure the woman of the house asked herself each time she mowed why she wanted such a showy front yard. Flower beds circled two small trees on either end of the house and around her mailbox and beside her garage. The red, white, and pink petunias and geraniums clung to life in this heat for love of this woman. No farmer would pick such a fight. There was a car no more than five years old in the drive behind the house. Farther behind the house stood a huge machine shed in addition to another metal barn, and two, six thousand-bushel grain bins—the country equivalent of tennis courts, Olympic pool, and a Maserati.

I tied Chief under one of three trees along a barbed-wire fence bordering the pasture east of the house. I didn't bother with the front door, which didn't look like it had been cracked loose this year. The house looked like everyone was at work, except for the car parked behind. I rang the doorbell and knocked on the rear sliding door. There was a faucet next it—so close. I could just use it. What if someone were inside and heard the squeak of the faucet handle and the white noise of running water? No one came. My cooling pump thumped in my chest. I pulled off my hat and jersey

knit brow band. I knocked and rang again and bent over with my
hands on my knees to keep from fainting.

I was walking away from the patio door when I heard the lock
click and the door slide open. "I'm sorry!" the woman exclaimed, "I
had my blow drier on, and I couldn't hear you." She looked
prepared to make a presentation to a bank board. She wore an aqua
business suit and a short, soft haircut, earrings, and matching, bulky
necklace, pantyhose and no shoes.

"I'm sorry to interrupt you. I'm riding cross country and wondered if I could have a couple of buckets of water for my horse."

"Of course you can! You must be so hot."

"It's not too bad. There's a breeze." Hot as I was, I only could
produce clichés, except to say, "I'll be running water over my
head."

"I should think so! You can use this faucet." She began to step
toward it.

"No, let me do that." I said. "I have to go get my horse's bucket,
anyway. I'll be right back."

"Help yourself. Is there anything else you need?"

"Nope, just water. Thank you!" I felt lighter and cooler already.

My comfort on this ride was relative mostly to my degree of
hope. I thought of it as a "hope index," rather than a heat index. I
hugged Chief's sweaty neck in the small patch of shade where I'd
parked him one hundred yards away and untied the wadded-up
vinyl bucket from the side of our saddlebags.

To my daily dismay, it always took twenty minutes to water my
horse, no less than four times a day, and all that time added up:

- Find a place to tie him.
- Remove his bit gently from between his teeth, clip it to
  the saddle, clip the reins to his halter, and tie the ends
  to a fence—then go knock and knock.
- Kneel and hold the bucket, while Chief drinks, so it
  won't fold over and spill. He drinks at least a bucket
  and a half, so there always are two trips from the
  hydrant.

- Wad it up and twist-tie it back to the saddle.
- Drench my head and fix my ponytail.
- Unzip my breast pocket and pull out my reading glasses and sweaty map, read it, put it all back.
- Don my headband, my hat, and tie it tight.
- Unclip his bit from the saddle and finagle it between his teeth. As usual, my gloves slip on the spinning trigger snaps, so I take off my gloves and start again, which is hard, because my gloves are wet and sticky.
- Clip the reins to his bit, untie him, put on my gloves, find my sunglasses in the grass, put the reins over his head, try to get him downhill of me, reach my foot up the height of my waist, climb aboard, and squeeze my boy into the road.
- *And merrily we roll along 'cause life is but a dream.*

Chief and I were pulling away when I heard the woman of the house call. She was jogging after us in her suit and a pair of running shoes she had pulled on and not tied. "I was trying to think what I could give you to eat." She handed up a Clif bar and two nectarines. "I don't know how good these are," she said of the fruit. I squeezed her clean hand with my wet glove.

How could I stop this trip and not meet another trim, middle-aged, suited-up woman who manages something major out here in some people's construct of nowhere? How do I let a stranger know she saved me by easing me into my next mile? She'd rifled her kitchen then tussled her hair and moistened her makeup in blistering heat to give me something, *anything* to take from her home to mine on the road. Two women—two bright lights on a squinting-bright day on Bates County's quilt of green and gold—lilted away from each other, eager to tell someone, anyone, what just happened.

Developmentally Perfect

By late afternoon of the twenty-eighth day of our trip, we paddled the gravel roads into scraggly hills in our north-westerly pursuit of home, now only three days away. Pastures secured their nutrients for winter. It already was winter to them, without rain. The blue sky and earsplitting bird calls, and ceaseless creaking of insects, and trees waving us on, supported our millions of cells in their quest for a drink and place to stay the night. As always, I feared we would spend the night in some ditch without water.

We rose from a scrubby hollow, and ahead, to my right, I spotted a perfectly round, pruned shrub near a fence where grass had been mowed all the way to the road—the first evidence of lawn care in hours. My heart jumped at the thought I might have found an industrious family that would consider me, if not convenient, at least mildly interesting as a guest.

All I could see of a home beyond the rise was a new, blue, metal roof and new gravel drive. Chief did not have to be directed to turn in. Its former incarnation as prairie farmhouse had been enhanced by an architect's expansion of both first and second floors with white wood siding and blue-gray bricks. Someone refused to let time and nature degrade this place. I dismounted behind the home and was about to stretch Chief's reins to knock on the glass back door when I heard, "Hallooo!"

I turned but could not locate the voice. It seemed to come from a loudspeaker.

"Halloo! Up here!" I looked up in the trees, and at least twenty-five feet off the ground, a boy of about twelve clung to a thin, main trunk.

"Oh! There you are! Hello."

"My sister's in there. You can knock." I would learn this voice belonged to Shane Kent, and I could relate—my Derek often could be found terrifyingly high in trees at that age.

A girl about fifteen came to the door with her little sister, whose age I couldn't discern. The smaller girl had large, gray eyes, round face, and a body like mine in prepubescence—all legs and arms and slight pooch at the belly. The teenager seemed a woman of thirty, the way she greeted me and guided her shuffling sister. I introduced myself and tried to explain the inexplicable—why I would ride so far in this heat.

"I'm Molly. I'll call my mother and make sure it's okay if you stay here," she said.

"I can easily go down the road. This might not be a good night for your parents."

I let Chief graze in the shade while I waited outside. Soon, Molly came out of the house, guiding her little sister with a hand on her shoulder.

"Jenny, stay right by me." Jenny, the younger, turned her shoulder away from Molly's hand and shuffled toward me quickly. I moved between her and Chief and funneled her toward his head.

"You can pet his neck like this," I said. The girl reached up and stroked him.

"My parents will be home in half an hour," Molly said.

I kept Chief saddled.

The couple arrived in two separate cars, their necks stretched forward and faces blank with suspense over what a horsewoman might look like who had ridden up after a month on the road. The traveler now was walking across their drive, and their special daughter was leading a horse. The couple looked wilted by the day's work. They both had dark hair with only a few strands of white and were dough-faced as sleepy toddlers after these past eight hours managing other people. I imagined their prom photo in a drawer somewhere inside—movie-star beautiful.

"I'm Lisa Stewart. Your daughter seems to have a way with horses."

The woman pressed her lips together with an expression of gratitude. She extended her hand, "Donna and Chad Kent."

"I apologize for barging in like this. I'm running out of steam and didn't know if you, or someone you know down the road, might have a place I could put my tent and horse for the night." The simple sentence blossomed into ten minutes of telegram-like descriptions that covered decades of all our lives.

Then Chad said, "Shane, help her put the horse in the stall. Molly, please grain him. We'll have supper for you later," he said to me.

"Remember to get ready for your ball game," Donna said to Shane.

"We'll be able to be more sociable in a couple of hours, after we finish helping a friend get their alfalfa in," Chad said. After they worked all day, they would drive to a field in ninety-five degree heat and haul small square bales of hay from the field for shares.

"There's a bathroom in an apartment through the barn," Chad said. "There's no hot water out there. You can come in for a shower after we come back. We should be back before dark."

Donna and Chad went inside and changed into different work clothes and drove off in a pickup pulling a flatbed trailer.

The children formed my audience for afternoon chores. Our locus became the driveway behind the house in front of the massive machine shed where a hydrant posed crane-like nearby. Just across the drive stood the low, wood barn and a couple of stalls. I led Chief around to a lone peach tree in the front yard, their mother's favorite of the two on their property, according to Molly. These peaches were the sweeter. The peach tree provided the only shade I could find that also had a soft bed of grass. Its branches hung droop-shouldered under the weight of hundreds of peaches. I dropped our saddlebags and led Chief back to the stall. Disburdened of his itchy pad and saddle, Chief stood rock still for his shower in the shade of the machine shed.

Without having been asked, Shane trotted to the hydrant and put his back into moving a one-hundred-foot-long hose. He jerked coil after coil to spread out the weight so he could drag the end to me. He worked as fast as he could—as I imagined his father and mother worked now. He strode and pulled like Bobbi Kleinschmidt, like my former, farmer husband, like I did when I was young, because we all in our youth had seen how it looks to use your legs and back, to get it done, to hear, "That's the way," or to hear no praise at all but receive the gift of a grown-up job.

Children out here grow up sitting on mother's lap in a pickup, creeping slowly, while Daddy kicks bales out of the bed in winter, or tosses cattle cubes during droughts. They pull up for the first time not on a coffee table but on a steering wheel or the truck window, waiting, while Mother clips the strings off big round bales and jerks them out from under the four-hundred-pound roll. These children sit and watch new calves doze in the sun or shake their heads and baby-hop in the pasture. They watch a calf find mother's teats the first time. They learn to wait, and look at things, and hear sounds, like a cow calling for its calf in the distance, the one Mom and Dad can't see in the herd. They've counted thirty-one cows and need thirty-two. The windows are down in the pickup. Everyone counts again. They are one cow short. "Listen," Dad says. A cow is bawling in the distance with big gasps between—a frantic mother. Dad puts the pickup in gear and drives over the rise. There she is. Dad taps the pickup horn. She looks up and stares. Dad honks again and begins a slow wide turn. The cow walks toward the pickup, unable to resist the idea of cattle cubes. She trots behind him over the rise, back to the herd, and finds her calf. In country like this, children strengthen their shoulders for football and softball, become the best interns in college, vice president of the company, groomed for COO, because the board knows they'll put their backs into every task they're given without complaining.

After his shower, Chief squeezed through the narrow stall door. He swirled up grain from a bucket, and when it was gone, he slept hard. Nothing could get him there.

When I'd wrung out my laundry, the girls took me upstairs to a second-floor deck to hang it on a clothesline with a pulley that stretched comically over a fifteen-foot dip beside the house and tied to a post in the adjacent field. Molly explained, "When they remodeled the house, Dad wanted to be able to drive his tractor out of the barn and go straight to the road, so we had to stretch the clothesline from up here so he could drive under it."

"Mom grew up in this house," Molly said. "My grandmother lives up the road that way, and I have aunts and uncles over here, and over that way." She pointed to the four directions.

"Mom and Dad work at Sioux Chief," Molly said. I had driven past that plant for thirty-five years on 71 Highway. It makes industrial plumbing fittings and products. I assumed their father was in management, and their mother seemed to be, too, by their clothes.

With my laundry drying, and my horse in his own container of heaven, I told the children I would use the restroom in the metal barn. I did not need to wait for a warm shower in their house. I entered the barn and stepped through the darkness among the tools and benches and equipment toward a door on the side wall. It opened upon a miracle—a bright, windowed, sheet rocked, and painted apartment with a kitchenette, and what appeared to be the family's pre-remodeling furniture—a bed, television, pool table, and bathroom with a shower. I took my bath from the sink with cold water and shampooed my hair twice by leaning into the shower.

People in the country have very many things and little time in which to enjoy them. Live poor, die rich is the farmer's financial plan.

Donna Kent and I leaned against one of two long kitchen counters, well after dark. I had eaten a pork cutlet dinner with my new little shadow, Jenny, at a small breakfast table in the kitchen. Donna cooked every day, twice a day, and made lunches. The kitchen could have been mine when my children were young: school papers, a few clean pans that needed to be put away, colored pencils, a notebook, a stack of mail, breakfast dishes in the drainer. The only difference between this and my past kitchens was her granite counters and new cabinets—and she had the KitchenAid mixer I always wanted.

"I only wish I had done it five years earlier," I was saying.

"Really?"

"I take bioidentical hormones. I can't even tell I've had a hysterectomy," I said. *Either I keep running into menopausal women on this trip, or I can't stop rejoicing over my blessed hormone replacement,* I thought.

"Well, that makes me feel better," Donna said.

"Don't put it off if you need it."

Donna was an elegant shift-of-a-woman—slender, pretty, and made, it seemed to me, of high-tensile fiber, like silk. She could transition from work to evening seamlessly. She had spent all day keeping her team on task to return home and produce her son's clean ball uniform and wrap her attention around the children who had waited all day for her leadership, and who needed relief from their day of independence, to be noticed, fed, and held accountable—to be prepared for adulthood.

Chad Kent came in from evening chores, while his wife and I talked, interrupted by occasional, indecipherable (to me) comments from the youngest. This man—like the concrete contractor on his Bobcat, and Jerry my first week—crinkled his eyes at a joke that seemed always to play at the edge of his mind, and why not have a sense of humor? How can you take yourself seriously when the whole world knows you through the redneck lens of country comedian Jeff Foxworthy (another brilliant man)? Or maybe through images of the doofuses who stand in a pond of floating cranberries on TV commercials written by twenty-five-year-old communications majors. Men like Chad Kent use global positioning systems to plot their fields, manage a hundred people, and direct engineers who make parts out of molds from CNC machines. This man could likely tell by feel how much moisture might be in his wheat or hay, had taught his son how to pitch a baseball, knows more good restaurants in Kansas City than I do, and thus holds a certain amount of air in his lungs for a snort at some irony. When you know you have to earn enough to keep your farm in the family, put two children through college, and save enough to care for the littlest the rest of her life, you stop worrying about what anyone else thinks.

Jenny was pulling my arm to come see more of her house, and her mother did not interrupt, perhaps for lack of energy or, more likely, to let Jenny feel like a grown-up girl. Her soft hand drew me into the family room, in front of the fireplace to review the blond, leather furniture. We padded in stocking feet over thick carpet down the hall, past the kitchen toward the laundry room. Her mother called after her, "Use your sentences!"

The girl led me with gesticulations and her index finger. I said, "Oh!" and "Yes!" Her eyes widened behind her glasses when she turned to witness my amazement. She flipped on the light to reveal the washer and drier. I let her lead me, as I let Chief lead me to the next clump of weeds and the next at the end of a day. She climbed the stairs, taking a step and bringing her second foot up to meet it, leaning forward on the cutting edge of balance. We toured each bedroom.

At the end of the hall near the stairs was the door leading to the deck outside from which the clothesline was anchored, which frightened me. The deck had no railing against the fifteen-foot drop on one side. She was leading me toward that door.

"Is it okay if you go out there?"

She nodded.

"Do you want to help me bring in my clothes?"

Her eyes grew big, and she grasped the doorknob and threw the door wide.

The sun had set minutes before, leaving the sky royal and peach. To the degree the sky mimicked asters in bloom and blushed at the act, the fields had lost their color and definition below. My wash hung straight down in the stillness that came between light and dark in this land. The sky drew my eyes to it. The first star of the evening pierced the atmosphere, as if we had awakened it.

No developmentally handicapped girl had led me through this house. This girl knew who she was and what she wanted. We stepped onto the deck. I placed my hand on her arm, afraid she might stub a toe and tumble off the edge. She swiveled her torso away from my touch. She pulled the clothesline around to bring my laundry near, unclipped it with one hand and held it toward me. I released the fear of her falling. I stretched out my arm. Jenny draped me with my laundry one piece at a time. Star after star appeared.

That night, the yard light did not reach my tent. I listened to coyotes skirt the house. A parent coyote sounded like a tornado siren far away. Then another joined with high, thin *oohhs* that moved from one auditory sector to the next through the fields. Suddenly their children got tickled and jumped and chirped like a flock of sparrows. Then they all hushed at once.

I heard a thud. Then another. Peaches falling.

Home Pasture

We had Etch-a-sketched our way north and west from the Kents' that morning through gloriously cool six o'clock and seven o'clock hours. By 8:00 AM, we were sweat-wet, sipping the last cool wafts that tossed through the farm-land, and we set ourselves to the heat and hourly showers from garden hoses if we found likely homes.

By mid-afternoon, we had reached our greatest challenge of the ride home, crossing 71 Highway, a four-lane vessel between Joplin, Missouri, and Kansas City, that carried cars and trucks with hardly a breath between them. Once on the west side of 71, we could skirt conservation areas and follow the grid of gravel roads into Kansas and finally to Chief's home pasture.

Every step today in the heat provided its own reward, *ca-closer, ca-closer, ca-closer.* No remaining bloom, tiny and woody, went unblessed by me for its will to survive the drought. The sky looked like it never had seen a cloud in its life. My horse felt hard and strong. He looked for monsters in hedgerows and searched farmsteads for clues to dark shapes and flipping soft things he was sure would spring at us. The world electrified my horse as much on day twenty-nine as on day one, when a strange man had to hold him to help me mount after llamas scared him into backing ten miles an hour. Or the second day when he sent me to the emergency room. I was quieter, though, more patient. Five hundred miles after I left on this trip, I'd returned from battle on a horse legged up and looking for foes, and I had never felt more powerful in my life, except when I was eight.

We drew close to 71 Highway on flat gravel beside beans prematurely golden in high spots where their roots dangled in dry dirt above a sinking stratum of moisture. We rode parallel to trembling 71 Highway, separated from it by a narrow strip of houses and trees, yet within its din. We could see occasional flashes of semis.

My sunglasses hurt the bones above my ears, so I took them off, then the sun made me put them back on. I ate jerky as I rode. We turned south, the opposite direction from which we should go, on an outer road that would take us to a blacktop that years ago crossed the highway. The Missouri Department of Transportation (MoDOT) had eliminated many access points to 71, and I hoped a local could say whether the road I thought of still crossed it. If so, we wouldn't have to ride the highway shoulder.

My heart pounded its code for air and water. I had stopped sweating by the time we reached a modular home. Retired military, I guessed, with flush brown lawn, sculpted cedar bushes, and pointy small pines. I could see the hydrant when I turned into the drive.

A couple ate a late lunch at their dining table just inside the front room window. I needed their water more than I hated to disturb them. Chief dropped his head to graze. Not far ahead was the blacktop I hoped would let me cross the four-lane and lead me to the gravel grid that would take Chief home to his friends. If not, perhaps this couple could tell me where I could cut onto the highway right of way.

They greeted me with country manners, which is to say they pretended there was nothing unusual about a woman, white around her mouth from heat, riding up on a horse. Of course, I could use their hydrant. No, I no longer could cross 71 where I wanted. Yes, that gap I saw back up the gravel, on which I had come, was clear—I could ride over the mound, through the trees, and walk beside thousands of semis and cars two miles to Archie and cross the highway there.

I drenched my head and scarf, watered my horse, sprayed his legs and belly, and we set off, back up the road to the gap I had seen beside the highway.

When we reached the highway and climbed through the tall weeds and ditch, I had to make a decision: Could I ride the miles along 71, or should I walk and lead my horse. Could I trust Chief to stay where I put him if I rode? What were the odds after four weeks he would see a flash in the trees that would send him sideways in front of a truck? Nil. He was traffic-wise. Still.

This ride had filled me with a knowledge that I was not alone, *All is well.* But it never said, "Nothing can hurt you." I could get myself killed—unless I gave up devising and did the next thing that compelled me. I didn't want to die so close to home, but more, how homicidal would it be to have a horse get away and kill someone else? I dismounted when we reached the 71 shoulder and began a lumpy, stumbling walk toward Archie.

I set myself against the heat as never before, with aching head and engorged temples toward the Archie café. I would have a pork tenderloin sandwich and onion rings and a chocolate malt in air-conditioning. I would tie my horse in the shade and let the jumpy bastard wait. I could take step after step in the howl of engines and backwash of trucks for that. I was sure after that I could ask one more time to camp—once more, each day, until we reached home.

Chief followed, head down. I lifted my hand to truckers and people in pickups who smiled and waved. I was a two-legged, pulsing heart. The roar and turbulence from spinning tires and blurring pistons and spinning shafts and whining belts created a four-lane wind tunnel that lit my horse and tightened my chest. The miles—how long they took, I don't remember. Only that I worried for my health, comforting myself that Buddhist monks had walked across mountains in winter, that a man stowed away in a jet cargo hold and survived, and that my body could do anything if I wanted it enough. I trained my mind on topping the hill at the overpass to the town of Archie and my café. At last, the embankment forming the overpass came. It would take ten minutes to top it and see Archie, population one thousand.

Faint and leg-weary, we finally reached the top of the overpass, and beyond it—nothing. Like a canyon in my chest. No Shell station on one side or BP on the other as I had remembered. No houses. No painted, cinder block café with an exhaust fan in back pumping out the smell of cooked hamburger. Nothing lay below where Archie had been but a field of beans, and an acre pond, and a small wood building that once had been someone's real-estate office. It was skirted by two pickups and men wearing work belts, apparently remodeling it. I bent, dumbstruck, confused, and put my hands on my knees to keep from fainting. To the men (if they looked up) I would comprise a black silhouette against the blanched sky of a tiny woman beside a big gelding, loaded with packs.

A highway sign said "AA." I might as well have stumbled out of a bar drunk, trying to remember where I parked my car, for all the sense that sign made. I had to get my horse to the pond behind the building for a drink and myself to the shade of that porch. There was nothing coming on AA. I led my horse across.

I wanted the work-belt-wearing men down the hill at the house to hold me, which I knew they would, with gazes of respect, and a daintiness, having me on their porch while they worked inside, probably using a minimum of curse words. I led my horse along the overpass down a steep embankment to the little building. It had a wood porch with overhang across the length of its front and a window on either side of a door in the middle. I asked the first man I saw if he would mind my dropping my saddle and resting in the shade of the porch for a while. The man wouldn't talk to me, but he went back into the house. Another man who could speak English came out and said it was fine. Make myself at home.

Chief acted weirdly upset. He swung and screamed. This building provided no home, that he could comprehend, so close to the highway. No horses, no outbuildings, no fences, no dogs or kids, only a porch support to tie him to and that was a bad idea as torqued as he was from his twisted nerves. I planned to unsaddle him and walk him through the field to the pond behind the building. I unbuckled our saddlebags one-handed while he swung in circles around me. I pulled off his saddle, and it fell to the ground. Right away he pulled me to coarse stubble someone had mowed around this place. He put his nose down and turned a circle around his front feet. He folded his knees and began to roll while I held his reins.

A man in a pickup drove like a banshee up the outer road and powered down to a stop sign at the top of the embankment. He wore a cowboy hat—a horseman with rope and rifle on a rack in his rear window, with "Hernandez" stenciled across the top. He craned his neck at my horse rolling with his bridle on and, nearby, my mound of saddle and packs. After Chief had scratched both of his sides on the ground and the top of his back twice, he stood and shook. I gathered his reins and led him toward the pond. On the way, I surprised a man relieving himself behind the building and pretended not to see him.

I stopped on the way to the pond to offer Chief some lush graze in a swale. He took one snatch and swung and anxiously pulled me.

You're getting close to home, aren't you?

Gradually, I came to understand that when we had climbed onto the shoulder along 71, I had turned the opposite direction from Archie, south instead of north.

It would take me twenty-four hours for my brain to cool and rest to figure why I did that.

I slipped my flip-phone from its holster on my thigh and dialed Bob as I walked. If I kept moving, I wouldn't faint. My heart pounded, and his phone rang in syncopation.

"Ts' Bob."

"Hi."

"Hi!"

"What are you doing?" I said.

"Oh, I don't know. Not a hell of a lot. Trying to get through some manuscripts."

"I need you to go rent a horse trailer and come get me."

"When?"

"Now."

"What happened?"

"I'm done."

"Are you sure?"

"It's too hot."

"Oh." Bob paused. He was considering whether later I might feel I'd let myself down if I quit so close to home. He sounded disappointed. "Do you want to think about it?"

"I got disoriented and just walked four miles out of my way. I am not asking one more person to camp."

"Okay, I'll see if I can find a trailer."

"I'm at Route AA and 71 Highway. Go back to A-1 Rental."

"Are you okay?"

"Yah. I have a good place to wait. A little building. I don't even know if I'm on the north or south side of the highway."

"71 runs north and south."

"Shit."

"It's okay."

"I gotta go. He's dragging me all over the place."

"You sure?"

"I'm happy with this. Would you hurry?"

I lay on my back on my poncho on the wood porch with my head on my saddlebags. The sun had moved enough there was a horse-sized patch of shade at the end of the porch, where I had tied Chief. He slept there with his head slung low.

After a time, the foreman walked out, and I got to my feet as quickly as I could. By then I had told the men about my trip, that my husband was coming.

"I noticed you're riding an Ortho-Flex."

Nobody else had said the brand of my saddle, an odd name, like they knew what it was.

"You know about Ortho-Flex?"

"Are you Lisa?"

"How did you know that?"

"My niece used to work for you. Maggie—used to be Bullock."

"You're kidding."

I lay back down on my rain poncho with Chief's saddle pad for cushion on the porch. My spine seemed to sink through the decking, through the gravel and dirt into the magma that had held me centered on my horse for a month. Chief slept tied near my head. His breath sounded like someone shoveling snow a block away.

A work truck came and went, exchanging one worker for another. I drifted nearly free of this trip, almost loose from my horse—a sixty-mile trailer ride home.

Enough breeze to cool my sweat found our porch in phrases. My heart no longer pounded but floated in a gap between the hard job of making the next mile and mounting, dismounting, straining at straps, splashing cold water on breasts, feeling in the dark for my headlamp, asking to stay—between that and my former life of writing patent portfolios and grants to cure *c. difficile*, and business plans for pork products and calling on buyers. I lay, undefinable, between the demands of my horse—and what?

When I am home, how will this warrior live?

Of greatest weight is the smallest detail: the mourned-for pull tab that came off the right-side zipper of my pommel bag. The greatest blessing: the Velcro patch to which I stuck my gloves hundreds of times and never lost a one.

I hover, a sheer fog above the grass. The men's boots thump beyond the wall. Their nail guns pop, and their voices smooth over each other with the deference of co-workers. Purple caution tape unspools along Dad's road, meaning No Trespassing, No Hunting. The morning sun warms my cheek like cancer knocking. Chief weaves under me from one side of the road to the other, so by noon I am tired of steering him straight. We rest in a ditch. When he kicks a fly off his belly, I bounce as on a wake that has come a long way from its boat. He looks up with soft, forward ears when he chews. Road dust makes my pen drag on the page. Cold awakens me—the best alarm. I am not crazy. I am crazy about this. I have no time for underwire bras or any other BS. A door opens when I knock, revealing the face of God or one just as good, for I had decided beforehand that's who lived there. I regret these callouses on my heels.

I hear a gunshot. Friendly fire—someone practicing against a strip pit. I hear gunfire every day. I lie in my tent. In pranayama, we are taught to receive the breath. Even my tent knows this.

Chief slows through a Cass County intersection. He begs to stop, and I let him look longingly left, then right, then behind. I kick and kick to get him going, a sluggish Harley. I'm pushing him too hard. He bolts. I am not pushing him hard enough.

An electric screwdriver grinds low then shrieks and strips the head. The pad I lie on smells like my hot horse, which comforts me.

Heavy clouds meter the dawn. Muddy boots and cold gloves are all I know. Dark lines in dew mark rabbit paths; Chief's muzzle submerged in an unspun salad of weeds—how do they taste to him after a night's crisping drizzle? I squat and snatch at grass with my hands beside his nose to try to relate. He tastes the bites I pick.

Everything goes away eventually: the heat rash around my ankles where wool socks ground my skin—because getting riled up gets old. When I sit, I can't clamp things between my thighs anymore, because my thighs don't meet. Even my thighs went away.

A retired Pentecostal preacher tells me his son-in-law uses every vacation to come from Virginia to help on his land and brings him United States cavalry artifacts he collects. His eyes grow wet, "I asked why he does this," said the preacher. "He said, *I have enough love in my heart for two fathers.*"

A retired couple near Filly, Missouri, walks me back to my horse after insisting I drink Coke with ice, which hurts my stomach. They show me where a tornado took their barn. "Our neighbors called us from our own cellar yelling, 'Where are you?'"

We stand in a ditch as if waiting for a bus. Chief bends his body toward me. I notice the horse fly and slap it. I unzip my pocket and two-finger my map and pull it out without spilling my compass and pen. The creases of my map have turned to velvet.

From Nathalene's yard I watch a frantic man on a tractor with brush hog wiggle it through a narrow gate. He has just raced home from work in town. He mows around his cows.

Chief can swat his whole body, shakes his mane side to side, dips his chin to his chest, kicks a forefoot to catch his fore-belly, kicks a hind foot to catch his rear belly, slaps his tail on his sides and rump and privates, stomps each foot, swings his teeth to his sides. I slap what I can; why let him work?

A Mennonite woman comes to the door after a long wait and my internal debate whether to use her faucet without asking. She wears a blue, floral print dress and black scarf and must have risen from a nap. In her nineties, she does not live alone, she says. "My son lives up the road." Her people came from Germany and Holland. She is a bent reed clutching the step rail. Her blue eyes sparkle with the Lord so close on this hill. The water never stops running rusty from her faucet, and I move on. I can't stop riding now—I am not through being loved yet.

I tie Chief to a fence for the night then step in Bill Cheshire's shower in a five-by-five-foot stall beside the outbuilding he's made into a house. He commutes ninety miles one way to Kansas City every day to work for the Postal Service. I'd interrupted him and his lover earlier. She was in from Arizona. Her parents had destroyed his love letters to her when she was a girl because he was "rodeo trash." He rode bulls fifteen years. He knows rodeo trash. He wasn't that. I shower in the small outdoor stall beside a plastic lawn chair where breakfast dishes are stacked, soon to be washed there, too.

"Ho-ho-ho!" jolted me. Not Santa. A carpenter slowing down his partner who was swinging a board. I opened my eyes and lifted my chin to look at Chief upside down, still asleep, tied to his post on the porch.

I sink into the cloud of a foam mattress under a creamy quilt with purple flowers and green leaves in the silence, out of the wind, with a ticking kitchen clock on the wall above the tiny aluminum sink in an air-conditioned, living-quarters horse trailer the Reynolds let me use. I cover someone else's pillow with my clean long-john top.

In Donna's shower, I raise my arms. Large wrinkles form above my tight nipples. I have my mother's skeleton, easy to see when I bathed her at ninety years and ninety-five pounds.

I use up half a mile approaching a house where I might ask to stay. Halfway down the lane, I feel scared and turn back.

I am Hopi—by osmosis—no past or future, only a state of becoming, a rug being weaved, like the young wife I once was, who left a young marriage. I was becoming; I see that now.

Duress of wind and sun quiet my mind, which fills with its own sound, and the dust, and the gravel track, and the long, thin road of my horse's neck. Zip it all out at night, and the mind lifts and blurs to a parade of scenes, this walking, dressing, freezing, packing, crush of tedium, holding my horse, thirst, discipline, lunch of jerky, his mouthing the bit, and swallow and grunt, the back of my knuckle against my raw eye, to turn toward home with hands that confine and free, guide and correct, soothe and console, to offer my horse the aisle between my fists, the middle way, the needle's eye.

Four hours later, late afternoon, Chief stood inside a stock trailer dripping with fear-founded, colic-inducing sweat, and every muscle trembled. Bob and I had parked in the drive of Chief's home pasture. I slipped into the narrow side door of the stock trailer and untied him. Bob unhooked the rear door to open the entire back end. He held it wide. I backed my horse. Chief took small steps and squatted his hind end, testing the floor behind him for the edge with the tip of each hind hoof. Chief found it and backed out and swung around upon the sight of his pasture. He whipped side to side, head in the clouds, and screamed so his whole body shook.

Loose in the pasture, now, Chief put his head down and scooped up the earth with arcing strides. The head of a black horse in the herd rose up in a far corner—Chief's best friend, Dreamer. Dreamer spun and leapt toward Chief with arcing, earth-eating strides. They careened toward each other and slid to stops, mid pasture, and performed for each other airs above the ground, then spun and galloped together up and over the rise.

The End

Acknowledgments

I would like to thank my publisher and editor, Tracy Million Simmons, for seeing the value in a book about a woman riding her horse home, describing the land and people she loves, and rediscovering herself in the process. Tracy's enthusiastic support and careful edits have made this book its best. I thank the editors of *I-70 Review*, Maryfrances Wagner, Greg Field, and Gary Lechliter, for publishing an early excerpt. Thanks especially go to Greg, Maryfrances, William and Sue Trowbridge, Trish Reeves and Lorna Wright, Catherine Browder and Randy Morris, HC and Val Palmer, Jo and Charles McDougall, Paul Temme and Loring Leifer, Tom Stroik and the late Michelle Boisseau for their friendship and encouragement during the writing of this book. Thank-you goes to my sister Nancy Simmons for her encouragement and my sister Donna Jackson for reading every word and encouraging me to keep going. Special thanks go to Rev. Heidi Alfrey, my mentor and guide. Without her, I never would have admitted to anyone that I wanted to take this trip, alone.

Thanks also go to Robert P. and Kathryn Jankus Day for their careful reading of the manuscript and for their comments and to Cynthia Beard for her expert cover design and textual proof reading. I deeply appreciate the careful reading and kind words and encouragement offered by Judy Blunt, Kelly Barth, Gary Dop, and James Hoy. I wish to acknowledge the Issa haiku quoted in the prologue, translated by Robert Hass.

Thanks also must go to my children's father, Len Brown, who

told me years ago that I could change the world with my writing, if only I would have confidence.

Without the kindness, openness, and trust of the families who allowed me to camp on their land, Chief and I would not have been able to take this trip. I thank them for being there for me, even though they did not expect to be. They did what I believe comes naturally to people—they made a place for a stranger among them. I have changed nearly all their names to respect their privacy.

My deepest appreciation goes to my children, Derek Brown and Natalie Kane, who have watched me write endless drafts of a memoir about my first horseback trip, and just as many of this memoir, always firm that I should, indeed, spend my time that way and that my book would be good.

Finally, I thank my husband, Robert J. Stewart, editor emeritus of *New Letters* magazine, where he was managing editor and editor-in-chief for forty-six years. Without his support I would not have taken this trip, and I could not have completed this book.

About the Author

Lisa D. Stewart is a commercial writer in Prairie Village, Kansas, who writes magazine articles, feasibility studies, business plans, grants, and marketing content. Between 1984 and 1999, she and her former husband created and grew Ortho-Flex Saddle Company, after a three thousand-mile horse-back  trip that taught them about the relationship between saddles and the biomechanics of the horse. The couple produced and sold patented saddles and tack in more than thirty countries. She has published more than one hundred articles on the topic of saddle fit. Lisa lives with her husband, Robert Stewart, editor emeritus of *New Letters* magazine at the University of Missouri-Kansas City.

WWW.MEADOWLARK-BOOKS.COM

Read

A Meadowlark Book

Nothing feels better than home

meadowlark-books.com

While we at Meadowlark Books love to travel, we also cherish our home time. We are nourished by our open prairies, our enormous skies, community, family, and friends. We are rooted in this land, and that is why Meadowlark Books publishes regional authors.

When you open one of our fiction books, you'll read delicious stories that are set in the Heartland. Settle in with a volume of poetry, and you'll remember just how much you love this place too—the landscape, its skies, the people.

Meadowlark Books publishes memoir, poetry, short stories, and novels. Read stories that began in the Heartland, that were written here. Add to your Meadowlark Book collection today.

Specializing in Books by Authors from the Heartland Since 2014

CPSIA information can be obtained
at www.ICGtesting.com
Printed in the USA
BVHW031044190720
584083BV00001B/135